TRANSLATION MULTIPLES

translation
TRANSNATION
SERIES EDITOR **EMILY APTER**

A list of titles in the series appears at the back of the book.

Translation Multiples

FROM GLOBAL CULTURE
TO POSTCOMMUNIST DEMOCRACY

KASIA SZYMANSKA

PRINCETON UNIVERSITY PRESS
PRINCETON & OXFORD

Copyright © 2025 by Princeton University Press

Princeton University Press is committed to the protection of copyright and the intellectual property our authors entrust to us. Copyright promotes the progress and integrity of knowledge created by humans. Thank you for supporting free speech and the global exchange of ideas by purchasing an authorized edition of this book. If you wish to reproduce or distribute any part of it in any form, please obtain permission.

Requests for permission to reproduce material from this work should be sent to permissions@press.princeton.edu

Published by Princeton University Press
41 William Street, Princeton, New Jersey 08540
99 Banbury Road, Oxford OX2 6JX

press.princeton.edu

GPSR Authorized Representative: Easy Access System Europe - Mustamäe tee 50, 10621 Tallinn, Estonia, gpsr.requests@easproject.com

All Rights Reserved

ISBN 9780691265469
ISBN (pbk.) 9780691265490
ISBN (e-book) 9780691265575

Library of Congress Control Number: 2024036061 (print) | 2024036062 (ebook)

British Library Cataloging-in-Publication Data is available

Editorial: Anne Savarese and James Collier
Production Editorial: Natalie Baan
Cover Design: Haley Jin Mee Chung
Production: Lauren Reese
Publicity: William Pagdatoon
Copyeditor: Norman Ware

This book has been composed in Minion 3

10 9 8 7 6 5 4 3 2 1

For Maya et al.

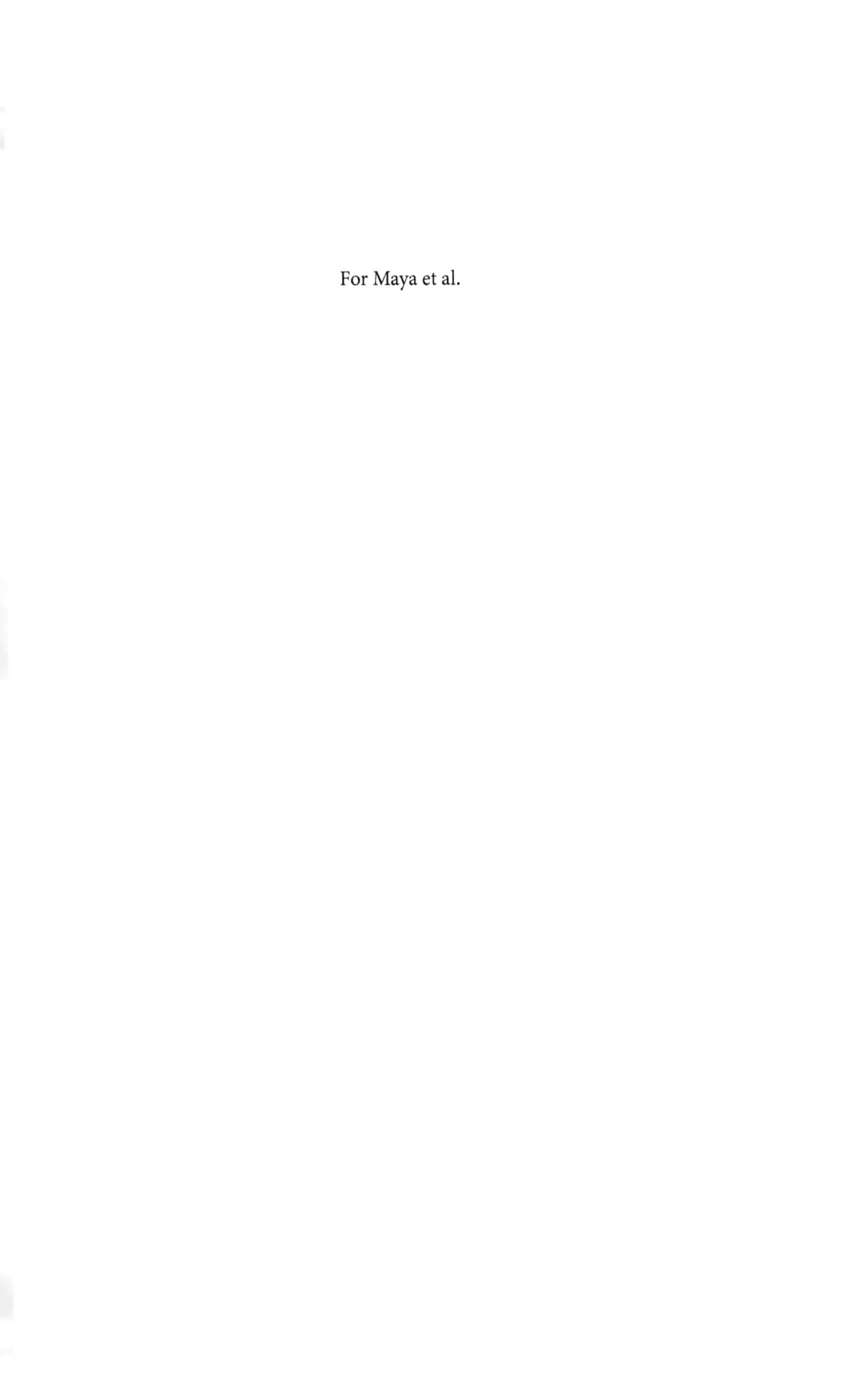

CONTENTS

List of Illustrations ix
Acknowledgments xi

Introduction 1

1 The Multiples Now 10
   Before a Conceit Is Born 10
   Translation Multiples Tell Their Own Story 19

2 Ethics of the Multiple 43
   Against the Grain 43
   The Metatranslation 50
   Pluralist Multiples 61

3 Inner Pluralism in the Wake of 1989 75
   Against the Spirit of Generalization 75
   Oratorium Moratorium 83
   Mister B., but How to Live? 94

4 Winding the Clockwork Orange Three Times 99
   The "2 in 1" in the Making 99
   The Mechanical and the Wind-Up Languages 111
   Multiples Going Round in Circles 121

5 Doing Brecht in Different Voices 132
Translation beyond the Barricade 132
Brecht in Translation Slams 144
The V-Effekt 156

Conclusion 161

Notes 169
Bibliography 195
Index 217

ILLUSTRATIONS

1.1. "VIA: The Diagram of Forking Paths" (2020) — 28
1.2. Alejandro Cesarco, "Untitled (Dante/Calvino)" (2004) — 31
2.1. A scene from Krzysztof Kieślowski's *Blind Chance* (1981–1987) — 72
2.2. The cover image for the Criterion Collection version of Kieślowski's *Blind Chance* — 72
4.1. The covers of Robert Stiller's translations of Anthony Burgess's *A Clockwork Orange*: version R (Russian) and version A (American), both published in 1999 — 101
4.2. The special 2017 double edition of versions A and R of *A Clockwork Orange* in Polish combined into one volume — 102
4.3. Posters of two theater plays based on Robert Stiller's translation double: *A Mechanical Orange* (1991, directed by Feliks Falk) and *A Wind-Up Orange* (2005, directed by Jan Klata) — 120
4.4. The first page of Robert Stiller's unfinished manuscript of "A Spring-Assisted Orange" (version N, German) alongside the late translator's commemorative picture — 129
5.1. The cover image of *Ten cały Brecht* (2012) — 134
5.2. Ryszard Krynicki's Polish translation of Brecht's poem "Die Lösung" in a regional bulletin of the Solidarity union (Lublin, 1981) — 138
5.3. A Solidarity poster with a poem by Bertolt Brecht in Polish (Gdańsk, 1980) — 139

ACKNOWLEDGMENTS

MORE THAN anything else, this book shows how meeting the right people and having meaningful conversations with them can metamorphose a project as it grows and pulsates. I am sincerely indebted to each and all of them.

I'd like to thank all of those who helped at different stages of the process, which involved (going sort of backward): navigating the logistics of book publishing, reading the manuscript and its parts in different forms, feeding me reading suggestions and sending materials from faraway places, supporting my doctoral and postdoctoral endeavors, and being role models in my life more generally. One person who has scored most points overall across all of the above categories is Adriana X. Jacobs, the best possible mentor, friend, and source of academic, poetic, and translatorial inspiration. Without you, Adriana, this book publication would never have come to fruition.

I am equally grateful to Emily Apter, who rooted for this project from the very first email we exchanged, offering her invaluable feedback on the book proposal and readers' reports as well as her generous support throughout the process overall. Here, I'd also like to give credit to the readers and reviewers of my book project in its different reincarnations: Adriana X. Jacobs, Rebecca Walkowitz, Matthew Reynolds, Stanley Bill, Maciej Jaworski, Tom Kuhn, Jan Fellerer, the late Jim Naughton, and Nina Taylor-Terlecka, as well as thank the three no longer anonymous readers of the manuscript (Susan Bassnett, Adrian Wanner, and Jacob Edmond) for their positive response and enthusiasm. Finally, many thanks to Norman Ware, Ingalo Thompson, Sam Burton, Sayantani Mitra, and Ágota Márton for great language suggestions on some of this book's sections.

Book writing may seem like a lonely and daunting task in its own right, and it'd be rather grim to not have had a chance to share my work in progress with a bunch of translation enthusiasts and members of various academic communities. In particular, I'm indebted to the Oxford Comparative Criticism and Translation (OCCT) research group for creating such a vibrant and inclusive space for discussing different modes and forms of translation, including those as quirky as the ones discussed in this book. Special thanks to the OCCT chair, Matthew Reynolds, but also to Eleni Philippou, Karolina Wątroba, Adriana X. Jacobs, Amy Xiaofan Li, Patrick McGuinness, and Ola Sidorkiewicz. Together with some of the OCCT members, I participated in the Global Humanities Institute on "Challenges of Translation" at Universidad de Santiago de Chile, which turned out to be yet another great forum for discussing "translation multiples" across languages and disciplines. These and other interesting conversations that unfolded on other occasions (e.g., during the CETRA Summer School at KU Leuven in Belgium, my short visit with the Princeton Society of Fellows, a "translation multiples" workshop I ran for the Queen's Translation Exchange at Oxford, and an outreach talk for the Polonium Foundation) shaped this book on several levels, not only in terms of the final case study selection. Thank you, Dirk Delabastita, David Bellos, Michael Wachtel, Irena Grudzińska-Gross, Nicola Thomas, Alex Braslavsky, Francesca Southerden, and Ola Sidorkiewicz for being there to engage and chat about my work. Then, I've had a chance to present fragments of this project at several conferences such as the American Comparative Literature Association (ACLA) Congress at UCLA and the Prismatic Translation conference at Oxford, and it was after my Oxford panel that an anonymous doctoral student approached me with a brilliant reading idea of his own—I am so sorry I've never thanked him for this little gem in person! Lastly, I have also been invited to give talks about translation multiples at the University of Bristol, Cardiff University, Trinity College Dublin's Long Room Hub, Queen's University Belfast, and the University of Warwick, with each being an eye-opening experience thanks to audiences comprising a mix of literary scholars, scholars and practitioners of translation, as well as the so-called general audience.

This book could never have been written without the very translators in question. Let me name a few to thank them for being so encouraging and patient during our correspondence and providing me with extra materials and helpful answers to all the tricky questions I had in store for them. My sincere gratitude goes to late Robert Stiller for making me privy to an unpublished section of his third version of Anthony Burgess's *A Clockwork Orange* before he passed away on December 10, 2016. Many thanks to him and his widow, Nina Stiller, the founder of the Foundation for Robert Stiller, for allowing me to release this iconic fragment in its work-in-progress format in print. Likewise, I'm grateful to Polish translators Edward Balcerzan, Piotr Sommer, Andrzej Kopacki, and Jerzy Jarniewicz, as well as to the creators of English translation multiples Hiroaki Sato, Caroline Bergvall, and Alejandro Cesarco for clarifying a few intriguing issues emerging from their projects. Special thanks go to Tom Kuhn, English translator of Bertolt Brecht's poetry, and Steve Parker, Brecht's biographer, whom I was able to consult on a few technical issues before publication.

More people I must mention work for several cultural and archival institutions in Poland. The list of names is long, but I'm immensely grateful to all of them for giving me access to crucial texts and visual materials. Many thanks to Teatr Nowy in Poznań (Poznań New Theatre), Wrocławski Teatr Współczesny (the Contemporary Theatre in Wrocław), Teatr im. Stefana Jaracza w Łodzi (the Stefan Jaracz Theatre in Łódź), Stowarzyszenie Autorów ZAiKS (the Polish Society of Authors and Composers), and Instytut Teatralny im. Zbigniewa Raszewskiego (the Zbigniew Raszewski Theatre Institute) for providing me with access to video recordings and transcripts of the performances mentioned in this book; to Archiwum Akt Nowych (the Central Archives of Modern Records) for examining relevant censored materials related to *Literatura na świecie* magazine; and to Europejskie Centrum Solidarności (the European Solidarity Centre) for providing high-resolution reproductions of Solidarity materials from their archives.

I've been also very lucky to have been supported financially by a number of academic institutions and research funding bodies, and I would like to thank them all for their support and for being ready to facilitate exchanges of thoughts in the United Kingdom and Europe, and across the Americas: Robinson College and Trinity Hall (Cambridge), three Oxford colleges (University College, St Hugh's College, and St Anne's College), the Faculty of Modern Languages at Oxford, the OCCT, the Centre for East European Language-Based Area Studies (CEELBAS), the British Comparative Literature Association (BCLA), the European Society for Translation Studies (EST), the Martha Cheung Award, Enterprise Ireland, Trinity College Dublin's School of Languages, Literatures and Cultural Studies, and the University of Manchester's School of Arts, Languages and Cultures.

Finally, and most importantly, this book is a tribute to individual people's creative minds, as well as to reading communities, whose team spirit and simple gestures of kindness are what we live for. It's sometimes accidental that someone, somewhere, by sheer happenstance knows of and is happy to share something that will later be included in someone else's book. I was fortunate enough to have met such people in good time and receive their generous suggestions, ideas, and even materials sent by post, photographed or scanned from their university and home libraries. Special thanks in this respect goes to Michael Benedikt (Oxford), Magdalena Cabaj (Toronto), Anna Cetera-Włodarczyk (Warsaw), Sandy Flint (Cambridge), Theo Hermans (London), Rosario Hubert (Connecticut), Henrike Lähnemann (Oxford), Joseph Lacey (Dublin), Barbara Spicer

(Scotland), Annegret Sturm (Geneva), Eduardo Thomson (Santiago), Joanna Trzeciak Huss (Cleveland), and Karolina Wątroba (Oxford). All of these people (and certainly many others) should be given credit for finding the time and energy to lend their hand to a colleague and friend in need. And last, but not least, I am truly indebted to my family—Maya, Krzys, my parents, and my sister Karolina—for always being there. They probably think they disturb me more often than help, but I also wouldn't be in the position to finish this book without them in the first place.

TRANSLATION MULTIPLES

Introduction

"I KNOW NOT who was the first lying author to construct the seventy cells at Alexandria, in which they were separated and yet all wrote the same words," wrote Jerome in "Preface to the Pentateuch" of the Vulgate, his Latin translation of the Bible.[1] He referred here to the famous case of the Septuagint, the erstwhile primary Greek version of the Hebrew Bible commissioned in the third century BCE to a group of seventy Jews of Alexandria. Jerome debunked what later became the core element of its myth: namely, the claim that all the learned translators would under divine inspiration come up with entirely identical translated texts, word after word, sentence after sentence, despite working simultaneously and independently in seventy isolated cells. There are more caveats to the legend as known and subsequently circulated. In fact, the number of Jews was not a round seventy but seventy-two (six men of each of twelve tribes); they did not translate into standard Greek but its spoken vehicular variant, Koine; they originally did not render the entire Old Testament but only its first five books (the Pentateuch); and so on.

The crucial aspect of this widely shared lore, questioned by Jerome in the fourth century CE, is the alleged convergence of seventy-two translation solutions that were said to be produced individually and in isolation. "For it is one thing to be a prophet, another to be an interpreter," soberly argued Jerome,[2] well aware of the translator's convoluted chains of decisions and arduous work, and later chosen as the patron saint of translators. To his mind, rather than being the result of miraculously synchronized interpretations from dozens of different people, the eventual Septuagint came into being as a product of the translators' collaborative work. The latter scenario actually corresponds to the earliest known record of the legend, a letter by Aristeas. It was only centuries later that Philo Judeus—the "first lying author" at whom Jerome pointed the finger—tacked the image of separate cells onto the story in order to strengthen the claim of the translation's divine inspiration.³ And it indeed made quite a difference to say that a few dozen translators did not cooperate over the final product, but somehow their individual readings cohered into what could be nothing else but one true and authorized translation of the Bible.

Besides its obvious scriptural significance, what was accomplished by this meeting of seventy-two translation minds into one? What consequences does it have on translation history and our contemporary understanding of what translation entails? It is safe to say that it could be one of the first moments in the history of textual practice when the "equivalence" between two texts in completely different languages is firmly established, legitimized, and justified with sufficient rhetorical power. Since a few dozen authorities, seventy-two competent interpreters approaching one text, reached exactly the same conclusions in their renderings, the identical fruit of their work must constitute the only faithful and authentic translation, supported by the highest authority imaginable. Radical as this case of imposing Equivalence with the capital *E* might sound from today's perspective, it is by no means an isolated one in translation and textual history. In principle, it finds its solid continuation in any institutional, political, or cultural mechanism of establishing the one and only translation equivalence in different historical contexts. These occurrences range from bilingual dictionaries with fixed interlingual one-to-one equivalents, to sworn authorized translations, to broader publishing practice and audience expectations making translators merge all potential variations into one ready-to-go translation product: a single finite text substituting for the original.

This book revolves around literary translations and conceptual works that do not conform to such norms and embody the exact reversal of the Septuagint's story. Instead of demonstrating how seventy-two translation attempts coalesce into one sanctioned rendering, the present discussion aims to turn the tables and swap the two sides of the equation. The question at stake here will be rather: how an original literary text can possibly diverge into seventy-two different variants. And when it does, how can such an unconventional multiplicity be displayed and embraced; in what way can it still be read as a coherent text, be it by one translator or poet or a team of several? And what follows: How can readers deal with similar instances of literary works with plural translatorial voices; is it possible to redefine our reading habits to be able to take full advantage of their rich reservoirs of meanings?

These questions are more pressing now than ever before. Translation multiples, this newly emerging genre of writing, has even developed its own artistic form and literary texture. These days, the multiples reside in conceptual books with plural translations or poems composed of different renderings of the same original. Translators, poets, and artists alike have come to expose the act of translation by producing different parallel variants, placing them next to each other as legitimate versions of the original, and presenting them as stand-alone artistic works. While doing so, the creators of multiples also want to tell their own story. The story can be deeply personal, visual, critical, or political; it can reflect on the nature of translation itself, its multiplicity, or any other artistic themes they set out to explore. A whole literary universe can be easily encapsulated in what might look like a series of dispersed translations—multiple translations that have been put together alongside each other for seemingly no reason.

This is of course not to say that the multiplicity of translation as such is something very unconventional. In fact, if we look a little bit closer, the tale of translation multiples is as old as time: plural variants lie dormant in any revised version by the same translator and every single retranslation of one work in a given language by different translators. There are translators who could ponder over alternative versions of their own rendering until doomsday—unless, of course, put under some external pressure (time, financial situation, next project, etc.) to cast what should ultimately be its final version on paper. Consecutive retranslators, too, tend to approach and reinterpret the original text differently from their predecessors; their varied readings of one work fork into multiple different paths depending on their personal and cultural background, interpretative lens, ideology, individually projected audience, and many other factors. This is partly why David Bellos humorously remarked: "Give a hundred competent translators a page to translate, and the chances of any two versions being identical are close to zero."[4] Bellos's assumption clearly jars with the Septuagint-like convergence, shaking and turning the concept of one true equivalence upside down. It is rather the infinite and inevitably multiple nature of translation that comes into play and ought to be treated as a default option. But still, even though such multifarious outcomes are in theory recognized or even taken for granted by literary and translation critics, the actual norms of translation production are a completely different matter. Hardly ever do several different renderings of the same work appear in print simultaneously, alerting readers to various possibilities and alternative translation solutions as well as manifesting how tentative and arbitrary each of them is. With a minor exception of scholarly editions and critical anthologies, the status quo rather leans toward the Septuagint convergence. For a range of reasons, it is more convenient to nourish the illusion that a given translation wholly represents the original it stands for. As many people before have pointed out, despite ongoing efforts to change this state of affairs, the function of translations and their mode of being in the majority of publishing cultures is still to be produced and read as substitutes for their originals.[5] And so this cultural status of translations, along with the respective pursuit of translation equivalence, governs prevailing praxis, apparently leaving little room for multiple variants and divergent readings of the original. A constant friction between the potentially plural and the prescriptively singular lies at the heart of literary translation.

In *Translation Multiples*, I discuss a wide range of contemporary literary works that against all odds fight for a different form of expression and display plural renderings of the same source text both in parallel to and on a par with one another. The examples of such multiples span the past few decades, beginning in the late twentieth century, and this book discusses several key examples focusing on two different contexts. First, it takes a broader outlook on the Anglophone literary scene. Translation multiples can offer a special shock therapy to the contemporary lingua franca, whose largely monolingual lens makes it necessary to debunk the myth of translation as a transparent medium and an unoriginal, secondary form of writing. Only the oft-quoted "three percent" of all books published the United States are translations, and a roughly matching number of translations are released yearly in the United Kingdom and Ireland.[6] With this lousy translation record as well as its expansive status of a global language, English is often lampooned for being oblivious to the creative resources of translation, let alone to translation coming in larger numbers and repetitions. This is also where authors of translation multiples and their gestures of pushing the envelope of the print format come into play most forcefully. Meddling with the audience's expectations, projects displaying plural renderings of one original lift the veil on the very act and process of translation, alert readers to its transformative powers, and expose different artistic idioms and language variants at play.

Second, this book zooms in on the minor culture of an emerging democracy, post-1989 Poland, where projects introducing multiplied translation variants with different ideological readings offered an essential platform for a pluralist political discussion after the transition from a totalitarian system. In these two literary cultures, a more globalized and a local one, translation activity occupies a completely different place. The almost proverbial "three-percent" figure does not really hold a candle to Poland's one-quarter of translated titles published yearly, a proportion closer to that of other European countries.[7] At the same time, while the English-language and Polish book industries are both governed by free-market publishing, the translation culture of post-1989 Poland needs to be seen in relation to its previous communist counterpart. What translation multiples flesh out in this context is a strong quantitative tension between two successive literary orders: the authoritative legacy of the state-driven publishing monopoly before 1989 on the one hand, and a more decentralized system from the 1990s onward on the other. The first often favored canonization, officially anointed translations, and often reeditions of the same translations rather than soliciting new renderings. The latter has provided—even if in theory and with some caveats—similar technical conditions for a larger number of translations to emerge and more interpretations to be voiced without imposing any ideological priorities. Translation multiples in post-1989 Poland, I argue, are a touchstone of the transition between these two literary orders. Abolishing the communist legacy in favor of a more pluralist system brought about a move from singularity to plurality, from one authoritative interpretation to multiple renderings treated as potential alternatives.

In the same vein, these globalized and local literary contexts do not really lend themselves to comparison in terms of geographical and linguistic scope. Languages involved in English translation multiples span a much wider and more diverse range: from Ancient Greek to French, German, and Italian, to Chinese and Japanese. Among contemporary translation multipliers, we find quite a mixed crowd: not only American and Canadian poets and writers but also a Norwegian French artist (Caroline Bergvall) and two Italian writers and editors (Eugenia Loffredo and Manuela Perteghella), all three based in the United Kingdom, as well as a German-born poet (Rosmarie Waldrop), a Japanese poet and translator (Hiroaki Sato), an Indian-born professor (Aijaz Ahmad), and a Uruguayan artist (Alejandro Cesarco), the last four based in the United States. It does not really matter whether the originals they wished to multiply come from iconic authors such as Ibycus, Wang Wei, and Dante, or more recent (avant-garde and modernist) poets such as Ernst Jandl and Chika Sagawa. What still links the authors of translation multiples is the gesture of welcoming and embracing the creative potential of translation in English. While speaking from the linguistically privileged end, they refract originals through the prism of the global language but also position themselves somewhat against the grain. Their multiples aim to expose the appropriative medium of global English and rebel against institutional and cultural efforts to standardize language. For this reason, some of the multiples explicitly aim to open up the translation scene to very different ways of using of English or writing in various types of Englishes.

Within this power relation, the postcommunist examples should be placed on the other side of the spectrum. They often underscore the Eastern European experience after the fall of communism, anchoring it in a very local political situation. At the same time, however, their creators also transgress the Polish local and ostensibly homogeneous context. In fact, one author, Stanisław Barańczak, was a dissident poet and US émigré who created his political multiples when teaching at Harvard. Another, Robert Stiller, was a Polish Jewish polyglot and translingual visionary. Others were translators affiliated with a liberal "world literature" magazine, which disseminated Western literature in multiplied translation before 1989. Yet, the postcommunist multiples are striking in how they position themselves against major languages and major political forces. In particular, they concentrate on the powerful European triad of English, French, and German, with some presence of Russian added to the mix, and take works originally written in these languages as the starting point of a pluralist discussion. This positioning against major cultures and translatorial intervention into their literary texts will also be key to understanding the subversive element in post-1989 projects. The multiples stray from the beaten pathway of either "assimilation" or "differentiation"—the two possible strategies identified by Pascale Casanova in the history of "small literatures"[8]—and look for a third way out. While they are vibrant and critical voices that come from a "minor literature," it is not the kind of minor literature that is written by minor writers fully in a major language (Deleuze and Guattari) nor fully in a minor language (Kronfeld).[9] The oppositional force of these "minor" projects of translation multiples lies in their linguistic in-betweenness. In generating diverse renderings of a work from a major Western language, the postcommunist translation multiples enter a polemic with the originals across languages, dismantle their alleged authority, and offer their own plural interlingual responses.

While these two distinct contexts pose a set of different questions for our understanding of translation multiples, this curious literary practice has emerged on the wave of similar artistic forces. Both these literary milieus treat the texture of translation multiples as an artistic and subversive idiom in its own right—even if to quite a different effect in some instances. Regardless of the geographical location, translation multiples have coincided with broader cultural trends: the gradually changing perception of literary translation and its recognition as a creative domain by both writers and academics. As most of the examples I focus on in the book span the past three or four decades, I also will discuss how these trends have informed the shift in thinking about the artistic potential of translation multiples. The practice of generating plural translation variants has not been so uncommon in other editorial contexts. In particular, scholarly publishing is known for its academic anthologies that present plural translations for pedagogical reasons: they place different renderings one after another to illuminate the original from different hermeneutic angles or to trace the reception of translated works or authors in multiple translations over time. While acknowledging the legacy of these editorial strategies, the translation multiples discussed in this book have entered a more artistic and experimental realm. They no longer see originals as the final anchors of meaning but rather treat them as a starting point into a much wider narrative. The critical reflection on the multiple nature of translation that they offer is no longer a by-product of scholarly exegesis but rather a creative principle binding all different variants together and turning their diversity into an artistic conceit.

In the first part of the book, I discuss the notion of translation multiples in the Anglophone context, placing them alongside other experimental practices in modernist and contemporary translation tradition. Whereas some experimental translations, in Sawako Nakayasu's words, "behave, or 'pass' as normal, traditional translations,"[10] the genre of creative multiplications and reiterations does not follow suit, resisting easy or passive reception. By subverting the usual one-to-one relationship between the original and its translation, the practice of multiplying translations rather tends to knock readers out of their routine of equating these two and taking one for the other. As translation multiples expose the process and act of translation by producing different parallel variants, their self-referential nature will also inform their longer literary lineage. Drawing on Oulipo-inspired ideas, I argue that the task of translation multiples is in accordance with that of metaliterature. While breaking the original into plural variants, they alert readers to the mediating subject and the act of creative transformation in the process.

The idea of translation ethics that underpins this understanding, discussed more thoroughly in chapter 2, will have a slightly different twist. A lot has been written about the ethics of translation, understood as fidelity toward original authors and source texts. This time, however, the ethics of the multiple will concern the receiving end of translation production: the reader. Instead of asking how to be "true" or "faithful" to the original, this book will open up literary translation to a range of reformulated questions testing in what way the literary genre of translation multiples can be valid for contemporary readers. Is it possible for a translator to signal to their audience the infinite spectrum of possibilities and so the tentative nature of a single translation choice? How can a translator break through the translation's "fourth wall" and the long-cherished illusion of treating translations as providing direct access to original meanings? How does acknowledging more than one legitimate reading of the original change the way we think about language—and global English with its many different varieties—and about society, on today's culturally diverse map? What does it mean to interpret and translate differently from someone else and accept this other reading, and what do these distinct ideas about the original tell us about our own position in the world?

Especially with an eye to these issues, I will move on to discuss in much more detail three instances of translation multiples in postcommunist Poland in the second part of the book. In chapters 3, 4, and 5, respectively, I will highlight how translation multiples could become a pluralist gesture in a newly emerging democracy drawing on the following examples: homophonic multiples of "La Marseillaise," the French anthem (1991); a double/triple rendering of Anthony Burgess's *A Clockwork Orange* published as a novelistic tie-in (1999); and a quadruple book with Bertolt Brecht's poetry in distinct readings by four translators from *Literatura na świecie* (Literature in the World), the leading Polish magazine on world literature in translation (2012). These three case studies, outlined chronologically, have made their way into this book for a number of reasons. First, they are particularly compelling manifestations of the art of translation multiples in Polish with its core idea of reading one original text from different interpretative and ideological angles. Second, they also map out the most prominent and controversial figures and translation experiments in the local literary practice of the past decades. Third, their creators have strongly been invested in the literary translation culture. As such, they had their say in shaping it through their own translation works, debates, and criticism, and their artistic personas have incarnated some of the most interesting features of this tradition. Finally, all of these translators and authors have in one way or another dealt with the country's communist past, often taking a stance through their translation practice on the political and cultural situation at the turn of 1989 and beyond.

It is probably no coincidence that these pluralist translation multiples came to fruition in the postcommunist world and often served as a form of artistic liberation and critical reevaluation of the past. At this juncture, I will suggest how in each of these cases a multiplicity of interpretative perspectives in translation could also be read in pluralist or democratic terms: as opening a forum for discussion and introducing different viewpoints in opposition to the communist legacy. Depending on the case, the idea of translation pluralism manifest in post-1989 translation multiples will also put forward agendas pertinent to recent cultural discourse in the country. These include, for instance: an ethical suspicion of language and an urge to pursue individual perspectives against totalizing discourses, a critical engagement with different political systems and the cyclical nature of history, an intellectual protest against partisan tribalism and political polarization with an emphasis on the totalitarian mindset with "either/or" and "friend or foe" binaries typical of the Cold War era, a revision of ideologically encumbered images, and an activist role of acknowledging multiple voices and viewpoints.

These themes, one by one, permeate consecutive literary works, but they also nourish the notion of translation multiples more broadly. With special reference to these cases and broader themes, I hope to demonstrate that this newly emerging literary genre, besides simply inviting the diversity of artistic articulations, activates and responds to broader social and ethical issues. Translation multiples that treat different readings, worldviews, and visions of society on a par with one another might be a remedy against totalized ideas in our times. This remedy is particularly necessary in the face of not only the antagonizing rhetoric in the ongoing bloody conflicts all over the world but also the rising tide of political tribalism more generally. These phenomena form the underbelly of Western democracies as well as of a country like Poland, which until recently was seen as part of central Europe's "illiberal revolt"[11] and is still very much torn by partisan divisions. As translation multiples promote polyphony and an open forum for discussion around various ideas, they equip their readers with a crucial critical tool for approaching textual and ideological difference. In the grand scheme of things, they also demonstrate how every act of translation and retranslation, reading and interpreting in different ways, is inherent to the human condition and to coexistence in a democratic society.

1

The Multiples Now

A poem should be equal to:
Not true.

—"ARS POETICA," BY ARCHIBALD MACLEISH

Before a Conceit Is Born

Multiple translation with different variants coming in series, chains, and reiterations feels less strange now than ever before. Digital publishing has established itself as a promising platform for offering plural renderings of a single literary work. Online literary journals can more easily release various takes on the same original without the fear of adding extra pages and generating extra shipping costs—a common problem when printing in hard copy.[1] In this sense, it might sound as if, owing to this technological advancement, we are witnessing a breakthrough in translation as it enters a new digital age of visual comparison, juxtaposition, and multiplication. Besides online journals such as the *Asymptote* and *Telephone* as well as websites such as Drunken Boat and Fleurs du mal,[2] a few recent projects have already used digital tools to trace how originals branch out into plural translation variants. One of them, for instance, took a scene from Shakespeare's *Othello* and traced its thirty-seven German renderings published between 1766 and 2012; another focused on various translations of Charlotte Brontë's novel *Jane Eyre* rendered into more than sixty languages in multiple versions.[3] Similar digital projects set out to examine the widest array of different variations, like many earlier projects had done in the traditional medium of print. Here, however, technologically driven approaches to the study of multiple translations clearly have an advantage over traditional comparative studies of translation series.[4] They make it possible not only to analyze and describe but to *see* and show students and nonprofessional readers of translations in a clear and efficient format how the same original words can play out in so many ways in a different language. Such an image, instantly prompted thanks to its digital tool kit, definitely works to the advantage of multiple translations. A couple, a dozen, tens of different variants can easily be brought together in one go.

Perhaps it is only in the age of digital production and reproduction that multiple translation can finally blossom.[5] However, as much as I support the idea of digital media facilitating multiplied and serial translation, I would like to dig deeper and look for other potential catalysts of translation multiples. In particular, the technological transition does not exhaustively inform the multiplied translation projects I will discuss in this book, most of which have appeared in the traditional medium of print. Surely, their creators in some sense attempted to overcome the publishing conventions and constraints that a traditional layout entails. Nonetheless, their artistic intuition to construct their works with such a richly differentiated palette of translations has clearly originated elsewhere. This raises more fundamental questions relevant to the strand of contemporary translation multiples discussed in this book: To what end did their creators multiply renderings of the same original work and place them next to each other? Why did they compose their poems or books out of various interlingual readings of a given source text? How do we read such works, and what is so special about them as opposed to other instances of experimental translation or conceptual writing?

If we look at translation history, translations of literary works are quintessentially multiple—as long as translators decide to approach the same source texts and retranslate them or revise their own previous attempts, different renderings will keep coming in series over time. Very rarely, however, are they brought together in this diverse spectrum and presented simultaneously in print. In this respect, Rebecca Walkowitz rightly singles out a more university-oriented practice of collecting different variants of translated works in scholarly compilations for pedagogical purposes.[6] It has indeed long been present in scholarly publishing, for instance in critical editions devoted to particular authors or works with more than one rendering in a given tradition. In such books, it is usually a third party that collects and edits different versions without the knowledge of the translators involved in order to either illuminate the original from different angles or to trace the history of its reception. This focus is especially redolent of whole critical series such as Penguin Classics' Poets in Translation, which demonstrate how the readings of classical and canonical writers (in this case, Horace, Ovid, Virgil, Dante, Charles Baudelaire, and others) changed over the centuries. Collections of this kind could often work as typical variorum editions. Whereas variorum editions (e.g., of Shakespearean plays or the Bible) keep track of any textual instabilities, processual changes, and editorial decisions in the production of original works, multiple translation editions work analogously by displaying a range of available translated variants of one text. In the face of these scattered viewings, the notion of one fixed translation equivalence can no longer be taken for granted. Variorum editions destabilize the original textual base—and the idea of text more broadly—by revealing any glitches, reworkings, and manipulations in the process of its making and delivering. This original instability, as Karen Emmerich argues, could be negotiated in any act of translation or textual proliferation.[7] However, variorum books composed of multiple translations more explicitly complicate this next step of bringing texts across two different literary languages. Dispersed in a halo of alternative "equivalences," translation here reflects numerous stylistic and interpretative takes of various historically situated translators, each activating different reservoirs of meaning.

At the same time, I should perhaps backtrack on the rough-grained distinction between the more "literary" or "creative" translation multiples and their more "scholarly" equivalents published by university presses. This book argues that contemporary translation multiples are a new literary genre that resides somewhere on the border between experimental translation and conceptual writing, leaving their more academic prototypes behind. At the same time, however, the creative idea underpinning translation multiples has inevitably drawn from the familiar academic apparatus surrounding translation. I would prefer to say that contemporary translation multiples playfully hijack and creatively rework the otherwise long-standing scholarly exegetic practice. And since that familiar practice sparks the artistic imagination of their creators, I still have to acknowledge their more traditional lineage. The very idea of unpacking the original in multiple ways has its roots in ubiquitous and age-old scholarly textual practices such as annotations, explanatory glosses, textual exegesis, and commentaries with alternative variants in footnotes, in brackets, or after slashes—all of which constitutes the long-standing tradition of tackling polysemy in source texts. In the European exegetic and philological practice, this has taken place in the contexts of closely related languages: for instance, early modern English translations of classical texts in which the margins of the page contained alternative variants to "make visible the multiplying potential of translation."[8] Likewise, a dissatisfaction with single-translation solutions has been also present in attempts to render non-European languages. It became a critical theme in I. A. Richards's *Mencius on the Mind: Experiments in Multiple*

Definition (1932), one of the most well-known and radical protests against automatic matchings of terms across languages and cultures, with multiple translations of definitions from the Chinese. Likewise, in David Hawkes's *A Little Primer of Tu Fu* (1967), different translation variants were meant to resolve what the author saw as the original ambiguity of Chinese verse.[9] In encircling and illuminating the plurality of meanings from various angles, translation acts here at its hermeneutic best.

What strikes me in these two contexts—translations from European and non-European languages—is that regardless of the perceived cultural and linguistic distance between different languages, the critical apparatus of translation, with its idea of multiplying glosses and parallel variants, works practically in the same way. In the case of "less related" languages such as Chinese, it becomes a rhetorical device to navigate through what is seen as insurmountable difference—to approach and approximate something that is so remote that it cannot be easily tamed through the appropriative medium of our language. In *Mencius on the Mind*, Richards objected to translating the Chinese thinker's terms one-to-one and instead suggested a whole "scheme of possibilities,"[10] a comparative exercise in multiple definition to overcome that distance. His parallel translation variants for different original expressions such as *hsing* ("nature," "human nature," "man," etc.) were an ostentatious act of resisting reading fixed concepts of the English language into the text and outmaneuvering easy translation matches. But all this was done explicitly in order to "understand and translate a work which belongs to a very different tradition from our own."[11] This assumed remoteness of Chinese culture concurred with the intuitions shared by Hawkes and other anthologists of Chinese lyrics. Providing more than one translation variant for some passages in his 1967 introductory book for nonspecialist readers, Hawkes tried to come to terms with what he identified as original indeterminacy and numerous possibilities of resolving it—each time only partially.[12]

Although it was often the perceived difficulty and ambiguity of the "oriental" language that led other anthologists and translators to similar conclusions,[13] distance between cultures could not be the only driving force for writers like Richards or Hawkes. In fact, the same point—about semantic ambiguities inscribed in words and terms—can be made about any language, at least one that did not develop in a vacuum. Subsequently, translation between any pair of languages (let alone communication within one language) will be prone to approximations of meanings and multiple possibilities of definition. It is true that some pairs have worked more closely and have established frameworks for mutual verbal exchanges throughout their shared history. Still, this does not erase the potential for ambiguity and polysemy in any of the words that have been in currency among past and contemporary users of the language.

Otherwise, it would be hard to explain the long-standing scholarly craft of translation glosses and multiple definitions, which have attempted to grasp a complexity of meaning between more closely related languages for centuries. It would be equally hard to justify the intellectual import of projects such as Barbara Cassin's *Dictionnaire des intraduisibles* (2004) and Emily Apter, Jacques Lezra, and Michael Wood's paradoxically translated edition of this, *Dictionary of Untranslatables* (2014); in these books, the editors and translators practically do the same thing as Richards but apply his appeal for multiple definition to a wide range of European languages. Cassin's original edited project and its English edition, too, resist smooth translation and instead collect chains of lengthy definitions, approximations, connotations, and interpretative contexts for understanding some key concepts and philosophical ideas that would be taken for granted in French or English. But this deconstructive instinct doesn't really need to originate from translations of abstract philosophical terms, nor does it have to come from the sense of cultural distance. In fact, the idea of shedding light on the original from as many perspectives as possible and providing more than one translation as a means of scholarly commentary can be much more intimate—it often starts at a more individual stage of working critically with texts written by other people, including those in other languages. Those of us working in comparative literature and modern languages who read literature written across languages but write in English or other vehicular languages will immediately recognize this nightmarish scenario and feeling of uneasiness. Your skin crawls when you have to quote a literary passage from a different language while making sure it fits your argument. Our decision is often not to cite it in the original but to provide a fair equivalent in the target language of writing (in my case in English, the common denominator of all languages these days)—a decision that might often require some extra tweaking. We try probing alternative renderings in search of the one that feels closest to our point and particular reading lens, or even come up with our own version in case no existing translation appears to fit the purpose. Either way, a given framework and specifically identified trait of the original text often dictates the terms of combing through possible variants and considering other translations than the one at hand. As a result of this procedure, a visible track record of different measures and multiple trials may be smuggled into the text. We leave a mark in the form of alternative propositions in brackets, enlisted in footnotes, divided by a slash, and so on. A sense of intellectual dissatisfaction with a single equivalent follows any in-depth reading whose findings have to be packed into one single formula. This is even more disheartening as they boil down to a combination of words and phrases, each of which constitutes a mere approximation of the original, written in a literary language systemically incongruous with the original language.

Now imagine that translators have the exact same dilemma for some words, lines, or sometimes even entire literary works. They come up with multiple versions in their heads, ponder over all possible choices, and sometimes even record them in their "translation memoirs"[14] (for instance, Daniel Hahn's *Catching Fire*)[15] or published "drafts" with side commentaries (for example, Joanna Trzeciak Huss's translations of Zuzanna Ginczanka's poems, including one titled "Side Commentary").[16] But otherwise, literary translators don't usually follow suit and do what academics do; they don't really place alternatives in footnotes, after slashes, or in brackets. Why wouldn't they just include all these versions, one after another, within their translated texts? This is where the dogma of translation as a single, well-rounded, and ready-to-read product comes into power. In his oft-quoted essay on "relevant translation," Jacques Derrida observed that a firm line is customarily drawn between academic and literary translation; the rule of thumb is that these types of textual practice should involve different degrees of quantitative equivalence to the source text. Thick translation with glosses and alternative variants, which "occurs daily in the university and in literary criticism," does not hold a candle to a translation formally equal to a work, "a translation worthy of the name."[17] But being formally and quantitatively equal to the original is a command that writers and translators have also struggled with. A well-known case in point is probably Vladimir Nabokov's infamous and intensely criticized translation of Pushkin's *Eugene Onegin*. It considerably extended the length of the original thanks to its "copious footnotes, footnotes reaching up like skyscrapers to the top of this or that page so as to leave only the gleam of one textual line between commentary and eternity."[18] Tangibly longer literary translations with footnotes, multiple solutions, or other markers of critical apparatus are lampooned for being pedantic, pedagogical, and nonliterary because they stop pretending they act on their own. They work against the audience's reading expectations—the habit of reading translations as primary literature—in that they too readily disclose their own interlingual and intertextual provenance.

Perhaps every literary translation to a degree includes criticism, gloss, and scholarship, as some would argue.[19] There is always something hermeneutic about translation, as it aims to explicate and comment on the literary work it simultaneously purports to represent. In fact, this argument could be easily reversed when speaking about translation multiples. Perhaps, besides an inherently academic element in every instance of literary translation, can we, likewise, search for an artistic one in its academic genre? In other words, there might be, after all, some creative potential dormant in the textual practice of translation criticism, with its tradition of glosses, encircling the originals from different analytic angles, squirreling multiple translations in anthologies, editing them collectively, and so on. Occasional fascination with translation apparatus creeps into modern translation books that experiment loosely with the convention. For instance, in *Yoko Tawada's Portrait of a Tongue: An Experimental Translation* (2013), Chantal Wright turns the commentary running in the margins of her rendering into a literary work as such. Others such as Aijaz Ahmad in *Ghazals of Ghalib* (1971), Hiroaki Sato in *One Hundred Frogs* (1983), Eliot Weinberger and Octavio Paz in *19 Ways of Looking at Wang Wei* (1987), Robert Wechsler in *Performing without a Stage* (1998), and Eugenia Loffredo and Manuela Perteghella in *One Poem in Search of a Translator* (2009) have combined the style of a translation workshop around a case study. In all these instances, the book concentrates on one work (Ghalib's Urdu love poetry, Matsuo Bashō's "old pond" haiku, Wang Wei's "deer park" poem, an excerpt from Homer's *The Iliad*, and Guillaume Apollinaire's "Les fenêtres," respectively) and applies to it a mixture of critical modes. These analytic tool kits may contain a philological lens, an editorial voice, an essayistic narrative, and an assemblage of creative responses to the poem. In some cases, the editors also resort to back-translations, an equally popular form of academic translation apparatus customarily used to record changes across the source and a different language version within one language as a common denominator. Cases in point may be Jon A. Lindseth and Alan Tannenbaum's *Alice in a World of Wonderlands* (2015), whose second volume displays an array of English back-translations of an eight-page excerpt from Chapter 7, "A Mad Tea-Party," of Lewis Carroll's *Alice in Wonderland* rendered across multiple languages; and Adam Thirlwell's chains of translations with each of "12 stories in 18 languages by 61 authors" going through an English version as a point of reference for English-speaking readers.[20] Otherwise, ensembles of artists and translators have fiddled with the format of single-author or single-work anthologies and edited volumes. For example, Daniel Halpern's *Dante's Inferno: Translations by Twenty Contemporary Poets* (1993) features multiple poets translating consecutive parts of Dante's work, while Michael Hofmann and James Lasdun, the editors of *After Ovid* (1994), commissioned English-language poets to engage in translation with Ovid's *Metamorphoses* and create a series of translation metamorphoses in its own right.

Many exciting translation projects of this kind, including translation multiples that I will introduce later, aim to challenge Derrida's "law of quantity" governing literary translation. Translation multiples in conceptual forms stay close to their scholarly lineage only insofar as they share the extended and multiplied editorial format. At the same time, they will also take these specific editorial and textual practices entrenched in translation culture to a completely new level. When multiplying translations of single words, passages, or whole works, both domains—the scholarly and the artistic—share the same intuition: that translation is never a finite and singular act, that there is never one "true" equivalent in a different language and literary culture, and that an inherent part of any translation process is pondering more than one legitimate interpretation of the original. At the same time, the artistic universe is governed by the same cultural, economic, or legal expectation that applies to most translations: that translation should be, ideally, a smooth read that conveys information equivalent to the original, and that it ought to substitute for its source text and reenact it for a foreign audience. What lies at the heart of similar multiplicative acts in multiplied translation is, therefore, friction between the prescriptively singular and the potentially plural. Whereas cultural and editorial standards customarily squeeze translation into an autonomous and ready-to-read product with only occasional discursive escapades, translation's immanently multiple nature kicks against this paradigm with more variants asking for their equal share.

Translation multiples clearly stand out in this respect as they openly appreciate translation's multiple nature, which otherwise remains behind the scenes. However, there is also something that distinguishes them from loosely dispersed compilations of different renderings put together for pedagogical purposes. First of all, as we will see in the next section, the emphasis shifts from the hermeneutic function of reconstructing meanings of the original to a more playful illumination of creative transformation. As this happens, some sort of formal conceit, overarching theme, or artistic reflection creeps into the texture of translation multiples. This is also what I call a "conceptual moment," a moment when separate translations no longer constitute dispersed, unrelated commentaries and approximations of original meanings. Instead, they become clustered together around a story that their author wants to tell us through the medium of translation. This story, a coherent narrative, can be deeply personal, visual, critical, or political—whether in relation to the nature of translation itself, to its multiplicity, or to any other artistic themes the story sets out to explore. Openly spelled out in some cases and more implicit in others, this conceptual quality, fueled by a broader critical intuition about the potential and the role of translation, is what characterizes more recent translation multiples. Reading them as conceptual artworks therefore marks an essential transition in their status.

Each contemporary genre of writing and phenomenon, however new and unique, has its unknown and quirky precursor somewhere back in the long history of literary activity. In a slightly provocative way, I will resort to one of them to introduce an imaginative framework for thinking about different sensual properties of contemporary translation multiples. A celebration of diversity inscribed in translation multiples in the present day was heralded by one of the most puzzling acrobatics of multiple translation. The unwitting harbinger of this genre is English chronicler and religious writer Sir Richard Baker, with his 1636 rendering of the Latin *Distichs of Cato*. Criticizing the attempt of his predecessor John Penkethman to translate Cato, Baker argued that "the words of one language cannot alwaies be reached by the very same words of another."[21] As a remedy to that incompatibility between English and Latin, he invented an alternative method in his *Cato Variegatus*. Translated with "variations of expressing in English verse," as the subtitle had it, this seventeenth-century rendering dismantled Cato's original couplets one by one through multiple English variants, in a number ranging from two to eighteen and with all enlisted one after another as "paraphrases or Collateral Conceits." In justifying his unconventional technique, or the "conceit of the Expressing" as he labeled it, Baker praised the potential of multiple translation, referring to the aesthetic ideal of pleasantly harmonious diversity in the world:

> This kinde of writing seems [...] not only an Exercise, but a Dillating of Invention; and if there were nothing else but the Variety; we see how much the Eye is delighted with varietie of colours in the same object; the Eare with variety of Descant upon the same Plaine song; & even Nature herselfe seemes delighted with it: [...] shee takes a pleasure in the variety of Formes.

Nourished by poetic conceits typical of seventeenth-century verse, Baker's variations on original lines reveal the complex process of negotiating between different interpretative choices and their literary realizations in English.[22] Conceptual variations and exercises in translation multiples such as *Cato Variegatus* make the scholarly and the literary merge into some hybrid borderland genre. In Baker's case, the aesthetically pleasing "variety of Formes" turned into a metacritical commentary on *The Distichs of Cato* and its multiplied viewing; and likewise, a multithreaded lesson about original works became inseparable from the act of indulging in different styles of verse translation.

While the two domains are inherently intertwined, Baker's "Collateral Conceits" also anticipated something more important. They point to the variety of approaches crucial to the contemporary acts of looking at, listening to, sensing, and critiquing different originals through the texture of translation multiples. Let us then look at, listen to, and stay attuned to the variety of forms in contemporary translation multiples. Although labeled "rare projects" by Walkowitz,[23] a strand of multiplied renderings of the same original passage or work brought together within one conceptual poem or book composed of multiples has come into being since the late twentieth century. While some of these cases test the texture of translation visually, and others aurally, somatically, or philosophically, all of them treat it as a springboard for reflection on the nature of literary language and its transformative power. In doing so, they treat the originals as a starting point into a much wider narrative.

Translation Multiples Tell Their Own Story

With an eye to these traits, let us plunge right into contemporary translation multiples published in the form of conceptual books and poems. Several examples keep recurring in literary criticism. To begin, we have Eliot Weinberger's *19 Ways of Looking at Wang Wei: How a Chinese Poem Is Translated* (1987), which compiles nineteen versions of a poem about a "deer park" by a ninth-century Chinese poet, including a transliteration, a character-by-character translation, and a series of different renderings—each with a commentary running on the right-hand page. There is Douglas R. Hofstadter's *Le Ton beau de Marot: In Praise of the Music of Language* (1997), eighty-eight translations of a sixteenth-century French poem by Clément Marot—created by Hofstadter himself, by Hofstadter in collaboration with others, and by friends, family members, colleagues, computer programs, and other people whose versions he solicited. Then, Caroline Bergvall, in her conceptual poem "VIA: 48 Dante Variations" (2000, 2005), puts together forty-seven opening tercets of Dante's *Inferno*, orders them alphabetically according to the first letter of the incipit in English, and couples each with the translation's author and date. It might seem at first glance that what links all these multiples is only the mere fact of compiling different renderings of one original. However, the fabric of serial translations in these works shapes up into a completely new overarching theme. The idea of multiplication becomes a pretext for expressing a sense of continuity and progression. Further translations arrive to embody consecutive afterlives of the original in various ever-changing forms.

Weinberger's *19 Ways of Looking at Wang Wei* completely redefined the scholarly convention of translation anthologies, tracing what Weinberger calls "19 incarnations" and "a nomadic life"[24] of a four-line verse by the eighth-century Chinese poet Wang Wei. The poem's title itself is already difficult to quote in

English translation, as it ranges from transliterations in the Latin alphabet to poetic phrases such as "The Form of the Deer," "Deep in the Mountain Wilderness," and "Deer Forest Hermitage." In a sense reformulating Walter Benjamin's understanding of translations as an original's afterlives into Buddhist categories, Weinberger explains on his part how "great poetry lives in a state of perpetual transformation, perpetual translation: the poem dies when it has no place to go."[25] As that journey unreels, it spans a phonetic transliteration, a character-by-character translation, and fourteen different verse renderings in English (as well as a Spanish[26] and a French version). It is the eponymous "19 ways"[27] of viewing the original that become the book's actual theme; even more so since, as Walkowitz rightly points out, "no original 'way' is presented" throughout the volume.[28] Weinberger underscores this concept in this title through sound: different Weis ("way-es") are a product of different *ways* of approaching this poem.[29]

What turns this volume into a conceptual translation multiple, however, is the idea of arranging consecutive renderings according to the act of "looking." For one thing, the book brings to the fore the visual aspect of Wang Wei's poetry[30] as well as that of the Chinese script with its "spatial relationships concretely portrayed" through the pictographic nature of ideograms.[31] This symbolically stretches the Chinese poem into more dimensions: the pictorial script is recast in language depending on various observation points, each limited by its singular perspective and blind spots. For another, it also echoes Wallace Stevens's cubist exercises in his imagist poem "Thirteen Ways of Looking at a Blackbird" and follows its technique by transposing the art of multiple viewing perspectives onto literary translation.[32] Differently framed, zoomed, and cropped snapshots of the original metamorphose the text analogously to the cubist's grammar of visual deconstruction, showing at the same time, as Baker wanted, "how much the Eye is delighted with varietie of colours in the same object." And so with a similar "Eye" metaphor at the back of his mind, Weinberger constructs a narrative around how different takes on the original couplet transform the perception of this short text. We can no longer be sure who is speaking throughout this translation multiple, depending on consecutive versions ("I hear," "we hear," "voices are heard," "yet—hear"), especially because, in fact, no one, or perhaps no human, appears to be there: "no one in sight," "no man is seen," "nobody ever comes," "I meet no one," "no glimpse of man," and so on. Where is the speaker, or where are the speakers, of this poem located, and what's their relation to the nonhumans and, indeed, to this ever-changing scenery? They seem to be facing a single "lonely" or "lone mountain" or "empty mountain," or otherwise they are positioned among "empty hills" or "empty mountains," or they may even be hidden somewhere "deep in the mountain wilderness." And we can't even know for sure what color exactly the moss is, as it scintillates with different shades, too, becoming "jade-green mosses," "dark green moss," "green moss," "shadowy moss," and so on, depending on the viewing perspective.

In the story that rounds off the Wang Wei translation multiples, Weinberger recounts his impression of Gary Snyder's translation, especially how he was puzzled by the word "above" referring to moss growing in the forest.[33] After his correspondence with the translator, it became apparent that Snyder (along with his Chinese teacher) visualized a different spatial arrangement in the poem: the original moss, according to his vantage point, grew up in the trees rather than on rocks on the ground. This elucidatory case of a reimagining of the poem eventually proved how Wang Wei's original "continued in a state of restless change" as various translators filtered it through their individual lenses. And while this final rendering seemed to satisfy Weinberger as a potential arrival point back in 1987, the 2016 reissue of the book "with more ways"[34] added to the list (numbered up to twenty-nine) proved that readers' excursion following Wang Wei's steps could be extended further as time went by.

While itself an exercise in poetic imagism, Weinberger's translation multiple may also be read along more pedagogical lines, blending elements of conceptual art and literary criticism. For one thing, just like variorum editions, *19 Ways of Looking at Wang Wei* records the history of the reception of Wang Wei's poem over several decades. According to Haun Saussy, this chronological sequence testifies to the changing image and voice of Chinese poetry in English since Ezra Pound's translations; as time progresses, readers of consecutive poems can better understand the scene in the deer park as the convoluted syntax gets simpler, the narrator retreats, and the focus shifts toward parallel and rhythmical constructions.[35] In reflecting on the historical evolution of this poetic idiom, Weinberger's translation multiples foreground how retranslations are indebted to previous versions by borrowing from existing solutions, but also how they implicitly critique their predecessors by offering a new quality in each innovation.[36] In this way, *19 Ways of Looking at Wang Wei* takes up the gauntlet to challenge a reductionist approach that tends to look at an individual translation out of its historical context and in abstraction from other versions. This is also why Weinberger attached a postscript to his book, where he caricatures the attitude of a "furious" professor who responded to his multiplied project in an angry letter and later confronted Weinberger in person.[37] According to Weinberger, the accurate, "philologically correct" crib of the Chinese poem by Peter A. Boodberg to which the professor referred resembles "Gerard Manley Hopkins on LSD." While Weinberger did not include this example in his numbered sequence of gradually transformed poems, he still presented it in full toward the end of the book (to be followed by "more ways" in the 2016 edition). By calling it "the strangest of the many Weis," Weinberger sidelined this version as a product of a too philological and pedantic approach; at the same time, despite this hierarchizing gesture, Weinberger gave it some room within the book and included it as a poetic curiosity, and as yet another fragment of Wei's convoluted route through various minds.

While Weinberger's ways of looking at Wang Wei cherish, in Baker's terms, the variety of the Eye, Douglas Hofstadter's book on translating Clément Marot's verse eighty-eight times principally explores the connection between the "Eare" and the "Forme." First published in 1996 as *Rhapsody on a Theme by Clément Marot*, with roughly half the final number of translations, the project then expanded into its full version of 1997, titled *Le Ton beau de Marot: In Praise of the Music of Language*. Having previously received the Pulitzer Prize for his *Gödel, Escher, Bach: An Eternal Golden Braid* (1979), which explored the common themes of symmetry, self-reference, and form across mathematics, art, and music, Hofstadter took up his next ambitious project with an eye to form and self-referentiality in translation. In these translation multiples, the act of reiterating Marot's poem many times stems from Hofstadter's interest in musical forms and the idea of a recurring musical theme, which becomes the book's organizing principle. This musical affinity is signaled in a few ways. First, the text known as "A une damoyselle malade" (To a Sick Damsel) or "Ma mignonne" (My Sweet), originally written by Marot in 1537, is treated here as musical notation that could be performed in at least eighty-eight different ways thanks to "the music of language" mentioned in the book's subtitle. The number of translations also alludes to the standard number of piano keys (eighty-eight); thereby, the idea of piano variations is also something that Hofstadter attunes us to hear. Whether emulating the looser structure of a "rhapsody" inspired by Sergei Rachmaninoff's *Rhapsody on a Theme of Paganini*[38] or "the rondo form, in which a given theme recurs periodically throughout a work,"[39] Hofstadter's book uses a musical narrative to construct his translation multiples around the original "pattern" or set of formal constraints he predefines. But this music of translation often ostentatiously goes against semantics. Hofstadter strongly criticized the camp of translators prioritizing the literal meaning, a manifesto that is perhaps most wittingly anticipated in the pun on *tombeau* (a grave) and *ton beau* (a beautiful tone) encoded into the book's cover. The image placed there (Marot's grave, *le tombeau de Marot*) reimagines the actual grave of the poet, which no longer exists.[40] It also alludes to the strand of musical or literary compositions commemorating the death of a notable person, especially in the French tradition,[41] for example Maurice Ravel's *Le tombeau de Couperin* (1919) or Stéphane Mallarmé's "Le tombeau de Baudelaire" and "Le tombeau d'Edgar Poe" (1914). At the same time, this grave, *le tombeau*, only seemingly clashes with the book's title (the beautiful tone of Marot, *le ton beau de Marot*) as the two merge in sound. It is in fact the beautiful tone of Hofstadter's translation exercises reviving the original forms that also symbolically restores Marot's memorial.

When constructing his narrative around multiple renderings, Hofstadter explicitly treats them as equally fascinating products of the mind's creativity: as he states, the question of "which one is the very best" and which ones should be rewarded with "gold, silver, and bronze medals" are "certainly not the point of the book—far from it."[42] These attempts range from various "literal" attempts debunking the notion of literalism in translation (2b–5b), to archaic and modern takes, to indirect renderings amid what he calls the "hall of mirrors" (50b–54b), to different takes by people with different professional backgrounds (French-English translators, colleagues, university students), his family members (mother, wife), as well as machine translators (65b–69b). In his parallel commentary and introductory chapters, Hofstadter also signals a few interpretative keys for reading his multiple experiment. He demonstrates how tentative each element of a translation series can be; in fact, knowing later attempts or versions by other people might completely change the original train of thought and translation process from the project's onset. In this sense, Hofstadter hints at the most essential purport of the book: "that every poem in [the] entire collection of 'Ma Mignonne''s is a translation of every other one,"[43] that any single translation is never abstracted from others and has to be seen as part of a natural extended progression, a variegated eternal braid—the multiple. One version can inspire another or influence it negatively by making the translator avoid overlaps in words,[44] but either way, the multiples are still all integrally interwoven.

In this spirit, *Le Ton beau de Marot* displays how each of Hofstadter's renderings is embedded in life and often depends on serendipity: his somewhat verbose and meticulous stories give a backdrop to the origins of different variants as they get intertwined with single occurrences, ideas, and decisions. As the project progresses, some of them become personal tributes to, for instance, his mother ("Mom in Yon," 70b) and, most poignantly, his deceased wife ("Carol Dear," 71b). It is especially the latter that influences the book's construction. Toward of the end of his work on the larger volume with Marot's translations, Carol Hofstadter comes to embody the titular "sick damsel." Her own rendering ("Chickadee," 72b) was tellingly placed as the ultimate version rounding off the whole sequence just before she died from brain cancer. In fact, the two final variants become a translatorial dialog between Douglas and Carol Hofstadter on the margins of Marot's poem. In his address to "Carol Dear," the husband explicitly consoles his wife after her surgery and offers her their favorite brand of Californian chocolates: "Have some See's!" Where the original text has Marot's own name inserted into the poem—"Car Clément / Le vous mande" (because Clément tells you to)—Hofstadter accordingly discloses the translator's identity: "Doug does need / His best pal, / So come, gal" (71b), replicating the poet's self-referential gesture. In her final response, "Chickadee" (72b), Carol Hofstadter envisions Marot's sick lady as a bird ensnared in a cage—rather than prison—which prevents it from flying away and fleeing the croup. In retrospect, this image could be read as a metaphor for the limitations of Carol's own body confining her movements and cognitive power, as the fatal tumor grew bigger. Adopting a very light-hearted tone, her final translation gets entangled with her own story as she bids farewell:

> Flu consumes
> Scrawny birds;
> Heed my words
> And take care.

Translation multiples in Hofstadter's project become the only recourse in dealing with death. They provide a smattering of continuity and a pretext for revival through repetition and reiteration. According to Peter Dayan: "[T]he sense of the importance of pattern, and of the preservation of pattern through the loss of the original matter in translation, is clearly wedded, in the book (just as content is wedded to form), to the way in which his wife, for him, remains alive, despite her physical disappearance."[45] Carol Hofstadter stays with the reader throughout the whole sequence as her version is also placed on the bookmark accompanying the book. This design suggests that Carol's voice guides all other renderings and resonates with them. At the same time, Hofstadter's own reverence for a pattern is solidified through recurring multiples; his meticulous braid of translations gives hope that the original is never lost as long as the power of language keeps resurrecting it over and over again. In a quest for eternity, Hofstadter's creative mind settles at no less than eighty-eight translations—perhaps pointing to yet another interpretation of the number 88 as a symbolic representation of infinity. The translation multiple is meant to extend its own structure endlessly as well as promise continuous revivals of the original form in a regenerative chain. In this sense, Hofstadter's sequence becomes a personal memorial (*tombeau*) to life marked with the epigraph: "To you, Carol, *ma mignonne*, from me, Doug, *ton beau*" (xxiv). Thanks to this translatorial rite, the afterlife promised by "Doug, *ton beau*" (Doug, your love), can come to fruition through form, a beautiful tone (*le ton beau*), which transcends and outlives its original body text.

A life journey along multiple twisted paths of different translations was also made by Caroline Bergvall, a poet and a multimedia artist whose work has often engaged with the idiom of translating, reworking, and rewriting. In her conceptual piece "VIA: 48 Dante Variations," first published as a sound performance in conjunction with the composer Ciarán Maher in 2000 and then, among others, in her poetry collection *Fig* (2005), she compiled forty-seven different English translations of the first three lines (terza rima) of Dante's *Inferno*.[46] Why does the title feature forty-eight versions, rather than forty-seven variations? When I first read this poem, it reminded me of the "hidden triangle" puzzle in which one has to count triangles in the image, but most people don't spot the biggest triangle encompassing all the little ones. This is also the way this translation multiple works: the final variation on Dante is the "big" one including all the little ones. Bergvall treats the whole poem, the very act of placing different translations next to each other and its performance, as the forty-eighth legitimate take on Dante.[47]

Another arguably unusual aspect of Bergvall's compilation is its arrangement. In putting the versions in alphabetical rather than chronological order, Bergvall rewrites traditional histories of reception and academic compilations of translations. Of course, her lyrical procedure is still clearly inspired by academic procedure. In her poem, she creatively emulates and reenacts the scholarly practice of ferreting in libraries and archives for research purposes. In her introduction to the 2005 version, Bergvall explains how she embarked on the project "to collate the opening lines of the *Inferno* translations as archived by the British Library up until May 2000."[48] Since the year 2000 marked the seventh centenary of Dante's commencing his own artistic journey, it could also become a sound cutoff date for her archival study. In an almost pedantic manner, Bergvall goes on to explicate her selection criteria for the forty-seven translations out of two hundred at hand and the way she framed the material. She adds for the record that two new translations were published after the cutoff. She switches to the passive voice when stating: "In all, 47 versions *were gathered*—once the two archived as missing, the one archived as under restoration and the multiple unaltered editions by the same translators *had been disregarded*" (my emphasis). In adopting this impersonal and methodical tone, Bergvall's commentary oscillates on the border of academese.

It is quite easy to find scholarly prototypes that Bergvall's poem could artistically appropriate. In 1957, the then president of the Dante Society, Ernest H. Wilkins, published "A Note on Translations of the *Divine Comedy* by Members of the Dante Society," whose textual shape is almost identical to and anticipates that of "VIA." Arranged numerically, the list contains renderings of *Inferno*'s first tercet introduced by the name of translator, date of publication, and form of rendition. The key difference, however, lies in the fact that all these variants are "listed in the order of their publication" (41), and not—like in Bergvall's case—alphabetically, following the first letter of the opening word. But then, is there any added value in Bergvall's exercise in this case? Her introduction and previous revisions would suggest that she found this organizing rule crucial to understanding her poem. In the earlier 2003 printed version of "VIA," she divides the sequence into two "series."[49] The first series consists solely of numbered translations, arranged alphabetically with no extra information. The second series immediately follows the first one and looks like a list of missing endnotes matching the names of translators and dates of publication with their respective variants. However, since these endnotes are not arranged by number but the translator's surname, their long list ends up in a seemingly random order: 20, 70, 46, and so on. In imposing the alphabetical arrangement on these two separate sequences, Bergvall fiddles with textual hierarchies and familiar principles of presenting translations. The alphabetical logic of cataloging plays havoc with the orderly apparatus of glossing translations with footnotes or endnotes. As the first one governs the other, it turns the scholarly order into a mix-up of disarranged annotations. At the same time, the identities of translators, even though pushed to the margins of the second series, still take precedence over the numerical order of references.

As Bergvall rewrote this poem in 2005 for her poetry collection *Fig*, she kept the alphabetical order as the poem's arranging principle but moved the figures of translators to the body text. Her cataloging gesture in this new, and what would become most often discussed, version of the poem lends itself to several readings. In rejecting the chronological order of publication, Bergvall dissented from the idea that multiple translation variants are there just to record the history of reception of the original text. As the alphabetical and the verbal principle prevailed, Bergvall rather suggested that translation should lead *via* language itself rather than history and time. Following this logic, readers of "VIA" would be first and foremost exposed to the literary medium of translation with its wandering and forking paths. And if so, where does this "via," the road, way, or path through (*via*) language, lead us? The actual fragment, reiterated and reenacted over and over again by different translators, features a speaker who admits to being halfway through the journey of life and to having lost the right path. As the translator's name and the date of publication follow each version, all these differently articulated statements appear to be voiced by different people with different dates marking the middle points of their own journeys.[50] Despite the numerical order and ostensible succession, there is in fact no progress throughout as each translator repeats the same scenario of going astray and not moving forward with their lives. Paradoxically, the only thing that changes here are the very words and images conveying this standstill. Though seemingly grinding to a halt, this translation multiple reveals the diversity of scenarios expressed in plural possibilities, in different means of expression and distinct literary idioms in English. Let us look at a small sample:

> 5. Halfway along the journey of our life
> I woke in wonder in a sunless wood
> For I had wandered from the narrow way
>
> (ZAPPULLA, 1998)
>
> 6. HALFWAY on our life's journey, in a wood,
> From the right path I found myself astray.
>
> (HEANEY, 1993)
>
> 7. Halfway through our trek in life
> I found myself in this dark wood,
> miles away from the right road.
>
> (ELLIS, 1994)

The sense of being lost is expressed in a kaleidoscope of possibilities. Even in the fragment quoted above, three translations juggle completely different images. Elio Zappulla describes the sudden realization of having lost one's way using Romantic poetics: the lyrical "I" in his translation "woke in wonder" as if experiencing an epiphany, waking up from a numb dream into spiritual recognition. This image is then confronted with the sober and transparent version in number 6,[51] where even the forest drops its symbolic darkness. The poem moves on with Steve Ellis's slangy version, whose perspective extends the journey spatially, placing the temporary stop in the long and arduous "trek" as far as "miles away" from the right "road" (rather than "path"). Three translations of the same stanza employ distinct cartographies and parameters to lead us to three differently mapped scenes.

28 CHAPTER 1

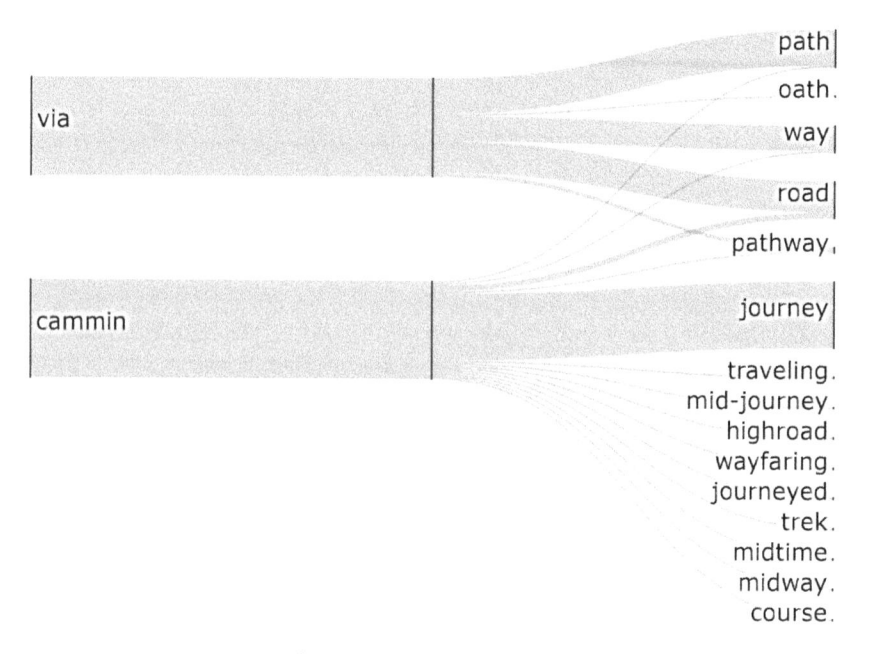

```
via  →  path
        oath
        way
        road
        pathway

cammin → journey
         traveling
         mid-journey
         highroad
         wayfaring
         journeyed
         trek
         midtime
         midway
         course
```

FIGURE 1.1. Kasia Szymanska and Krzys Brzezinski, "VIA: The Diagram of Forking Paths" (2020), showing how frequently different English translations of the words "via" and "cammin(o)" appear in Caroline Bergvall's poem "VIA." Note that the word "oath" for "via" (path) from Warburton Mayer Pike's 1881 version in number 43 was mistyped by Bergvall in the poem.

If we zoom out from this small sample to the whole sequence, each of these single words, phrases, and images will take us along similarly meandering routes. Let us take only two key words in the original Italian: "cammin(o)" (walk, way) and "via" (path, route), which Bergvall's multiple reiterates forty-seven times each (see fig. 1.1). In a distant reading of the poem, we can see how often the translators followed different routes when approaching just these two words and how many times they unexpectedly crossed paths. If we sketched a graph for each language unit or image in the sequence, Bergvall's poem would itself turn into a dark forest with thousands of forking paths. Some paths might be better trod, with a bigger group of translators heading in similar directions, while other translators wander off elsewhere. Still, despite the apparent linear sequence of Bergvall's multiple, the actual journey through its language leads astray on purpose. It tricks the poem's readers into a maze of multiple possibilities, making the reading process a lateral, rhizomatic experience.

Just like these two words forked in multiple directions, so did different ideas on what it actually means to get lost. In the course of the poem, "la diritta via," the ultimate aim and point of reference for all wanderings, also vanished from sight. Owing to a congregation of subjective and biased counselors, we are still none the wiser when listening about ways, paths, or roads that have all bent to different individual standards. They can be "direct," "straight," or "narrow" (emphasis on the shape); "straightforward" (emphasis on the ease of travel); or "true," "right," or "rightful" (emphasis on the moral trajectory). If at all, these diverse and individually defined goals in life must be understood and experienced at one remove. In Bergvall's own variation on Dante, her forty-eighth journey through all the previous reenactments and feelings of getting lost in the middle of different lives becomes exactly such a holistic but also very private act of comparison and recapitulation. Aged thirty-seven herself at the time, Bergvall stressed that the date of the poem's publication coincided with "Dante's 35th year or so-called point of midlife." And thus, while Weinberger includes his impressions and letters in his book and Hofstadter deals with his traumatic loss, Bergvall's ostensibly impersonal juxtaposition, too, reveals a deeply personal facet. It is her voice speaking from behind the multiples that provides a rationale for putting them together. In interweaving a subjective running commentary into her conceptual poem, Bergvall surrenders to a dynamic and transitional course of life with all its differently signposted routes.

As much as we can think of translation multiples in terms of voice and performance, using their material texture can also lead to picturing them in a very visual fashion. When juxtaposed next to one another, they visibly differ in shape, length, and sometimes arrangement on the page. Simply *seeing* the multiplicity of forms and various possibilities out there may be both aesthetically pleasing but also more challenging to process. It shouldn't come as a surprise that creators of translation multiples have also found this aspect particularly inspiring. In 2004, a Uruguayan artist based in New York, Alejandro Cesarco, came up with an idea similar to Bergvall's, though independently from her. He collected ten different English translations of *Inferno*'s first canto, a very diverse set that spanned over a century, and placed them alongside one another in his series of prints "Untitled (Dante/Calvino)" (see fig. 1.2), which were later displayed at the 2012 Deutsche Guggenheim's *Found in Translation* exhibition. The prints presented whole first pages from each of the translations, and each was headed with the title of one chapter from Italo Calvino's *If on a Winter's Night a Traveler*, a novel with a blatantly self-reflexive narrative composition. By bringing these two Italian classics together—one visually, the other allusively—Cesarco drew a parallel between translators and readers. Allusive captions commenting on the linguistic diversity in the series of printouts transposed "Calvino's postmodern understanding of an activated reader on the role of Dante's translators."[52] On the one hand, the captions bring to mind the seven readers from the penultimate chapter of Calvino's novel who stand for the audience's differently nuanced expectations. As these readers start sharing their views on reading, it becomes apparent that their preferences can never be reconciled. On the other hand, we observe a chain of visually and linguistically variegated renderings of *The Divine Comedy*'s first canto, into which each translator inevitably inserts their reading self. The effects of their distinct readings also cannot be reconciled in that they clearly never match one another. At the same time, we cannot be sure to what extent transformations that have taken place over a century are merely a result of the translator's interpretative preferences. Are there perhaps other forces and grand schemes, some sort of zeitgeist, that leave an indelible mark on the pliable and ever-changing language?

Either way, what this series of prints nicely visualizes is how translation multiples can redefine our reading practice. Cesarco is known for his artistic projects bringing to the fore textual elements that are customarily pushed aside and not treated as seriously as the main text. A few years earlier, in 2000, his exhibition *Index* displayed pages with an index for an imaginary book; that exhibition as well as subsequent ones focusing on different imaginary indexes encouraged viewers to read a nonexistent text *à rebours* by thinking of potential links to indexed words. In 2006, his exhibition *Footnotes* was a showcase of a series of footnotes placed on the bottom of a wall; such placement referred to an invisible text above. In these cases, Cesarco challenged viewers' reading habits. Just like no one reads only indexes, no one really reads footnotes for their own sake (except for readers of Nabokov's *Pale Fire*, or of Gibbon's *Decline and Fall of the Roman Empire* perhaps); everyone prefers to skip them in favor of the main text. But then again, what really is the main text, and how can it be separated from its constitutive elements? Analogous points could be made about reading multiple translations. It is not really customary to read more than one translation of the same work at one go, let alone read multiple translations one after another. No one really goes to a bookshop to search for several translations of the same work in order to cherish "the variety of Formes," as Baker would have it. But if that's the case, then who gets to decide which translation lands on our desks, when each of them is different from one another and none of them can be, by definition, equivalent to the original? Displaying and visualizing material connections and textual alternatives that usually remain behind the scenes, Cesarco alerts readers to the limitations of their comfort zone and cognitive laziness.

FIGURE 1.2. Alejandro Cesarco, "Untitled (Dante/Calvino)" (2004). Courtesy of the author.

The visual texture of translation multiples, in particular the potential of their seriality and spatial relations, is also where they can reinstate their own plurality most tangibly. Generated plural versions across a book's "turnable" pages, linear arrangements of translation series, and accumulated variations of one text spread out on a single page all exploit the potential of printed form and visual arts for their own purposes. Of course, the seriality of translations is and will be more and more efficiently facilitated by digital publishing, and it is in that context that Walkowitz mentions cases such as Uljana Wolf's bilingual *Falsche Freunde* (False Friends) and Augusto de Campos's concrete poetry in the 2010 and 2011 issues of the journal *Telephone*.[53] At the same time, one could also think of earlier projects in the North American context for which granting more space to multiple translations in print became intertwined with the projects' "bookish" format or simply their standard page layout. I will later discuss an example from *Chain* (1994–2005), a New York–based magazine printed in one thousand copies per issue, whose 2003 issue "Translucinación" featured poets such as Charles

Bernstein, Caroline Bergvall, and Rosmarie Waldrop who engaged with chains of translations, multilingual juxtapositions, and variations on Oulipo works. But the same could also apply to the 2000 volume *Reft and Light: Poems by Ernst Jandl with Multiple Versions by American Poets* edited by Waldrop[54] and three books with Bashō "frog haiku" multiples: Hiroaki Sato's "Translating into English" from *One Hundred Frogs* (1983), Gary Barwin and Derek Beaulieu's *Frogments from the Frag Pool* (2005), and Steve McCaffery's *The Basho Variations* (2007).[55] I would argue that in these cases the possibility of arranging translation multiples on the page or on consecutive pages contributes to the whole artistic effect. Translation multiples become visually and tangibly serial and ornamental, and they often start acting as visual poetry in their own right. Arranged in chains and patterns, they comment on their own plurality and bring to the fore quantitative tensions that are probably not visible at first glance.

This is certainly true of Waldrop's *Reft and Light*, in which translation multiples are a method of coming to terms with the linguistic and spatial experimentation of Ernst Jandl, an Austrian postwar visual poet. While poet-translators in the volume negotiate between sound, image, and lyrical form, they often collectively produce more than one English version for each poem in German. Translation multiples conveniently come to the rescue in this venture: "[H]ere is an experiment: several American poets respond to each poem so that the original is encircled by multiple English analogues."[56] Tackling the original from different angles, according to Waldrop, could at least make it possible "for the procedures to be imitated." But it is striking how the whole "experiment" in multiple translations also transposed Jandl's visual and linguistic procedures into the texture of translation and its material arrangement. In a few instances, a formal trick of reiterating different "encircling" attempts cleverly interact with the layout and graphic space within the volume. This is, for example, the case with the original poem titled "reihe" (row/series), consisting of ten misheard consecutive numerals (from one to ten) shaped in a word-per-verse column. As various poets reiterate it in their own variants,[57] the poem enters a multiplied "series" on its own—a translation series with differently played-out multiples. Three of these different renderings placed next to each other are each titled "series" (Benjamin Friedlander, Laynie Browne, Martine Bellen); another one mishears the "series" into "cherries," "ceres," "seers," "jerries," and "cerise" (Ray diPalma), triggering five respective sequences of translation; others extend the potential renderings into 4 × 4 or 9 × 10 tables (Julie Patton, Lytle Shaw), making a host of misheard words resonate with one another in numerous directions. In ostentatiously multiplying the original "series" of misheard numerals, Waldrop's ensemble implies that their generated series of translations contain similar instances of mishearings and misheard sequences that may equally occur in the translation process. Since these long chains of deliberate "mistranslations" spread both around the page and across pages, they often take advantage of the original minimalist form and fiddle with its material shape. As the book abounds with miscellaneous renderings throughout, the poets assemble translation multiples into ornaments and textual patterns, and thus create a form of visual translation poetry in its own right (39–40, 55, 57).[58] These new lateral ways of reading the multiples make us rethink the standard order of reading from top to bottom, from left to right, or from original to translation. Instead, they invite us to indulge in meticulously arranged translation multiples, navigating the series in reverted orders, and indeed, as Jandl would have it, reading from "reft to light."

A similar visual potential of multiples has become a driving force for creative renderings of Bashō's frog haiku over the past decades. This famous haiku is primarily known in the oft-quoted translation from 1952 by R. H. Blyth, which reads as follows:

>The old pond;
>A frog jumps in—
>The sound of the water.[59]

The generative potential of this haiku comes into play, for example, in the already mentioned *One Hundred Frogs* with its chains of frog translations, encompassing self-contained multiples across genres such as "Ten Variations on Bashō's 'Frog and Pond' Haiku" by William Matheson and limerick and sonnet versions by Alfred H. Marks, to mention but a few. It also involves projects from the Canadian avant-garde poetry scene building on famous multimodal translations by bpNichol and Dom Sylvester Houédard,[60] namely the aforementioned *Frogments from the Frag Pool* (2005) by Gary Barwin and Derek Beaulieu and *The Basho Variations* by Steve McCaffery (2007). While these texts amount to visual and conceptual poems in their own right, putting together such artistic gems also provides a decorative feast for the eyes. The books literally teem with haiku multiples as if the frog jumping into an ancient pond over and over again intended to leave multiple water ripples—marks of its constantly recurring presence.

It is also only due to multiple frogs in translation that quantitative ambiguities already inscribed in the original are brought to the fore. The tensions occur with regard to singularity and plurality. First, the translation multiples place the allegedly singular frog against its translated descendants, while in fact the number of frog(s) in the original Japanese is already unclear (*kawazu* can mean both "frog" and "frogs"). Second, the multiples ostensibly juxtapose the single original and plural translated versions, even though Bashō had actually revised the original, producing more than one textual base to be translated in the first place. Then, another apparent contrast can be seen between the haiku's minimalist form and its extended chain of translated transformations—something that offers an interesting twist on the original longer form, *renga*, with haiku serving only as its constituent part.[61] Finally, since there is an apparent tension between the haiku's individual authorship and the collaborative crowd of translators, the multiples revise another preconception about the author's singularity. The collectiveness is already embedded in the original writing context of Bashō's haiku, as it was created during the so-called frog contest (*kawazu awase*), a gathering of poets writing on the subject of frogs. And thus, even though every new frog hopping into the ancient pond "plops into oblivion" in its singularity, according to one of Cyril Patterson's renderings,[62] the visual succession still inculcates some sense of continuity. Each of these jumps becomes a modest contribution to the long tradition of conversing with the Bashō poem, with translators each time reading and approaching it anew.

In the same vein, visual and spatial relations underpin another case of multiples that take Guillaume Apollinaire's "Les fenêtres" (The Windows) as their point of departure. In their book *One Poem in Search of a Translator*, Eugenia Loffredo and Manuela Perteghella invited twelve translators and artists to explore the poem's original multimodality in plural renderings.[63] Since Apollinaire had been inspired by a series of Robert Delaunay's geometrical paintings under the same title (*Les fenêtres*, 1912–1913), the multiples based on his poem recast the image of windows into translation in several ways. Similarly to Weinberger's cubist ways of looking at Wang Wei, Apollinaire's translators open the original windows onto a palette of scintillating images. Some of the translators create more than one rendering to offer multiple viewings of the poem from different vantage points (e.g., Tom Paulin's "The Windows" 1, 2, and 3). Some follow Apollinaire's own poetics and his poem's ekphrastic use of colors as they refract the original sequence of red, green, and yellow into prismatic multimodal translations. This is the case with George Szirtes's "Three Windows," Maggie O'Sullivan's "Windows Opening," and Martin Sorrell's "Windows," all of which engage with the texture, shape, and color of Apollinaire's windows to further establish a visual and conceptual affinity with the original paintings. The cubist composition and simultaneity present in Delaunay's paintings such as *Simultaneous Windows on the City* and *Windows Open Simultaneously* (1912) are reimagined into the multiplicity of different translations. As plural renderings are exhibited next to one another in the volume, this sense of simultaneity and continuity could justify a reorientation of perspective in our reading practice. This is why Loffredo and Perteghella in their introduction explicitly invite readers to embark on this "translational journey" in whichever order they want, since the book should not be necessarily read in a linear fashion.[64]

While very much anchored in the visual dimension of textual reiterations, such a perpetual process of unfolding the original into variegated sequences and assemblages also sparks reflection on a more metaphoric aspect of translation multiples. Like a reel of film with changing frames, their construction becomes a capacious figure for a quest for language or travel through time, with translation and its different forms leaving an imprint on our experience. This is the case when Weinberger speaks of "reincarnations" and "nomadic life," Bergvall leads us along *via*, "a life path," and Loffredo and Perteghella take us on a "translational journey." Translation multiples send us on long treks and faraway travels, propel the sense of continuity or movement forward, and extend our horizon spatially and historically. In looking at all renderings together and seeing each of them in context, readers understand how the pieces of the puzzle fit together. Reading multiples always means observing from a better vantage point and with a wider vision.

Not unlike Bergvall and Weinberger, Sawako Nakayasu in her poetic cycle "Promenade"[65] from *Mouth: Eats Color; Translations, Anti-Translations, and Originals* (2011) also imagines her translation multiple as a sort of physical and mental travel. In approaching the original Japanese poem by Chika Sagawa under the same title, Nakayasu reenacts her walk on the eponymous "promenade" at least seventeen times. Her seventeen translations of the same poem are enlisted as versions 1–9, A–C, and a few others with markers in other scripts, some with no subtitles and some with elaborate ones (e.g., "Pass the hand over a life as fleeting as the dew)." As a result of this procedure, the cycle in the volume spans various language combinations mixing English, French, and Japanese, as well as different scripts (the Latin alphabet, and kanji and katakana, the Japanese phonetic script used for foreign pronunciation). According to Irina Holca, Nakayasu also included other experimental versions into the mix, such as one that is likely a result of "typing English words with a Japanese keyboard."[66] When read against Nakayasu's other book of Sagawa translations titled *The Collected Poems of Chika Sagawa* (2015, 2020), it is clear that the "Promenade" cycle gave her leeway to both extend Sagawa's multilingual poetics in translation as well as reimagine her modernist work through multiplied renderings of one poem. In fact, Nakayasu treated *Mouth: Eats Color* as her alternative take on Sagawa, which explicitly "foregrounds the multilingual."[67] In her introduction to Sagawa's 2015 collection, she further commented on Sagawa's original multilingual writing: Sagawa's poetry combined Japanese with words in Portuguese, Dutch, German, French, and English, which went against the Meiji-era and early twentieth-century "institutional efforts to standardize the Japanese language."[68] Just like in Sagawa's case, Nakayasu's translations also go against the grain: some of these densely multilingual renderings are definitely hard to read and may appear impenetrable, especially for a largely monolingual audience of global English. It is through the potentially laborious process of sequential and comparative reading across these more and less "difficult" versions that individual elements of the multilingual puzzle may come together. In some instances, translations that are less multilingual may shed light on those that are more, as some English variations of terms or transliterated concepts such as "hitomi" and "higurashi" come to the rescue and fill in the gaps in understanding.

While wedded to the idea of difficult multilingualism, Nakayasu also wanted, in her own words, to "blow it up" and abstract herself from "certain established ideas about translation."[69] Well aware that her translations of Sagawa are "only one out of a myriad ways that each poem might be rendered in English,"[70] she especially wanted to let go of the usual "one-to-one relationship: one translation per poem."[71] Stretching out this narrow convention, Nakayasu composed her cycle of over a dozen variants, each reflecting the repeated experience of seemingly the same place, every day at the same time. The cycle visibly juggles different forms of conveying the same point in time ("trois o'clock," "午後三時," "three o'clock afternoon," "3:00pm," "three-time meridian," "15:00") and registers distinct ways of capturing the unique twists and impressions of what happened during the walk on the titular promenade. On the one hand, these translation multiples still lend themselves to multilingual reading: perhaps all these versions reflect what is going on in the brain of a multilingual person who sees the world through a mix of idioms, metaphors, and images across different languages. On the other hand, spreading a fan of possible scenarios, Nakayasu brings to the fore the transformative power of translation as well as its arbitrariness and serendipity. Depending on the vantage point, perspective, and style employed in a single rendering, the same poem could change and scintillate with different images—just like a different detail can catch the eye during a regular walk in a familiar place. In this way, Nakayasu's multiples with her personal viewings of the "promenade" stretch out into a long passage through translation, a never-ending walk on the promenade in its own right.

In one of the "Promenade" versions, a prose poem modeled on a meticulous report, Nakayasu also smuggles in a self-referential question giving a cue of her translation procedure: "[W]hy take things so literally?"[72] Allowing herself to not pack the translated poem into one exact, finite version, Nakayasu treats the recurring possibility of expressing the poem anew as leeway for imagining alternative stories with different endings to the passing day: "Sunset bound" ("Purmunaado 1"), "Sun late capping promise" ("Purmunaado 5"), "Promise me no day" ("Purmunaado 6"), "Some promise-less day comes to an end" ("Promenade A"), "The day makes no promises, regardless of season" ("Promenade" [Report]). Translation multiples pave the way for Nakayasu to reimagine and relive the same walk over and over again through time. As the speaker rewinds and replays the same scene, she each time learns something new about her registered memories and responses to the scene, and also about herself. This possibility is granted to her thanks to the tranquil progression of translation multiples, which reward her for waiting for yet another chance and hoping for some sort of continuation. "I am a promise that goes beyond a single day," ends one of the multiples, "Purmunaado 9." Again, we are not sure whether this promise of duration comes from the poem's speaker or refers to the almost transcendental act of repetition through translation.

When authors of translation multiples interweave their personal stories into the matter of translation, they usually embrace the diversity of reading as a constructive and creative form of expression. But there is also a flip side to that coin. Sometimes a more pessimistic reckoning comes to the fore: for some of us, the act of multiplying can be distracting and alienating; the multiples place their readers at several removes from the text. Since it is impossible to retrieve original senses, what else are we left with? A more critical strand of translation multiples dwells on similar questions, arguing that translation does not facilitate communication across languages, but on the contrary, it always leaves us with misunderstanding and a sense of dissatisfaction. This might be the case in the translation multiple by Allison Cobb and Jen Coleman entitled "Come Out of Works: A Physical Translation."[73] This collaborative project appeared in the previously mentioned 2003 issue of *Chain* magazine, "Translucinación," edited by Jena Osman and Juliana Spahr. The translator duo focus on a fragment from the Chinese philosopher Chuang Tzu. With the help of Burton Watson's 1964 literal translation, the authors transform Chuang Tzu's text into six English poetic renderings, each time approaching the original differently "through the fog of physical world."[74] Their series of Chuang Tzu translations involves different senses in the original's reception and generates multiple oblique and veiled readings, for instance "with the Noise of the Shower Running," "from Behind Smeared Glasses," and "Hearing Chuang Tzu While Not Looking at the Writing Page," to mention a few. The translators consciously follow the lessons of the philosopher, who saw the Tao through the world's physical features such as animals and landscapes. In taking his original ideas as a credo, Cobb and Coleman transpose them into their own "physical translation" by means of their own bodies. They rely on hearing, sight, and physical movement—all anchored in the present day but also impeded by contemporary devices and material objects: a shower, a cell phone, a street, a check-cashing office, smeared glasses. With the help of other distractors, the boundaries of sense and cognition obscure the translation multiple in the same way Chuang Tzu would understand it: "[T]he lessons of Chuang Tzu were shaped and obscured by the passing of time and boundaries of language."[75] It is therefore the visceral and multisensory reading that inevitably blurs and distorts the original; it filters the text through the translator's own sensual apparatus.

To a certain extent, this idea questions the possibility of reaching a "somatic equivalence" in translation as postulated by Douglas Robinson in his book *The Translator's Turn*.[76] By the same token, it might partly echo Clive Scott's longstanding agenda of sensual and phenomenological variations of French and German poetry.[77] For Scott, the experience of reading a poem in a different language can be dismantled in various ways, including a focus on prosodic, rhythmical, and visual qualities, and then creatively translated into various graphical, spatial, and visceral markers (e.g., doodles, a bolded font). Cobb and Coleman, however, treat their exercise in senses with a more skeptical aim. In their multiples of Chuang Tzu, their "physical translation" no longer provides various artistic means of recording the richness and variety of experiencing a poem. What we get instead are fragmentary lines ("A bird look day"), clunky misappropriations ("You shall music in the wild / Fly off or dive / to the fish and thrive. Or die."), and hectic, almost frenzied multiple creations ("all creatures come out of works," "creatures come to the mysterious works," "produce produce produce / mysterious works go back to them"). This exercise in physical translation sets a boundary between the text and its reader, the interpreter who is always doomed to fail. The phenomenological take on Chuang Tzu provides a deliberately limiting paradigm of various distracted and never exhaustive approaches; it highlights how "physical translation," just like "physical world," can draw us away from experiencing the equivalent of Tao in our times, whatever it may be.

Anne Carson takes an equally skeptical stance in her "A Fragment of Ibykos Translated Six Ways," later included in the book *Nay Rather* (2014). In this translational collage, Carson renders a passage of Ibycus's poem[78] first literally and then by employing various limited vocabularies as verbal filters, such as John Donne's poem, Bertolt Brecht's FBI file, Samuel Beckett's play, Gustav Janouch's

Conversations with Kafka, signs in the London Underground, and a manual for her microwave. In Ibycus's original, a luxuriant garden standing for the organic growth of love in young women is contrasted with the speaker's own unsettled and harrowing desire illustrated by a fervent Thracian wind. In her constrained rewritings of the poem, Carson explores other ostensibly conflicted phenomena over time, starting with a woman's nature and marriage contracts (filtered through Donne's "Woman's Constancy"), through the tension between an individual— "the subject"—and the state apparatus with all its official classifications (a variation on Brecht's FBI file), through life and death (a variation on Beckett's *Endgame*), and ending with the difference between heating and defrosting food (a variation on the new Emerson 1,000-watt microwave oven). As the poem unfolds, subsequent narrating minds are torn apart and preoccupied with a host of dramatic issues revolving around feminism, human liberty, existentialism, travel and movement, and consumerism. In the process, readers can notice how different reiterations map a progress toward more modern language, officialese, and even technical, dehumanized idiom.

Even though the Ibycus multiples at first glance look completely different from one another in terms of language and poetics, Carson anchors them in a scaffolding of unchanged elements throughout the series. All renderings follow a similar grammatical and rhetorical pattern, spread over several linguistic signposts: "and [...] beneath," introducing some hidden meanings; the contrastive connectives "on the one hand ... on the other hand," dramatizing the poem's recurring antithesis;[79] and a very distinctly rendered English phrase "nay rather," continuing the sharply sketched contrast with an elaborate image ("like [...] accompanied by ..."). This schematic frame smoothly propels a stream of thoughts and ideas into the succeeding reiterations. And how easily does literary language slip into clichés, "stock phrases" (from the variation on Kafka), and convenient fillers providing lexical padding to the rhetorical scaffoldings! In this radical exercise, consecutive translators rush to transpose Ibycus's inner conflict into their own dilemmas and the ills of their times, applying a constrained set of categories and overused phrases. In a sense, Carson implies that Ibycus's metaphors of garden and wind, which themselves might wax banal from today's perspective, have found modern equivalents in hackneyed phrases such as "mind the gap," "expect delays," "please turn to page," "I shouldn't think so," and "flip the pieces halfway through," all familiar from different textual universes. By weighing and equating these parallel worlds, Carson could also suggest that the language of poetry has gradually exhausted its linguistic resources over time. Ibycus's original rhetorical matrix acts here almost like an ancient prototype of a poetry generator gone wrong. In the final iteration, even the microwave's manual ends up reproducing a dramatic conflict in a chain of beautiful-sounding phrases. Introducing ostensibly antithetical ideas about the fast preparation of food, a dilemma redolent of the contemporary lifestyle, this variant manages to squeeze alliterations and rhythmic fricatives out of phrases such as "steak sauce [...] sprinkled with paprika" and "properly position the [...] popcorn popper." How do these images and poetic sequences compare to those of Ibycus? How do they *translate* into each other and to what extent are all other variants "translated" in the traditional sense of the word, to take Anne Carson's title at face value?

In 2013, Carson incorporated this translation exercise into the ending of her republished essay "Variations on the Right to Remain Silent." Arguing how one language cannot be exactly rendered into another, she dooms her travels between these distinct lexicons to the inevitable act of translating into clichés and "wrong words."[80] Carson's starting point for the essay is the interlingual trial of the illiterate Joan of Arc, which allowed the judges to manipulate Joan's statements by translating them into convenient formulas. In discussing this case alongside her translation multiple, Carson makes a strong point about the rhetorical and causative power of language, always working at someone's expense. The recurring theme of "A Fragment of Ibykos Translated Six Ways" is different acts of naming, pigeonholing, and translating into categories, which can bear very concrete consequences. The institution of marriage from the variation on Donne is one of "those contracts": lovers are supposed to "foreswear the persons that [they] were" and change their legal status by means of a pronounced "vow." Brecht's files create a range of names for "subjects" whose true identities are "suitably paraphrased" into the FBI's quirky classifications ("known Communists," "Mr & Mrs Bert Brecht," "a certain Frenchman," "an unknown man," "an unknown woman"). In the variation on Gustav Janouch's *Conversations*, Kafka's words (as reported by Janouch, as translated by Goronwy Rees, as rewritten by Carson through Ibycus) refer directly to "modern armies, / accompanied by lightly spoken phrases." Equipped with fixed terms and clichés, these armies can change the course of history by sleight of hand. In laying claim to validity and relevance for real actions, translations between different words intervene in the histories, identities, and statuses hidden underneath them. By forcing the cliché onto the individual, these modern armies come into power "where everything human [has been betrayed]," as Carson's editorial interpolation hastens to tell us to fill a gap in the original fragmentary text.

While Carson's reiterations might not meet traditional translation norms philologically speaking, the title of the poem still features the Ancient Greek poet as "translated six ways." Not giving herself any slack with another "softer" term (rewritten, transformed, adapted?), Carson consciously makes a statement about the practice of translation with all its baggage of standards and expectations. Furthermore, as the text is said to be translated "six ways," we cannot be exactly sure which texts out of seven identically marked renderings she has in mind. Should we exclude one variant from the list of six translations, or do the ways of translating denote verbal transfers between any two versions? Either way, by acknowledging the exercise as legitimate ways of translating, we have to accept, in Rosalind Harvey's words, that "the arbitrary act of shifting from one sign system to another—here made beautifully explicit—is a deadly serious game with no right answer."[81] But the question here arises: In which case do we more readily accept this arbitrariness? Should the final microwave version be treated on an equal footing with the first philologically rendered Ibycus? Which wrong words in fact get us farther from Ibycus, an author who is already remote to us temporarily and linguistically: the ones filtered through the poetic diction of John Donne and others, or Carson's own philological translation in contemporary English, which is supposed to stand for an accurate, literal version of expressive means belonging to Ancient Greek? After all, we no longer have access to that world and need to restore a whole literary universe from nonmatching elements of our own familiar reality. In other words, all these bits and pieces might, too, end up forcing Ibycus's world into a series of convenient clichés. And it looks like the only thing we can do "in the event that all the captions are not correct," as Brecht's FBI files instruct us, is to simply turn to a different page.

It is curious to see the same exercise in the contemporary English of the London tube stops and signs:

> At the excess fare window, on the one hand, the king's bakers,
> ditching old shepherds for new elephants,
> where east and west [cross north]
> and beneath black friars forbidden from barking in church,
> angels
> mind the gap.
> On the other hand,
> a multi-ride ticket does not send me padding southwark.
> Nay rather, like the seven sisters [. . .].

This translation of Ibycus reads almost like a legend or an old tale, but it is in fact composed of hidden proper names: the names of stops on the London Underground. King's Cross, Baker Street, Shepherd's Bush, Elephant & Castle,

Blackfriars, Barking, Angel, Paddington, Southwark, Seven Sisters—all very specific places on the London map—have lost their source referents and no longer send us back to the original historical and geographical markers. This part of the poem is therefore made of pure signs (quite literally, the signs visible every day in the London Underground). Although they have now gained a new semantic function and direct the movements and actions of millions of people daily, their true meanings have been radically redefined. In the same way, the meanings of words in Ancient Greek fade out when taken out of the original context and appropriated through a violent narrative power of translation. In order to make sense of classical originals, translators need to force loose snippets of a bygone world into a full-fledged and consistent story. This is something that Carson had courageously opposed many times before, in particular in her ostentatiously fragmented renderings of Sappho and in advocating "the right to remain silent" and refraining from translation. At the end of the day, incommensurable dictionaries from these translation multiples are doomed to be "untranslatable" in the traditional sense of the word, a conjecture that Carson puts forward through the radical gesture of generating more and more jarring mismatches.

In all of these conceptual works, translation multiples play first fiddle. They completely redefine the familiar academic practice of compiling several variants and encircling the original in a hermeneutic quest for the meaning. As they enter a more experimental realm, poets and artists staying behind the multiples more and more boldly lay claim to the textual practices typical of the scholarly domain; they step more confidently into what had previously been the primary, if not exclusive, territory of multiplied translations. In this way, under the banner of translation multiples, these authors unfold a much wider narrative. Through their personal stories and responses to the multiple nature of translation, they give vent to their delights and creative outbursts but also voice their fears, traumas, and skepticism. They see the multiples as a journey, as promise of continuity or progress, a liberating force, a visual and experimental zone, but also as a way of testing translation's own possibilities and limitations. This is the story that translation multiples courageously keep telling beyond the letter of the translation.

2

Ethics of the Multiple

This kind of experiment would have its philosophical usefulness.
—*MULTIPLES*, BY ADAM THIRLWELL

Against the Grain

Translation multiples are not easy reads; they require attuning oneself to a new reading mode. As they veer off from familiar patterns of representation, they expose all the procedural machinery and inner workings that otherwise remain behind the scenes. While these works most often reside in conceptual books and poems composed of multiples in print, their authors are openly dissatisfied with the usual editorial practice of producing single and ready-to-read translations. They consciously go beyond what Sawako Nakayasu calls the "one-to-one relationship"[1] between original and translation and ask for more space in print. In the current publishing culture that favors single translations, this becomes a subversive gesture.

At the same time, even though translation multiples are literary products of the global lingua franca, they also question its unfair rules and biases. While the circulation of translated literature in English is palpably limited, translation multiples demand more airtime and visibility. They not only want to hijack the attention of English readers by reinventing the format of the conceptual book and the idea of verse. Oscillating between conceptual writing and literary translation, they also reinstate the position of translation as something equally or even more creative than what passes as "original writing." While no one has really written a manifesto of translation multiples, these works go against the grain and undermine many cultural norms and expectations, starting with the very "law of quantity" mentioned by Jacques Derrida. But, in fact, the subversive potential of multiples could also be better seen in a bigger picture of "experimental translations"[2] and in relation to previous projects of the kind. What the multiples have to offer now is also to continue the works of those before them.

The subversive genre of translation multiples is not an isolated case in twentieth-century Anglophone and European literary production. In fact, some "experimental" translation procedures revisit a range of literary and translation legacies. In particular, we can think here of the avant-garde, the modernist translation innovations under the aegis of Ezra Pound, the Oulipo with their notion of constrained writing, the Fluxus movement with their chance operations, and the American L-A-N-G-U-A-G-E poets with their focus on the uses of language. In her *Unoriginal Genius*, Marjorie Perloff argues that the current "unoriginal" creative writing became the new rear guard (*arrière-garde*), renewing previous avant-garde discourses and trying to complete the mission especially by the poetic means of reinvention, rewriting, citation, or, indeed, translation.[3] This argument was continued by Kenneth Goldsmith in *Against Expression*[4] and then Jacob Edmond in his *Make It the Same*, both of whom link the vanguard ideas of artistic replication, "cut-and-paste" literature, and reiterative poetics to global cultural change and new media technologies. In turn, translation at the service of literary production in the new age would therefore serve as a full-fledged artistic idiom that tests our assumptions about language, creativity, and originality just like modernist literature could. This is particularly true of experimental translations "in the age of algorithmic production," as argued by Lily Robert-Foley.[5] By transgressing translation norms, experimental translations keep moving the boundaries even further and redefine the rules of the game.

But in fact, each of the strands of experimental translation attacked from a different side and had its own enemy to unhorse. For instance, throughout the twentieth and twenty-first centuries we have witnessed the emergence of homophonic translations. The most oft-quoted examples across different languages include Semyon Kirsanov's "Osen" (1925), Ernst Jandl's "oberflächenübersetzung" (surface translation) (1964), Louis and Celia Zukofsky's *Catullus* (1969), and several projects by Charles Bernstein. The aim of these translations is to challenge the schematic distinction between semantics and sound in poetry. Because the starting point for any homophonic procedure is always the sonic and prosodic realization of an original in a different language, not its discursive content, homophonic renderings explicitly throw doubt on the fetish of literal accuracy in the translation of poetry. Similarly, chance operations have gradually encroached into the realm of literary translation. Cases such as Jackson Mac Low's experiments of the 1950s, David Cameron's *Flowers of Bad* (2007), and Christian Hawkey's *Ventrakl* (2010) all applied the idea of randomization and even destructive force to transferring a text (randomly piercing, splitting it) into a different linguistic and literary context. Similar procedures have debunked the belief that translation is always the coherent and determinate series of conscious and independent decisions made by the translator. Erasure techniques in literary translation, more specifically (e.g., Jonathan Safran Foer's *Tree of Codes*, 2010, and Christian Hawkey and Uljana Wolf's *Sonne from Ort*, 2012), have also played on the fading memory of older texts. They have called into question any possibility of resurrecting bygone literary worlds in the modern context through linguistically neutral transposition.

Then, we can also come across series of recursive translations also known as the game of the "telephone" (in the US) or "Chinese whispers" (in the UK), which has been featured in cases such as Walter Arndt's "chain of traducers" in his *Pushkin Threefold* (1972) and more recently Adam Thirlwell's *Multiples* (2013). These translation chains ostentatiously put literary texts in a state of constant interlingual metamorphosis, exposing the translation's inevitably transformative nature. Then, there are also a few intralingual translation projects in the contemporary scene (such as Paul Legault's English-English translations of Emily Dickinson, 2012, and of Shakespeare, collaboratively edited with Sharmila Cohen, 2012). These set out to make us uneasy about how translation is understood, between what kind of "languages" it occurs, and whether it always involves translating "the Other." Finally, we also experience a revival of artistic pseudotranslations such as Jack Spicer's *After Lorca* (1957), Christopher Reid's translations of a nonexistent eastern European poet, *Katerina Brac* (1985), and Kent Johnson's translations of a nonexistent Hiroshima survivor, Araki Yasusada, in the 1990s. On the one hand, these works have dismantled the notion of authorship and simplistic distinctions between original writing and translation, showing how the two always merge in one creative act. On the other hand, they also reveal that translation acts as a deeply political projection of an "imagined" translated persona, and so it is inevitably entangled in intercultural and racial politics of representation.[6]

While provoking heated debates and debunking a handful of translation myths, some of these controversial or unconventional techniques are also not entirely new. In fact, if we look more closely, we can find that most of them had been anticipated well before modernism. For instance, homophonic translations have their roots in macaronic verse, parodist adaptions of the Bible, humorous puns, and presumed misunderstandings of foreign phrases, all dating back to the early modern period.[7] What is now referred to as intralingual translation follows the earlier example of many other paraphrases, retellings, parodies, adaptations, transformations, and so on. Pseudotranslations, too, are as old as time. Some argue that the first works intentionally using the narrative structure of pseudotranslation were Cervantes's *Don Quixote* and Montesquieu's *Persian Letters*. More generally, they piggyback on the long-standing tradition of literary hoaxes, *fakelore*, and apocryphal writing in the spirit of James Macpherson.[8] Only recently do they reinvent themselves to fiddle with translation norms and the idiom of *translationese* more consciously. Also, as I mentioned earlier in this chapter, even contemporary and digital translation multiples had their unwitting harbingers much earlier. The scholarly and artistic intuitions of translators such as Richard Baker and I. A. Richards, as well as the whole editorial universe of translation criticism and editing, also feeds into what we might see from today's perspective as translation multiples. Nonetheless, it is the increasing self-reflexivity and self-consciousness in coherent literary narratives and conceptual approaches that make a difference and take the multiples to a completely new level. When placed in the ranks of similar experimental works, translation multiples, too, go beyond their age-old prototypes and precursors, abandoning their purely hermeneutic and scholarly kinship. Openly questioning what passes as "standard" modes of translation and turning it into a mode of expression is what makes current nonstandard translations lean more decisively toward Perloff's rear guard.

In fact, some creators have thought of themselves as contributing to a new and somewhat subversive culture of translation. For instance, Hawkey positioned his *Ventrakl* in relation to other experimental translations,[9] which is also what Legault picked up on in his review of the book: "The nonstandard translation has its own traditions as Hawkey, in his introduction, points to the work of Jack Spicer, Louis Zukofsky, Anne Carson, and David Cameron."[10] By using the umbrella term "nonstandard translation," Legault connects the dots between different unconventional occurrences in recent American translation history—pseudotranslations, homophonic translations, fragmented rewriting, and chance operations—and groups all of them in one vaguely sketched but probably intuitive category. The historically and culturally defined notion of what is seen as "standard" translation at a certain moment in time usually has clearly marked and widely accepted boundaries. All other types of translation practices are thus doomed to be jettisoned beyond it and placed into a residuary subset evading or opposing expectations about what a translation should look like. The proliferation of various labels for this strand of translation practices also indicates how critics and translators themselves have struggled to find proper terms to classify it, a situation that Nakayasu subtly mocks in her verbal compound: "what I might call experimental-radical-innovative-what-have-you translations of poetry."[11] In the meantime, a few other descriptions have appeared in various places including the "experimental" translations transposed from relevant literary currents as well as the slightly edgy strand of "transgressive translations"[12] or "extreme translation,"[13] "radical translations,"[14] "sensationalist translations,"[15] and "avant-garde translations."[16] Searching for accurate terms, Josef Horáček also proposed calling Zukofsky's *Catullus* a "difficult translation"[17]—a term aligned with Leonard Diepeveen's *The Difficulties of Modernism* (2013) but at the same time remotely echoing Charles Bernstein's "attack of difficult poems" from his 2011 book's title. Some creative translators have also stressed the previously signaled subversive nature of their works, which in practice boils down to being misfits within the "proper" translation paradigm. While Hawkey wrote about "willful mistranslations"[18] and Cameron called his poems "false translations,"[19] Nakayasu almost took it a step further. In her self-founded press, tellingly named Rogue Factorial, she released her translations and "anti-translations" of Chika Sagawa's poems, as the book's subtitle hints: *Translations, Anti-Translations, and Originals* (2012). Such negations and contrastive metaphors add to overall attempts to overturn the prevailing idea of literary translation. As Nakayasu explained in her interview with Thomas Fink:

> My subtitle is a gesture towards acknowledging that some of the pieces here would make (some) people nod and say, "This is a translation." And some of the pieces here would make (some) people shake their heads and say, "This is not a translation" or, "This is doing something that a translation should not do." Those are the anti-translations.[20]

Regardless of how well grounded these binary oppositions actually are, the translators still have an inkling of their renderings being incongruous with predominant translation models. They are willing to produce such experimental works against the current, even if this has to be via independent publishing presses (e.g., Ugly Duckling Presse, Rogue Factorial, Action Books, Telephone Books, Portobello Books), art galleries, or low-cost literary magazines with limited print runs (e.g., *Chain*). Such avant-garde spirit goes far beyond mere provocativeness. It comes from a more profound aesthetic stance; "nonstandard" translations are meant to critique certain expectations and beliefs about the medium of translation, its economy and cultural significance. And they keep doing that regardless of available channels and against all odds.

Placed within this subversive strand, translation multiples bring "nonstandard" or "experimental" ways of translating to the fore in at least two ways: first, as mentioned before, by straining traditional publication formats and their widely accepted low number of translations per book, and second, by embracing a wider range of potentially "nonstandard" or less conventional styles and languages. These tendencies rub up against many institutional constraints governing translation practice, such as who has the privilege to translate and publish translation, on the one hand, and various forms of linguistic exclusion and prejudice in publishing and translation criticism, on the other. Already half a century ago, British poet Nicholas Moore signaled these aspects of institutional and social contexts of translation production in a literary hoax involving translation multiples. In 1968, he hijacked George Steiner's translation competition in the *Sunday Times* by submitting ostentatiously different versions of Baudelaire's poem "Je suis comme le roi" (I'm Like the King) under various pseudonyms and signed with different (mostly) UK-based postcodes. Moore then published his *Spleen* (1973) in book format, displaying his thirty-one entries and revealing the ruse.[21] Similarly to Fernando Pessoa writing as various literary personas, Moore-the-translator also enacts distinct speaking voices in his volume. The poems' signatures range from different versions of himself living under different addresses, both men and women, academics representing different disciplines (Oxford's "Department of Romance," Leicester's English faculty, etc.), and members of the public with different institutional affiliations ("Go-Karts and Strip Arts Council," "The Society of Multiple Injuries," "The Poetrie Diabblers' Union," etc.). Though quite roguish in its intention, this experiment with translators' different credentials also raises a few nontrivial questions. Does it matter whether the poem is translated by an English literature specialist, a Romance philologist, or a self-taught poet? Does it make any difference when someone translates from the position of a French scholar at Oxford as opposed to offering a new rendering as an unknown Baudelaire amateur from Kent? If certain texts are judged and accepted on the basis of the translator's educational background, language profile, and reputation, then we may also end up reading them differently as a result of a similar framing. In this sense, the multiplicity of accepted and displayed versions actively makes us reflect on the assumptions about who has the institutional right to translate and in what way.

As more and more versions unfold, many other constraints governing literary translation production will need to be revisited. Some publishing circles may be dogmatic about whether translators ought to be academically trained in a certain language area, be native speakers of the target language,[22] or translate into a mainstream version of the (English) language by arriving at the most idiomatic choices possible. In fact, quite a few of the translation multiples in discussion explicitly object to similar, fixed ideas, and especially to normative language politics and institutional efforts to standardize language. Just like Chika Sagawa protested against Meiji-era language policies, so did Nakayasu's "Promenade" ostentatiously stretch the monolingual boundaries of contemporary American English with a gamut of multilingual passages, foreignized phrases, and transliterations. In the same vein, Caroline Bergvall—herself not a native speaker of English—also championed the variety of Englishes with their different pronunciations and translations. Both her audio recording of "VIA" (delivered with her characteristic accent) as well as its celebration of multiple idioms in translation across time and space combat monolithic ideas about the English language. This also ties in with the agenda of another, more recent translation multiple, Michael Cooperson's *Impostures: Fifty Rogue's Tales Translated Fifty Ways* (2020), which explicitly showcases different varieties of global English such as Scots, Indian, Jamaican, and Singaporean creole ("Singlish") in different renderings of prose narratives by the Arabic poet al-Ḥarīrī. Surely Cooperson's *Impostures* are still enrooted in the ludic tradition of rogue storytelling as they erupt into a concord of playful styles, sociolects, and specialized jargons such as management speak, legalese, and thieves' cant. But as these multiples allude to al-Ḥarīrī's own experimentation with the formal type of Arabic he used,[23] they also dismantle what may otherwise not pass as standard English. In this sense, the multiples give voice to different ways of speaking and translating, including some marginalized idioms and otherwise unrecognized language variants that emerge in writing. By eroding the idea of standard (global) English through translation, some of these projects may eventually lead to the decentering of mainstream translation discourse.

This also brings us back to the question of linguistic exclusion and prejudice, especially with relation to nationality, ethnicity, and the idea of "nativeness." For instance, introducing ethno-specific varieties among translations into English can lead to recognizing and consolidating these variants as full-fledged languages of artistic expression. This is the case with Cooperson's *Impostures*, which places standard written English versions alongside various spoken variants typically associated with underprivileged communities. Extending this symbolic representation to more diverse languages, his book with translation multiples aims to elevate the status of communities that "have suffered everything from ridicule to persecution for speaking as they do."[24] In this way, some translation multiples have the potential of revisiting and standing up to historical and contemporary forms of language violence, which are also inherently linked to cultural prejudice and racism. Yet another translation multiple, Brandon Som's "Oulipo"

(2014), which offers eighteen different homophonic translations from Li Bai's quatrain in Chinese, addresses these issues while musing on the idea of Chinese American belonging.[25] In his aural multiples across Chinese and English, Som smuggles into English an array of Chinese-imbued words, forms, and sounds, which also replicate the direction of travel of his grandfather, a "paper-son" Chinese who immigrated to the United States illegally. By defamiliarizing American English through ambiguously interlingual forms (wan, mien, sun, thong) and other exoticized borrowings (mahjongg, junco, sarong),[26] Som's poem symbolically addresses historical and contemporary racism against migrants in the United States, in particular Chinese Americans. In the same vein, Bergvall's act of multiplying translations in her "VIA" can also be seen as defying the xenophobic acts of policing linguistic and political borders. In his reading of "VIA," Jacob Edmond places "VIA" alongside Bergvall's other politically motivated projects such as the poetic book *Drift*, a meditation on forced exile, the refugee crisis, and migrant tragedies at sea.[27] By celebrating different "Englishes" in translation, Bergvall's "VIA" implicitly nods toward the increasingly more diverse linguistic landscape of the United Kingdom. This gesture may resonate even more strongly now in the post-Brexit community, with its narrowing definition of Englishness.

While opposing similar forms of monolingualism and bigotry, translation multiples openly go against the grain and stray from well-trodden paths. They resist prevailing publishing standards, mainstream forms of expression in writing and translation, and monolithic ideas about language and culture. Aligned with the agenda of "experimental translations," their subversive potential manifests itself in similarly defiant acts: they can put pressure on some institutional constraints governing literary translation production, they can redefine tensions between the familiar and the foreign, and they can dismantle the idea of standard (global) English by acknowledging different variants of the language used by diverse communities. In this sense, translation multiples continue the rear-guard spirit. They fight their battles in revisited interstitial spaces while also boldly encroaching into new, unexplored territories.

The Metatranslation

Translation multiples displaying the plurality of the same original text have also emerged on the wave of increasingly frequent literary experiments. Many other twentieth-century renderings of poetry draw their translation techniques from recognizable modernist poetic models, including impressionist, constructivist, cubist, and conceptual ones, to mention a few.[28] In this respect, translation multiples seem no different, as they could be seen as reconstructing the Oulipian multiplicative procedures and treating translation as a special type of constrained writing, namely, writing constrained by some correspondence to the original. This idea definitely lays the foundations for Douglas Hofstadter's *Le Ton beau de Marot*. It is probably not without reason that the author devoted a large portion of his narrative to English, German, Dutch, and Italian translations of Georges Perec's *La disparation* and Raymond Queneau's *Exercices de style*. For Hofstadter, the formal constraints he identified in Marot's original poem molded a creative matrix for multiple translation castings or, following his own metaphor, uncovered a "mineralogical display featuring sparkling crystals" that glowed with different colors and took on an array of shapes.[29] Similarly, Marjorie Perloff diagnosed "the Oulipo factor" in the procedural poetics of Bergvall's "VIA," especially in Bergvall's desire to demonstrate "the power of the poetic word."[30] According to Perloff, the poem could be easily interpreted alongside artistic works such as Christian Bök's *Eunoia* (2001) and Harry Mathews's "35 Variations on a Theme from Shakespeare" (1999). In the first case, Bök wrote each chapter exclusively using words with one particular vowel, a constraint reflected in the titular "eunoia," apparently the shortest English word containing all five vowels and literally meaning "beautiful thinking." In the second one, Mathews transposed the famous line "To be, or not to be, that is the question" into a series of what he labeled as "amplified," "reductive," "permuted," "isomorphic," or "interfered" versions. In the same vein, Perloff would probably also agree about further similarities with a more recently published poetry collection by Paul Hoover, titled *Sonnet 56* (2009), which consists of fifty-six versions of Shakespeare's sonnet of that number in different forms, including a villanelle, a ballad, a prose poem, and an epitaph, to mention a few.

Although Perloff was correct in establishing this conceptual relationship with the writing of the Oulipo group, we should ask what exactly this correspondence entails for the very fact of translation, which distinguished Bergvall's case from the latter ones.[31] Translation multiples are not only about rewriting the same work in different styles with a range of formal constraints. They also act as bearers of some truths about translation that may be overlooked at first glance. Translations that are conventionally believed to accurately and slavishly represent an original in a different language break the source text into dozens of splinters and multiple "equivalences." As things fall apart, the idea of equivalence cannot hold, either. It is revealed that all these different variants equally stand for the prototype and have actually been read as legitimate translation equivalents in different contexts regardless of constantly changing interpretative approaches and artistic stances. The inevitable multiplicity of these variants could also come from one creative mind when translation is in the making: the process of pondering and probing different translation possibilities and then showing them all without prioritizing any single final version lies at the heart of "procedural poetics." Referring to her multiples in "Promenade," Nakayasu admitted that she expected her readers to follow her act of "shifting the emphasis from product (the complete, perfect, final translation) to process (everything that happens on the way to the product)."[32] But although placing together and comparing different versions recorded "the considerations and questions going through a translator's mind in the moment of translation, which was definitely an intended effect," she was not sure "if the average reader is interested in doing that kind of work."[33] But it doesn't really matter if the reader actually does their homework and diligently compares all the variants. It is still the mere fact of bringing them all together and dismantling the one-to-one relationship with the source text that often does the trick and might give "average readers" a mild shock therapy.

In Raymond Queneau's *Exercices de style* (1947), the concept is also quite simple: an anecdote about a man on a bus who gets into an argument with another passenger is told ninety-nine times, each time emphasizing different parts of the story and describing the event from various angles in radically different styles (including metaphorical, oneiric, epistolary, emphatic, first-person or third-person narrative, the passive voice, different tenses, and so on). Queneau toys with multiple modes of storytelling. In his exercises, different narrators leave an individual imprint of their fabular styles on each version, deconstructing what is assumed to be the original story in ninety-nine completely dissimilar texts. Such a multithreaded performance in Queneau's narrative collage, as Karen L. Taylor remarks, "was supposedly inspired by a symphony that gave him the idea of writing variations on a theme."[34] Indeed, the idea of writing literary variations on a theme, which developed from musical form, has become a recognizable genre of writing as such.[35] It found its way into Queneau's exercises as a framing device for all the vocal improvisations on the original story line. A similar premise lies behind all translation multiples, as they are composed of narratives revolving around an original theme. In some cases, they concentrate on leitmotifs and catchy tunes that everyone plays on a loop and hums without knowing the original lyrics. This is the case with Wang Wei, whose "deer park" has almost become a literary cliché and an evergreen example of multiplicity in translation in the Anglo-American tradition. Bergvall's Dantes also come in "variations" in the title ("48 Dante Variations") explicitly because the opening lines of *Inferno* sound very familiar to the Anglophone ear, having been previously translated into English at least two hundred times. In the same vein, the idea of variation is inscribed into the inevitably multiple nature of Bashō's frog haiku in the English-language tradition. In his book entitled *The Basho Variations*, Steve McCaffery comes up with different takes in the style of Queneau or the Oulipo group more generally. He reiterates the well-known frog haiku through the mouth of radically dissimilar Bashōs, such as the "gastronomic," "philosophical," "dialogic," and "kinetic" ones, each time entertaining readers with more and more playful departures from the popular lines. Similarly, in Hiroaki Sato's *One Hundred Frogs*, William Matheson's sequence of three variants is published under the title "Ten Variations on Bashō's 'Pond and Frog' Haiku," suggesting that it belongs to a longer cycle. It was, however, not the editor, Hiroaki Sato, who chose three out of ten available variations. In fact, Matheson himself sent this seemingly incomplete poem for the volume, most probably treating the idea of multiple variations on the theme of Bashō's haiku as, in Sato's words, "an affectation or else a literary device."[36] This subtle hint marks the existent convention of writing after Bashō, which can never be exhausted. Matheson's own and many other variations more broadly feed into this strand treating the frog pond as a reservoir of renewable generative potential.

The notion of "variations," exercises in various styles, and improvisations around a recurring theme have been directly fueled by preceding and concurrent musical practices, both classical and modern. Although Hofstadter embarked on his translation multiples with a freer form of a rhapsody in mind and then reframed the sequence imagining a more cyclical structure of a musical rondo, the main driving force of his project is the idea of musical variations. In his book, repetition and pattern are musically reinstated through rhythm and form as the original theme recurs in differently sounding variants. We can consequently think of variation as inherently inscribed in several musical forms as well as defining the practice of literary translation repeated over time. Just like the "theme" serves as a constituent element of a musical composition, the recurring idea of an "original" lies behind all the different translation variants in a succession. But Hofstadter also conflated this formal understanding of variation in music with a broader reflection on the relationship between translation and performing an original score. He first compared different variants to "performances of Chopin's etudes in the media of string quartet, woodwind quartet, brass quartet, and barbershop quartet—each one faithful and unfaithful in its own way to the original."[37] He also recast the metaphor of translations as individual piano interpretations of composed masterpieces, just like in Vladimir Horowitz's own take on Chopin's works.[38] In this respect, translation multiples could also be thought of in terms of classical standards played in different concert versions by different performers. Each performer is an active reader of the original score and leaves a creative imprint on its individual interpretation and reenactment.

But there's still more to it. The emergence of jazz, aleatory, and improvised music in the twentieth century paved the way for a range of alternatives to the same musical piece by one musician. Some jazz recordings offer more than one equally legitimate variant simultaneously. For example, the 12-inch LP version of Bud Powell's album *The Amazing Bud Powell* (vol. 1) from 1956 features three alternate master takes on "Un Poco Loco," all of which are included as equally legitimate variants. Likewise, two albums with different improvisations of the same musical pieces by Ornette Coleman, entitled, respectively, *Sound Museum: Hidden Man* and *Sound Museum: Three Women*, were both released under the same record label in 1996. Already back in the 1960s, Glenn Gould championed an alternative take on musical recordings: he imagined that new technology would make it possible to offer to the listener not one but a series of variant performances they could choose from and assemble their own creative performance.[39] Similar ideas and productions not only make it possible to track more than one musical interpretation or improvisation of a given piece. They also challenge the very idea of "the original score" by opening the chance of understanding and performing it differently and anew. In doing so, they institutionalize the simultaneous presence of these different variants and performances within one musical production. And to think about it along more philosophical lines, the score itself has to be actualized in performance; it depends on being performed and reinvented. Without individual musicians playing it over and over again, the score would not be brought to life and would remain inaccessible to the auditors. While in some famous cases we cannot tell whether the original score even exists,[40] in others, especially more recently, the original score's authority is undermined in favor of individual performances. In particular, Nicholas Cook critiqued what he called "Plato's curse,"[41] a musicological fixation on the original score as the ultimate reservoir of meaning in music. Instead, he postulates thinking of music as intrinsically performative. By proclaiming the death of the original score, he thereby suggests yet another variation of the death of the author. But whether we think of readers, narrative mediators, translators, or musical performers, debunking the myth of the "original" works in a very similar manner. If we return to Queneau's ninety-nine exercises, we in fact do not have a choice but to observe that we, too, lack access to the original score. There is no default story or any unmediated document on what has actually happened. In fact, the "naught" or "hundredth" version that waits to be reported to round off the odd number of exercises ostentatiously goes missing in the thick of narrations;[42] it has already been filtered by different interpreters and subsequent retellers of the event. It would not be of much help, either, if those on the receiving end of the story had witnessed the actual occurrence themselves. Their account would still differ from the previous ones and be unreliable.

Reflection on the way of observing and narrating what passes as the original object is of course redolent of many twentieth-century metaworks belonging to the postmodern genres of metadrama, metafilm, and metaliterature. In deconstructing the "essence," these self-reflexive works have questioned the neutral mediation of narration, often by exposing what has lately been called "the Rashomon effect" after Akira Kurosawa's 1950 film, namely, the nonoverlapping and even contradictory interpretations of the same event by different witnesses. Similarly, these nonidentical accounts can vary within one interpretative mind depending on the sensual impression, contextual setting, mode, and position of observation. T. J. Clark's *The Sight of Death* (2000) comes to mind, in which the author recorded his constantly shifting responses to the same painting by Nicolas Poussin every day for a year—just like Nakayasu registered translatorial impressions from her repeated walks on the promenade. Conceptually affiliated with Queneau's exercises, similar metaworks that juggle multiple points of view make the audience rethink categories such as the original object, occurrence, and text. In doing so, they boldly alert readers to the mediation of the narrator in the process; they also question the neutral relationship between reality and its representation in art and literature. The task of translation multiples is very similar in this respect; it is aligned with metacritical reflections on unreliable, biased, framed, and contextually situated narratives. Translation multiples, too, could work as a metatranslation:[43] they make contemporary readers more sensitive toward related features within the domain of translation. By offering more than one legitimate translation variant, they reveal the translator's mediation and actively creative part in retelling the original. At the same time, they also contradict the still entrenched belief among single-translation readers that it is enough to read one translation, as it offers one sanctioned and authorized truth about the source text. But following the dispersion of readings and renderings, this idea has to be verified. What has so far appeared as a straightforward, neutral, and objective relationship between the original and its rewriting in a different language and literary culture can no longer be taken at face value.

Insisting on a platform for multiple possibilities and creative transformations in translation might sound like preaching to the converted—in particular, for many translators as well as translation critics and teachers for whom this is all bread and butter. Following the rise of translation studies as a separate discipline with its target-oriented approach and more focus on retranslations, academic awareness of translation's complexity and transformative power has significantly increased. Literary translation in particular is no longer perceived and analyzed in terms of mechanical matchings, a calculus of losses and gains, normative linguistic equivalence, or one-to-one representation. These ideas have been constantly fading away and sinking into oblivion in favor of alternative ways of thinking about translation: "the creation of connections, contiguities, and contextures in and through translation."[44] Translators and translation critics have come to appreciate the multifarious and transgressive aspects of literary translation. New journals and groups dedicated to international literature and the creative practice of translation are being formed and fueled by translation aficionados. While the University of Rochester is home to the Three Percent program, "the fine northamerican city of Rochester" has recently become a hub of the Outranspo (Ouvroir de Translation Potencial) group founded by Camille Bloomfield, Rachel Galvin, and Pablo Martín Ruiz.[45] Inspired by the Oulipo group and continuing its experimental and translingual mission,[46] Outranspo explicitly postulates to debunk reductive beliefs about the lack of creativity in translation practice. In their foundational act, a trilingual manifesto written across English, Spanish, and French, the ensemble states that they are interested in translation as "a stammering reservoir of sublime—though totally incestuous—marriages between languages, the creative, un-lucrative site of glowballization, the very real crucible of a universal potentiality for human and cultural interaction."[47] By giving a new lease on life to a gamut of experimental translation techniques, Outranspo has provocatively meddled with fixed translation norms. In a series of what would be conventionally deemed as "bad translations," they rewrote Donald Trump's hateful tweets "using the gift of translational foreignness."[48] In a series of Oulipian exercises, "35 Variations on a Theme from Translatology," Outranspo's affiliate member Ian Monk chose to reiterate no other phrase but the infamous: "To translate is to betray." As "traduttore-traditore" is the usual mantra of translation criticism, Monk playfully mocked the normative approach to translation in a series of ironic commandments such as: "To write it in another tongue's a crime" and "The act of passing from one idiom to another is equivalent to high treason."

Nonetheless, no matter how vibrant and transgressive their tenets, similar initiatives do not necessarily lead to significantly wider awareness and ideas among the reading public. In the global literary market, literary translations are more readily being produced to replace and stand for original texts. Their role in some readers' eyes could really boil down to that of SparkNotes; translations are there to provide convenient one-click approximations of originals just for the asking. Translator activists and writers do wish to change this misperception by campaigning for raising translators' visibility in the publishing industry. On September 30, 2021, the globally celebrated International Translation Day, Jennifer Croft and Mark Haddon released an open letter on the UK's Society of Authors website in which they appealed to writers to seek cover credits for their translators (#TranslatorsOnTheCover) with their publishers. In April 2023, the PEN America Translation Committee released "The 2023 Manifesto on Literary Translation" calling to action all parties involved in the industry such as authors, publishers, teachers, editors, and critics, as well as readers, to recognize translation as "a specialized form of writing that emphasizes the myriad interpretations available."[49] In the same vein, institutional efforts to promote the art of literary translation in the United States and the United Kingdom through a range of publishing venues, translation series, and prizes go back at least to the late twentieth century; this apparent trend has recently led Lawrence Venuti, the erstwhile proclaimer of the translator's invisibility, to write more optimistically about the times of "new visibility."[50] Some institutions and book distributors have also championed the art of translation, marketing "literature in translation" as a distinct genre on its own in order to elevate its status, while PEN and Man Booker have established special prizes for literary translations (the PEN Translation Prize, the PEN Poetry in Translation Prize, the Man Booker International Prize), awarding either both the original author and translator or just the translator for their creative work. But can this prize-giving politics also have the countereffect of suggesting to more traditional readers that translated literature is somehow of a lesser category compared to original writing; that it needs a separate section among PEN's genres (fiction, nonfiction, poetry, drama, multigenre, translation)? It shouldn't—and I do agree that translation is a special and incredibly creative literary work in its own right—but it potentially could. And this is also where the task of translation reviewers and critics comes in. Instead of judging "good" and "bad" translations, spotting flowing and wooden passages, praising translations for rendering the original's "spirit," "tone," and other vague categories, they should all drop whatever they're doing now and go write and teach about multiple translation. We need more voices that reveal this multiplicity and diverse power; we need more projects that help us understand how translation transforms our reading and how it changes us, too.

In the recent anthology *Into English* (2017), Martha Collins, one of the volume's two editors who put together multiple translations of twenty-five different poems, points to a paltry number of existing books of the kind. She suggests that this body of resources, with some cases hedged by limited access or a low print run, "made the need for a new anthology seem even more pressing."[51] In fact, Collins and Kevin Prufer's project partly builds on the lesson that translation multiples can teach readers as well as translators, academics, lecturers of translation theory, and translation critics. Spanning twenty-five poems in multiple languages brought into English in multiple translations (usually three versions each) and commented on by twenty-five translators, this book celebrates the multiplicity not only of translations and their individual readings but also of their commentators. Here, the artistic element to be found in translation triplets unexpectedly spreads into essays by translation critics, too, as they get their heads round these multiples—each in a different way and in their own distinct voice. As translators and translation critics discuss multiple renderings of a chosen poem, their aesthetic biases come to the fore. The critics often reveal their personal investment in the source leitmotifs and images insofar as they replicate them in their own analytic categories. This is visible in the titles coined after poetic phrases from the originals, but also in their writing style attuned to what they see as the distinct trait of the discussed verse. For example, Willis Barnstone becomes very possessive of his erotic interpretation of a poem by St. John of the Cross, reluctantly measuring other translations against his passionate reading; Carl Phillips's slightly moralistic conclusion about Virgil's translations jibes with the poem's didactic quality; Arthur Sze straightforwardly and calmly comes to terms with the "untranslatability" of Taoist spontaneity and peace of mind; and Cole Swensen toys with Baudelaire's pranksters in a very tongue-in-cheek manner. In one of the most palpable records of this mutual kinship, a very somatic and haptic reading of Wisława Szymborska's "Torture(s)," Alissa Valles does not shy away from talking about her deeply personal responses ("I feel," "I favor," "I prefer") and aesthetic biases ("rhythmically, I lean toward the latter"). And more, she activates all her senses and even rehearses some of the physical descriptions from the poem ("I find myself throwing up my arms as well as my hands"), letting herself be "tortured" by different possible reactions in translation.[52]

These translation critics, who are often translators themselves, embrace their subjective responses and admit how their own ideas about the original poem inform their ensuing discussion of multiple renderings. In other words, they often measure their experience of approaching plural renderings against that personal and highly subjective reading of the original. By no means is this an exhaustive approach to translation, but it also openly does not aspire to being such. But what this "chorus in celebration of international poetry and translation" can teach readers are several crucial things. First, the multiplicity of paths and parallel lives of one poem in translation shows how many innovative and artistic things, as well as entirely arbitrary ones, happen to one poem as it travels "into English." Second, it also makes us think about how different readings and renderings are prioritized in personal readings of different critics. This consequently raises the following questions: Who favors one variant over another—and why? Who is in a position to lobby on behalf of a favorite? Which of the variants finally gets selected as the final version to be published in a book or anthology and praised as a "good" translation? And this ties in with the third lesson to be learned from *Into English*: while the dynamic between multiple variants may intersect with discussions about aesthetic preferences and artistic values, it is equally enmeshed in the politics of publishing and the economy of power relations; these may in turn lead to competition and differentiation as key factors governing the production, tumultuous coexistence, and criticism of retranslations.[53] However, what we see in *Into English* is much closer to what Sharon Deane-Cox calls "a dialogue of difference," an approach that puts forward a less antagonistic relationship between the multiples.[54] Perhaps the stance of translation critics and translators alike may shift in this direction in the future, if it hasn't started at least budging already.

Surely, we may also have to speak of different forms and various degrees of how this dialogue manifests itself in translation multiples and other projects celebrating different translation approaches. While recognizing a plurality of possibilities in principle, translators, editors, and critics can still be tempted to introduce some level of hierarchization and comment on differentiating qualities within their multiples. For example, Eliot Weinberger's *19 Ways of Looking at Wang Wei* clearly dismisses a pedantic and philologically correct version of the poem in favor of more creative attempts that formed part of his Buddhist journey. Even though Weinberger did place the "strangest of the many Weis" in the volume, it was not given a number in the sequence of nineteen (and later twenty-nine) and was therefore placed somehow in the margins. In the same vein, Douglas Hofstadter's emphasis on form and sound over sense might have led to sidelining more philological and literal approaches to translation. We may say that Weinberger and Hofstadter each had an axe to grind in their selection of more innovative and wide-ranging variants that stayed in opposition to the previous traditional models and well-trodden paths. In this sense, while the multiples may try to achieve some level of equality between the texts and give recognition to as many of them as possible, the selection of variants and their representation is never completely free of bias. However, rather than dwelling on potential asymmetries of hierarchies within the multiples, which are inherently inscribed in any human and textual interaction, I instead propose to prioritize the postulate of *multiplicity over singularity* in similar projects. Let me explain why multiplicity, even though not offering an ideally equal distribution and representation of options, is still key to understanding the ethical project of translation multiples.

The call for translation multiples is of ethical relevance because the practice of displaying alternative variants communicates the crucial message that there is no single dominating option. This message conveys an imperative of nondomination and plurality in translation; at the same time, it can be seen as a continuation of Gilles Deleuze and Félix Guattari's philosophy of multiplicity and multivalent rhizomes, which has spread to many other disciplines.[55] Translation multiples also abolish cognitive binaries and show that the idea of multitude in translation cannot be sliced up into single and well-rounded elements: there is always some continuity on a spectrum of translation choices, some unfinished procedural thought in the making, oscillation between apparent completeness and potentiality. Similarly, there is no abstract idea of the translation of a work but always multiple renderings and variations, each different from the others. The universe of translation is exactly composed of these differences and not of the single, totalized ideas of truthful translations.[56] Arguably, translators could highlight the singularity of their own attempt on this spectrum of difference in their introductions, footnotes, and commentaries accompanying their work. Nonetheless, it is only in translation multiples that this diversity and multiplicity come through most forcefully and tangibly. In all other cases, there is still some risk of mistaking a single translation for truth.

The dangers of single, totalizing translation is very disturbingly illustrated in the celebrated Greek film by Yorgos Lanthimos, *Dogtooth* (*Κυνόδοντας*, 2009). While it hardly qualifies as a film about literary translation, *Dogtooth* still shocks by a range of tellingly parabolic depictions. In the film, a despotic father who has invented an entirely closed society for his long-imprisoned, oblivious children constantly controls them by "translating" the foreign world for them into his own infantilized categories. The mortal enemies of the household are cats visiting the garden; a child is able to leave the house only when their canine tooth ("dogtooth") falls out; and new words have to be learned from tapes recorded by the parents. The children's vocabulary is limited by their cognitive horizons, namely, the borders of the house: "sea" is a leather chair from the living room, "shotgun" is a type of bird, and so on. In one of the scenes, the father exercises a simultaneous translation of Frank Sinatra's performance of the song "Fly Me to the Moon" into Greek. In his usual manipulative matter, he reinvents all the lyrics one by one;

he pretends that the vocalist is the children's late grandfather expressing love to the family and convincing them all to stay strong together. Enjoying his monopoly over truth in translation, the father clearly manipulates his translation to further his evil goals and takes advantage of his children's lack of command of the English language. Unless confronted by other interpreters with their alternative readings, he can continue to cherish the uncontested and exclusive license for translation. Without other voices of protest, he keeps the children in the dark, blinded by his totalizing illusion.

Deconstructing such a monopoly for one totalizing point of view lies at the core of what I understand to be the ethical aspect of translation multiples, the metatranslation. Only when exposed to multiple variants do readers get to see a wider spectrum of possibilities—all with their wide-ranging and winding stories, "variety of Formes," and differently developed interpretations. In *Dogtooth*, too, listening to other voices eventually proves the only way out and slowly starts fracturing the father's authoritative kingdom. This turn of events follows the visit of a guest from outside who intrudes into the family and plants a seed of doubt in the children's minds. Similarly, by being exposed to different interpretations, the readers of translation multiples have no choice but to revise and suspend their belief about one truthful representation of original senses.[57] As multiples break the magic spell of the one-to-one substitution of the original, the idea of translation gets dismantled into a rhizome of transformations and individual voices. Of course, in the global culture of language powers, these projects might not stop the fast consumption of translations as substitutes of source texts from other languages. But they might at least act as a thorn in the side of the language monopoly. Forcing readers out of their comfort zone, irritating them with translation's procedural inconclusiveness, and making them *see* more is well within reach. This is what should be the task of translation multiples now.

Pluralist Multiples

Translation multiples have continued to challenge the monopoly of one totalizing point of view since the late twentieth century through global English in a range of Anglophone contexts; they have served various artistic and ethical purposes in several projects and moments in time. The task of undermining a single authoritative voice through multiples can also be shared across different cultures, and it has also fallen on the fertile ground of the postcommunist intellectual scene. Starting with the symbolic date of 1989, the end of communism in Eastern Europe later followed by the collapse of the Soviet Union, countries such as

Poland still had their own despotic patriarch to overturn—just like the children in Lanthimos's *Dogtooth*. The political transition from a totalitarian regime to a pluralist system did not happen overnight and went on to resonate with many spheres of cultural and literary life years after 1989. Translation multiples created in this political context are among the best testaments to this changing landscape. On the one hand, their creators had to deal with many fears and uncertainties lying ahead; on the other hand, they cohered around a strong resistance toward the difficult legacy of the former communist regime. The echoes of the totalitarian paradigm still haunted the creators of the Polish multiples as they attempted to dismantle the norm of producing only one true reading of an original. Instead, the authors of postcommunist translation multiples put on the table plural different takes on original texts and explicitly engaged with alternative viewpoints. This gesture emanates from a broader ethical agenda emerging from the post-1989 reality. The act of producing, welcoming, and recognizing more than one interpretation and point of view opens the original up to different ideas. Translation multiples can provide a pluralist forum for critiquing distinct stances and visions. The ideas in question relate to the surrounding political reality, the cyclical course of history, anti-imperial resistance, ideologically biased interpretations of literary works, and many other facets of the present and the past. In this way, in the milieu of postcommunist democracy, translation multiples embrace other missions, too. As they break through the illusion of one-to-one equivalence, they also discredit beliefs in one monolithic truth about society, one authentic ideology, and one ideal system.

In the Polish context, similar gestures carry larger cultural resonances on many levels. Contrary to the English-speaking world, literary translation in Poland has occupied a considerably more prominent space within literary and cultural discourse, amounting to one-quarter of yearly book production in the past few decades. This relative difference, accompanied by the rapidly changing translation landscape in the late twentieth century, brings translation multiples if not to the public spotlight then at least to the forefront of literary and cultural discourse. The backstory of postcommunist translation multiples, however, is much more complex, with other historical and political factors to be considered when assessing this genre of writing in the newly emerging reality. The most apparent shift at stake is between the two publishing paradigms and two different systems of translation production and circulation. Translation multiples discussed in this book emerged in the wake of the postcommunist transition from state-run centralized publishing to the newly established decentralized free-market system, which has, technically speaking, created more leeway and practical opportunity for releasing plural translations. This again comes with a few caveats. The difference between the communist framework, which, roughly speaking, favored one authoritative translation, and the post-1989 system, which allowed for plural versions, may not be as clear-cut when approached in purely quantitative terms and may not translate into absolute numbers for every individual work. In other words, this is not to suggest that the communist state-run press would always permit only one single rendering while the post-1989 market effortlessly yielded multiple equally legitimate and acknowledged versions.[58] What I understand was behind this tension between the singular and the multiple across the two political frameworks is much more multilayered and contextually entangled. With regard to literary translation production, different facets of this dynamic span several trends and political factors. Let me map out at least a few of them, namely: the publishing infrastructure, its centralization or lack thereof, the inclination toward canonization, the publishing pace, the general volume of translation production, the question of copyrights, official and unofficial channels of translation production and distribution, and potential frictions between them.

Before 1989, official translations in Poland were solicited by a limited number of coordinated state presses (around sixty major ones, approximately one hundred in total).[59] Just like in many other states in the region,[60] publishing venues in the Polish People's Republic were subject to state control, centralized planning, and production monopoly (due to limited resources and restricted access to paper) pretty much until the 1970s, when an alternative channel—underground publishing—emerged. Since all official publishing was party controlled, it all had to go through authorization from the Censorship Office,[61] a process that was in place until 1990, when preventive censorship was officially abolished.[62] Furthermore, even though Poland permitted a much higher volume of literary traffic than other countries in the Eastern Bloc,[63] it is important to note that the selection of works to be translated into Polish outside of the Soviet Union was still policed by the state. And these works had to be purchased with foreign currency allocated by the state (or else smuggled illegally), which restricted translation production and distribution channels for foreign literature in ways similar to the situation in many other countries in the bloc.[64] Furthermore, the translation practice and everyday lives of literary translators in the Polish People's Republic were also affected by the activities of the security services.[65] And while literary translation in the Soviet Union and its satellite countries was often perceived as a safe haven as opposed to original writing,[66] many literary translators were also writers in their own right and could often not escape psychological pressure and other repercussions while being on the state's radar.[67] Especially in the early years of communist rule, it was not unheard of for literary translators to be explicitly denied the right to translate or be included in the official publication of distribution channels.[68] These forms of quantitative and qualitative limitations exerted by the state's ideological patronage upon translation practice at that time were embedded within the general context of the publishing culture and political climate in communist states. In my understanding, these trends as well as other acts of policing literary production through the official channels that I am about to discuss did impose technical, ideological, economic, and psychological constraints on the emergence of the multiples.

My telegraphic overview above does not exhaust the list of all technical hurdles encountered in the communist production of literature, which also ricocheted into literary translation. In terms of publishing mechanisms that can limit the actual translation numbers in the production process, there are other factors hindering the flow of retranslations (or other competing versions) to be considered. In particular, the communist publishing system tended to canonize translation practices as a result of the state's ideological program as well as the overall longer book production process. The policy of canonizing some foreign authors (while jettisoning others out of the publishing agenda) as well as homogenizing their image in translation for ideological reasons was characteristic of a number of Soviet states as well as other satellite states during the communist period.[69] This process entailed the selection of authors to be translated as well as preventive censorship, both of which already limit the range of authors in translation available to readers. The process of canon formation in literary translation was perhaps most explicitly reflected in the emergence and consolidation of "World Classics" series published by official state-run presses, which presented themselves as authoritative translations of "canonical" authors. For instance, as Nataliia Rudnytska points out, major Soviet publishing houses operating during the late socialism period launched series of world classics with great panache and considerable print runs; she mentions Biblioteka Vsemirnoi Literatury (the Library of World Literature) from Khudozhestvennaya Literatura, which published two hundred volumes with three hundred thousand copies each, as a case in point.[70] A similar mechanism could be seen in the Czechoslovak context, where a high number of similar "world classics" were included in publishing plans in order to ensure that the working class had access to the literary trove of other traditions.[71] This is also why translations of authors who were accepted as "canonical" became fertile ground for the state's ideological and cultural policies—and why the state could be reluctant to see their image complicated by alternative perspectives outside the series. In the USSR, for instance, Shakespeare in particular grew to become an international symbol of unity among the Soviet republics; while individual works overall may have been translated more than once, translations of Shakespeare as a large-scale enterprise were still subject to the pressure of aesthetic and ideological homogenization, as all "directive[s] for the dominant style of production, translation, and interpretation came from Moscow."[72] This practice with regard to Shakespeare was further extended to the Soviet Union's "colonizing" mission to other socialist countries; in communist Romania, for instance, commissioning a new official translation of Shakespeare became a key priority, resulting in a monumental eight-volume edition of translations published over the course of the years 1953–1960, with each volume released in twenty thousand copies and distributed to all public libraries and schools.[73] In the Polish context, even though at least a few translators of Shakespeare entered the stage and completed their translations at different points under the patronage of the communist state,[74] the homogenizing mechanisms were still present in the practice of serial publishing. In the later years of the socialist state, a single figure (Maciej Słomczyński) effectively became the key translator commissioned to render all works singlehandedly for the series with the Wydawnictwo Literackie state press; this development was believed to reflect the publisher's preference for a single translator over a varied team to ensure consistency in a Shakespeare translation series.[75]

A by-product of similar canonizing and homogenizing practices was state publishing's penchant for an authoritative translation (even if not always the only one at hand), which would stay in distribution for decades. Looking at other translations from the period, we can trace analogous stories throughout other commanding series of "literary classics" from official presses that tended to anoint one translation and reissue it in consecutive reprintings rather than commission a new alternative. This holds true for many translations in the mainstream series of "classic" fiction books entitled Biblioteka Klasyki Polskiej i Obcej (the Library of Polish and Foreign Classics) released by the State Publishing Institute (Państwowy Instytut Wydawniczy, or PIW), with individual titles reaching print runs of over fifty thousand copies.[76] The scenario for some translations released in this series panned out as follows: the same "canonical" translation was recycled from the 1950s to the late 1980s in the form of multiple reprintings of one official rendering, an uninterrupted streak that would then break into at least three different renderings after 1989. The most extreme examples of this trend were translations of Charlotte Brontë's *Jane Eyre*, Gustave Flaubert's *Madame Bovary*, and Fyodor Dostoyevsky's *Crime and Punishment*. In each case, there were at least ten reprintings of one "canonical" translation in Polish published by the state press between 1945 and 1989, whereas three or more competing renderings entered circulation after 1989. Why recycling the same translation for decades rather than commissioning a new one was a more viable option for state presses can be explained by the relatively high production outlays and the long duration of book production in the communist publishing order. Editors in state publishing institutions had a great say in the translation process, all the way from commissioning translators to curating textual material, overseeing the translation process, and working on the final textual shape. This is also why a book-length translation could be in the hands of the translator and editors for a period of several years.[77] For instance, it took the official publisher as long as ten years to work on and release a Polish translation of Günter Grass's *The Tin Drum*.[78] The publication process for book translations involved a lot of meticulous work and careful editing, with different aspects relegated to an elaborate team of editors, proofreaders, and book formatters. And so, once finally ready, the same carefully procured translation could be then reissued in consecutive editions for decades with no incentive and no need for a competitive alternative.

The sluggish pace of the communist publishing system stands in stark contrast to the literary market in the post-1989 order governed by the fast speed and cheap process of book production.[79] The postcommunist transition created an entirely different working environment for literary translators, who had to keep pace with the new timeline and whose profession was now in such high demand that it also had to be more easily accessed by wider circles of translation adepts.[80] New private publishing houses in Poland mushroomed after the fall of communism, their number in the mid-1990s reaching twenty times that of the former state-run counterparts.[81] At the same time, many of the previous state-run institutions proved to be too unwieldy to survive in the new reality.[82] This shift happened on the wave of political and economic transformation, the opening of borders, and the removal of previously imposed ideological constraints throughout the 1990s, a series of developments similar to what occurred in many other countries in the region.[83] The Polish literary market experienced a sharp rise in book numbers in absolute terms in this period, and the proportion of translations also increased considerably even within this generally growing publication volume, if not doubled overall.[84] Dubbed by some as "overabundance" or "oversaturation" in the translation market,[85] this influx of newly published titles and the rapid growth of translations in the 1990s partly had to do with a booming interest in filling in the gaps in the Polish cultural scene, especially with translations from English-language literature (often more popular genres from the United States). A similar pique of interest in this literary transfer was characteristic of the whole region after the collapse of the Soviet Union, where the number of politically driven translations from Russian into respective regional languages plummeted in favor of English coming to prominence.[86] In the Polish context, however, the ballooning of the book market and the rising translation production were also accompanied by what Michał Borodo calls "the proliferation of new translations of classics."[87] This trend in particular—besides the dramatic changes in the general publishing scene—nourished the production of multiple alternatives vis-à-vis the previously established translations of novels such as the aforementioned *Jane Eyre*, *Madame Bovary*, and *Crime and Punishment* that had been meticulously prepared by the PIW state press. The roaring 1990s were characterized by low production costs and the liberalization of the publishing industry, which in response to high demand for foreign titles created economic incentives to commission new translations in the private publishing sector. Perhaps unsurprisingly, the 1990s bore the fruit of many other translatorial multiplications of the kind. To add a few examples to the pool: at least four new translations of Mark Twain's *Tom Sawyer* and four new translations of Frances Hodgson Burnett's *The Secret Garden* appeared in the decade following the fall of communism, and so did at least nine translations of Carlo Collodi's *Pinocchio* (with two of them released simultaneously in 1994) as well as at least eight translations of Antoine de Saint-Exupéry's *Le petit prince* (reaching a total of twelve available in circulation).[88]

At the same time, some of the post-1989 multiple translations included instances of revamping older renderings and reintroducing these previously forgotten versions into circulation. In this way, many publishing houses could capitalize on similar "oldies" entering the public domain following the release of the Copyright and Related Rights Act in 1994. This act had quite surprising effects on the proliferation of translations in Poland. On the one hand, the act consolidated the intellectual property rights of authors in ways that could be potentially seen as constraining the production of multiple translations. Venuti and others have argued that the institutionalization of copyrights prioritizes the economic interests of authors and circumscribes translation to a "narrow space."[89] This form of intellectual property allows literary estates (often represented by the authors' heirs) to police the translation production either by imposing high fees or by limiting translations altogether;[90] some of the most infamous examples of this practice involve the estates of Joseph Brodsky, James Joyce, and Bertolt Brecht.[91] In the thick of the translation boom in postcommunist Poland, however, the 1994 Copyright Act might have complicated this general consensus on copyright's impact on translation. In fact, the extension of the period of copyright from twenty-five to fifty years (for both original authors and translators) paradoxically led to introducing more translation variants into circulation. Due to this change, it was now more profitable for publishers to find low-cost alternatives rather than cover the rights to republish previous "canonical" translations that were still under copyright.[92] But even when the copyright expired, publishers were still obliged to donate 5 to 8 percent of the wholesale price to a fund supporting literature. In practice, this meant that reintroducing the oldies into circulation was only the second-best option. It was financially more viable to commission brand new translations, the most economical and popular approach on the table.[93] As a result of this incentive, the proliferation of new translations in the free-market publishing order turned out to become a rather counterintuitive twist of the 1994 Copyright Act in Poland. Owing to the act's inclusion of translation copyrights and the subsequent high demand for new translations, some scholars even go as far as to argue that the act in fact empowered literary translators active in the 1990s, or at least made their bargaining position stronger than before.[94] Regardless of the overall assessment of its influence on the profession, this legal development contributed to the emergence of plural alternative translations of many foreign works in the literary market. Just like other political and economic developments in the publishing climate after the fall communism, it created further technical opportunities for multiple translations to enter the market almost simultaneously and sometimes virtually overnight.

It was only in the 1990s that the Polish publishing culture underwent more abrupt and dramatic changes, which laid the economic and institutional foundations for plural translations; these changes ushered in a period of liberalization of the publishing market following the removal of preventive censorship in 1990 and led to the democratization of the profession of translation, the faster pace of book production, the rapid growth of translations overall (including the proliferation of new translations of "classics"), the 1994 Copyright Law, and many other developments as discussed above. In the meantime, however, the Polish publishing industry did go through one interim stage, an episode that adds yet another element to this political puzzle and that also needs discussing in the context of translation alternatives that were sometimes available even before the symbolic watershed year of 1989. While the official circulation enjoyed an exclusive monopoly over publishing literature (including that in translation), its uncontested position started eroding in 1976, when it became possible to publish works underground—without the interference of the censor or the need for the state's permission—via an alternative, unofficial channel.[95] A series of anti-regime protests and strikes led to the establishment of the so-called second circulation (the equivalent of Russian "samizdat")[96] and eventually to the emergence of the Solidarity movement in 1980. While much smaller in scale than the official circulation, Poland's underground publishing did provide an anti-regime platform for books that could bypass the official infrastructure. In some instances, the two publishing sectors could even produce two translation alternatives intended for different audiences: this was the case with Jerzy Kosiński's sexually explicit *Steps*, first released in 1988 in the underground to be followed by an alternative version from the "official" translator in 1989.[97] Another example is the "anticommunist" translations of Bertolt Brecht's poetry, which aimed to compete with the poet's official pro-regime image, a case further discussed in chapter 5. According to Robert Looby, publishing practices in the underground "industry" in some ways mirrored those of the official industry in the late 1970s and throughout the 1980s: both of these sectors had their own idiosyncratic selection criteria (representing two ideologically opposite agendas), both were subject to the relatively lenient approach of censors during this period, and both had their own alternative production infrastructures, distribution channels, and target audiences.[98] This state of affairs does not mean, however, that the two circulations were really in conversation with each other or functioned in peaceful coexistence, acknowledging each other's publications. State institutions still dominated the literary scene, actively suppressing independent outlets and restricting the circulation of their materials. Underground publications in turn offered dissident counternarratives to contradict the official media, party-led propaganda, and state censorship. It was particularly in the years following the 1981 declaration of martial law that the clandestine distribution of printed works became one of the key driving forces of the political opposition. Those Solidarity members who avoided detention set up a range of printing shops distributing books and periodicals, but also posters, postcards, and stamps. As the social and intellectual life in Poland at the time was extremely polarized along partisan lines, the publishing sector also got inevitably enmeshed in ideological clashes fueled by the ongoing pro-government campaign or, on the other side of the barricades, constant anti-regime activities.

So even though the underground publishing initiatives provided an alternative platform to the official translation channels, their positioning in strict opposition to the state-run publishers had considerable side effects. Functioning in a state of constant war with the regime, the "second" circulation's activity was still dictated by its antagonistic stance toward mainstream publishing venues, which would sometimes translate into further biases and tribalist blinkers.[99] Similar discursive binaries in the years preceding 1989 add more nuance to the institutional tensions between the singular and the multiple across the communist and postcommunist cultural orders. In the grand scheme of things, the Polish translation multiples that entered the scene after 1989 had to defy the legacy of the totalitarian regime in many different realms of literary and intellectual life. But as the political and cultural landscape shifted, their creators also needed to look for new ways out of the ideological impasse and tried to disentangle the Cold War rhetoric of the goodies and the baddies, us versus them. This is also why, besides merely bidding farewell to the mainstream political line repeated from the rostrums, the translation multiples from the following three chapters of this volume also aim to challenge the persistent binaries of "either/or." And even if not all the tensions between the singular and the multiple across the two political orders are so clear-cut when assessed in hindsight from today's perspective, the focus of the following chapters will be on how the creators of the postcommunist translation multiples understood this dynamic and how they approached it in their own artistic projects. And they managed to unpack it, as I will discuss, in many wide-ranging and nontrivial ways: by weighing the assumptions of two opposite paradigms and pointing to their individual limitations, by reconciling them, by muddying the waters by suggesting alternatives, or by explicitly moving beyond the ideologized readings altogether.

These intuitions were direct and immediate responses to the new post-1989 reality but also could have had their roots in the earlier period of intense polarization, during which it became necessary to reconcile the two feuding narratives. As the Solidarity movement rose to prominence, however, it was not so obvious that artistic gestures whose premise might be similar to that of the postcommunist translation multiples would be welcome in a society torn apart by ideological war. The story of Krzysztof Kieślowski's film *Przypadek*, a cinematic forerunner and unwitting harbinger of the key Polish multiples, might illustrate how high the stakes were at the time. Known to a wider public for his *Three Colors*, *The Double Life of Véronique*, and *The Decalogue*, Kieślowski produced the earlier *Przypadek* (customarily translated as *Blind Chance*) in 1981. Analogously to other films shot and released during the Solidarity period of 1980–1981, *Blind Chance* was banned by the Polish authorities and had to wait for its delayed premiere in a censored form a few years later (on January 10, 1987). The title literally translates as "coincidence" or "case" (as in case study), and the plotline was indeed constructed as a study of three parallel scenarios initiated by a random event. The story revolves around the different life paths of Witek, the young protagonist, who decides to catch a train to Warsaw after his father's death (see fig. 2.1.). As he runs across the platform, he crashes into a man with a beer. This moment is a starting point for three speculative scenarios: depending on whether Witek catches the train or not, and whether he meets a friend on the train or a railway guard on the platform, his story unfolds in three different directions. In the first scenario, Witek gets involved in the Communist Party and becomes a state apparatchik; in the second, he turns into a religious anticommunist and works clandestinely in underground publishing; and in the final version, he completely withdraws from political concerns and wants to lead a private, apolitical life. In each of these "variations on Fate," as Marek Haltof calls them,[100] the original story starts with the same scene, but a little accident on the way changes the protagonist's life forever.

What significance does *Blind Chance* bear for thinking about postcommunist translation multiples? The film goes through three different variants of the same biography, or three alternative life paths of one man. The question arises whether Witek is the same person in all three scenarios or, in other words, if he is the same original "self" translated into three different chains of events and coincidental circumstances (see fig. 2.2). If that's the case, then how could the same person possibly grow into a regime supporter while also having the potential of becoming an anticommunist dissident in his parallel life? Witek, perhaps controversially, remains a good-natured and decent man regardless of the trajectory he has accidently started following. By anchoring Witek at the heart of three stories and studying all of them on equal footing, Kieślowski seemed to suggest that the good could still reside on both sides of the political barricades in the conflicted Poland of the 1980s. The unfavorable reception of the film at the time left no doubt as to the possibility of accepting this balanced and impartial account. Critics could not come to terms with Kieślowski's unbiased narrative, which lacked a pronounced political line. Already at the script stage, his project was attacked by official critics for antistate demagogy, whereas Solidarity reviewers later accused Kieślowski of being a socialist filmmaker.[101] If the director truly wished to "throw down the gauntlet on his divided homeland" and create a "post-political film,"[102] then his *Blind Chance* was a visionary attempt that nonetheless arrived too early. In the bipolar world of the 1980s, the film's multiplied composition only teased out the contradictions dormant in the Polish collective psyche. In a restless society marked by political tribalism, it was impossible to reconcile all the differently thinking and acting Witeks.

This historical and cultural backdrop is key to understanding the ethical resonance of postcommunist translation multiples in the local context of political events in the region of east-central Europe. Other analogous examples might be governed by similar formal principles, just like *Blind Chance* was said to inspire other analogously constructed films, such as Peter Howitt's *Sliding Doors* and Tom

FIGURE 2.1. A movie still of the repeated scene from Krzysztof Kieślowski's *Blind Chance* (1981–1987), which becomes a point of departure for three different life paths of the protagonist, Witek.

FIGURE 2.2. The cover image by Gérard Dubois for the Criterion Collection version of Kieślowski's *Blind Chance*. Courtesy of the Criterion Collection.

Tykwer's *Run Lola Run* (both 1998).[103] However, the unique import of Kieślowski's film and the postcommunist multiples is their showing a way out of the ideological impasse on the wave of political transition in the region. In this respect, *Blind Chance* also differs from the previously mentioned *Rashomon* by Akira Kurosawa, even though both display multiple hypothetical stories. While the latter offers different speculative interpretations and unreliable accounts of an original event, *Blind Chance* toys with the idea that all the stories can be easily translated into action, depending on political circumstances. In the world of postcommunist multiples, Kieślowski's three scenarios could work as equally legitimate worldviews and political actions, or as politically possible worlds existing in parallel with one another. In other instances, resorting to the sphere of the apolitical might also be a way of looking beyond the totalized discourse of the 1980s, as the final scenario tentatively suggests. Still, opposing the total can only happen through seeing the multiple in its broadest possible spectrum; considering and acknowledging more than one viable scenario at a time is indispensable for a truly pluralist project. Translation multiples share the same intuition as *Blind Chance*, while they also complicate Cold War narratives about Eastern European countries in a similar way. The stories behind translation multiples never boil down to the easy distinction between being pro-democratic and therefore pro-American on the one hand, versus being pro-communist and therefore pro-Soviet on the other. The post-1989 reality offers more nuanced challenges and complex perspectives on past legacies as well as on the unification of Eastern Europe with the Western world. Even though the Soviets were gone, and some Western history books about the region might have complacently stopped at this point, there was no happy ending to the transformation story besides a handful of unknowns. This is yet another lesson to be learned from the translation multiples discussed in this book. As they diverge from the total, they might search in different directions and find answers other than what's expected.

In the following chapters, I trace three case studies, all published after the political watershed of 1989. That specific year, marking the end of the communist system in Eastern Europe, was a symbolic point of reference for poets and creators of translation multiples, though it was just the beginning of the transformation process. In the Polish context, it was the year during which, over a period of two months from February to April, the state held Roundtable Talks, a series of peaceful negotiations between the former communist government and Solidarity representatives. However, it was not until October 27, 1991, that Poland held its first entirely free and democratic elections since the fall of communism. In the same year, Stanisław Barańczak published his homophonic translation multiple "Oratorium Moratorium," based on the French national anthem, "La Marseillaise," which I discuss in chapter 3. Though responding directly to the fall of communism in Eastern Europe and the Western reaction to this chain of events, his translation multiple proved to be a well-timed commentary on the fledgling postcommunist democracy. In the same year, Robert Stiller started working on his second translation variant of Anthony Burgess's *A Clockwork Orange*. His double or even triple translation project, which is examined in chapter 4, aimed to unmask a vicious circle of recurring totalitarian systems and acted as a bearer of bad news about the ongoing political cycle. The third variant of this translation multiple, commenting on Germany's role in European history, was still a work in progress as Poland accessed the European Union in 2004. Finally, almost a quarter century after 1989, four poets and translators took up the challenge of de-ideologizing the poetry of Bertolt Brecht and discarding his previously manipulated and biased readings. In chapter 5, I introduce their 2012 project of translating Brecht in four different ways in search of a sphere beyond the pre-1989 political tribalism or perhaps even outside the political altogether. At this juncture, I also suggest how the ethics of the multiple can be translated into an openly dialectical discussion around the original author. With these broader issues at stake, the following three chapters demonstrate how the pluralist undercurrents of postcommunist projects add yet another layer to the ethical task of translation multiples. In all these cases, undermining the canonized authority of the original by accepting plural interpretations becomes a democratic gesture targeting the totalitarian legacy. Translation multiples in this context have the potential of acknowledging other individual points of view and teaching us how to coexist in society with full responsibility.

3

Inner Pluralism
in the Wake of 1989

IOSIF BRODSKY: The boy is a genius, Stasiek, ya?
CZESŁAW MIŁOSZ: Fantastic.
IOSIF BRODSKY: What he does in translation rates absolutely remarkable.[1]

Against the Spirit of Generalization

The Polish poet and critic (and Harvard professor) Stanisław Barańczak sent a letter to Czesław Miłosz dated April 15, 1986. Part of a relatively regular correspondence about literary matters between the two authors and émigrés, this letter discusses the manuscript of Miłosz's cycle "Six Lectures in Verse." The cycle of six poems, published in 1987 in Polish and the year after in English, follows a series of six lectures given by Miłosz as Charles Eliot Norton Professor of Poetry at Harvard University in 1981–1982 and later collected in his book *The Witness of Poetry* (1983). While Barańczak praised the poetic cycle and advised his senior colleague on the choice of its title, he got particularly fixated on one line from "Lecture IV." As he wrote to Miłosz: "I read the sentence 'The true enemy of man is generalization' as a central sentence of the work and at the same as the key to your poetry."[2] A few years later, in his 1993 review of Miłosz's poetic cycle written for the *Harvard Review*, Barańczak would uphold his opinion. This "most crucial statement," according to him, best summarized Miłosz's poetic creed and his technique of a moving camera that zooms into single events. Opposing the spirit of generalization, Miłosz's "synecdochic" vision instead breaks up "the panoramic image of an anonymous dehumanized mass into individual vignettes, close-ups, and details."[3] Its focus on what is tangible and concrete can split any totalizing and all-encompassing narrative into plural perspectives and individual stories.

Between Barańczak's two commentaries on Miłosz's poetic formula, in 1986 and 1993, political and cultural life in Eastern Europe turned upside down. As the communist system collapsed and the Soviet Union dissolved, some of the battles had already been won, but others remained to be redefined for a new future. Since literature and art were said to retreat from political engagement, Barańczak reiterated Miłosz's sentence to point to other challenges in the wake of 1989. In his talk "Poetry and the Spirit of Generalization" held in Austria in 1992, Barańczak warned that the poet's mission should not terminate with the end of political pressure.[4] As he reformulated Miłosz's line to guide artists and intellectuals during the challenging times to come, he also employed it in his own poetry and translation practice. This is true, too, of his curious homophonic translation multiple published in 1991, "Oratorium Moratorium," which I treat as a literary testimony to this critical reflection. An immediate response to the political reality in post-1989 Eastern Europe, this translation multiple accorded with the poet's call for plural voices and his critique of any one-sided account of history. At the same time, the ostensibly insignificant, but also unprecedented, idea of multiplying different translation variants in a literary text grew somewhat organically alongside Barańczak's own creative work. His translation multiples could be seen as a continuation of his earlier writing and essays on the ethical role of poetry from before 1989. Then, this strand of socially engaged interlingual experiments might be a paragon of the satirical strand of nonsense poetry reinvented for the early 1990s. Finally, they are also informed by his translation criticism and a broader agenda of presenting translations from multiple individual angles. In putting all these contexts on the table, I will shed light on the intellectual trends and artistic tendencies that informed the radical bent of Barańczak's translation multiples.

Why would the creative work of a US-based professor and critic be significant for the transition period between the 1980s and 1990s in Poland? Unlike his senior colleague Miłosz, Stanisław Barańczak is not familiar to an American reader in his capacity as poet. Many might recognize Barańczak's name from other aspects of his intellectual activity since he moved to the United States to take up a position at Harvard's Slavic Department in 1981. From that time, he was known primarily as a cotranslator of Polish poetry, for instance with Clare Cavanagh (of a PEN-awarded collection of Wisława Szymborska's work and the anthology of poetry *Spoiling Cannibals' Fun: Polish Poetry of the Last Two Decades of Communist Rule*, 1991) and with Seamus Heaney (of the Polish Renaissance poet Jan

Kochanowski). Others might have come across his name among promoters of Polish literature and literary critics owing to his two books of essays with Harvard University Press: a study on Zbigniew Herbert, *A Fugitive from Utopia* (1987), and a collection of inquisitive musings on cultural life under totalitarian rule, *Breathing under Water and Other East European Essays* (1990). But his name might also vaguely ring a bell in the context of Miłosz's 1965 anthology *Postwar Polish Poetry*, which became a model of political engagement for American writers throughout the 1960s and 1970s. Although Barańczak was too young to be included in the first edition of that book, Miłosz republished a selection from dispersed translations of Barańczak's poetry[5] in the third, expanded edition in 1985. Presented as a "preeminently political" poet,[6] Barańczak was lumped together with others in a rather congealed category of the "Polish school of poetry."[7] That pigeonhole already contained much more recognizable names at the time such as Miłosz himself, Wisława Szymborska, Adam Zagajewski, and Zbigniew Herbert. However, Barańczak represented the next generation of Polish poets whose work was more language oriented, a trait that might not have traveled well across languages. Despite his publishing a partly self-translated collection, *The Weight of the Body* (1989),[8] and being anointed by Miłosz as a "fantastic genius" and "shaman,"[9] Barańczak's literary work remained largely unknown in the Anglophone world.

In the meantime, on the other side of the Atlantic, Barańczak was one of the leading poets and central intellectual figures of late twentieth-century Poland. He played first fiddle in the 1968 poetic generation clustered under the umbrella term "Nowa Fala" (New Wave). This literary movement was born out of the antiregime protests of students and intellectuals in March 1968; these were followed by workers' riots in December 1970 and resulted in a range of oppositionist initiatives including strikes in 1976, the previously mentioned foundation of underground publishing, and finally the emergence of Solidarity. Barańczak—a cofounder of the human rights group Workers' Defense Committee (KOR), a lecturer at the independent educational institution called the Flying University, and one of the key anticommunist activists—soon joined the list of officially banned authors. His poetry targeted the hollow and uniform language of newspeak, officialese, and propaganda by, as he would write, "calling every word as a false witness"[10] and examining "the word in a state of suspicion."[11] In 1970, he formulated the New Wave program in his manifesto, appealing for poetry that critically and inquisitively confronts the political and linguistic discourses of oppression.[12] As Barańczak's texts were intermittently banned from official print from 1977 onward, they were instead released in the underground press or by publishing houses abroad, especially in London or Paris. In this way, Barańczak and many other writers of the anti-regime faction tried to operate in a gray area and somehow "breathe under water," as he called that condition in his essays published later in the United States. After his enforced dismissal from his university position in Poland, he was offered a temporary academic post at Harvard. However, the authorities of the Polish People's Republic hindered the process of issuing his passport, tediously delaying it for years. After Barańczak made it to the United States in 1981, and martial law was imposed in Poland in December the same year, he never moved back to his home country. He taught at Harvard until the late 1990s and continued to live in Massachusetts until his death in 2014.

This backstory is key to understanding Barańczak's positioning between two countries and his involvement in the intellectual life on both sides of the Atlantic on the eve of 1989. His translation multiples and other interlingual experiments published prolifically in the early 1990s were a creative by-product of this in-betweenness. While Miłosz was Poland's official cultural attaché, Barańczak's role was less formal in this respect: he actively mediated between English and his mother tongue, cotranslating Polish poetry into English but also bringing into Polish thick volumes of Anglophone poetry and drama spanning a few centuries and hundreds of authors with radically different styles. Though aware of the incongruity of two different linguistic worlds, Barańczak saw this Polish-English cultural transfer as a liberating pursuit. What might have appeared to some as "a split personality" was seen by him as a "profoundly advantageous multivalent consciousness" and an "authentic inner pluralism, openness to multiple values co-existing in the world."[13] Barańczak put this gesture of embracing multiple values into practice by integrating the translation of other literary traditions into the public sphere. From the 1990s, his guest talks on translation in Poland would gather crowds, translation seminars were formed, and literary critics had their say in translation debates in the most significant cultural newspapers. "You just needed to have an opinion on Barańczak's translations so you would study them carefully and critically," reminisced Magda Heydel.[14] Barańczak's translations became a cultural phenomenon in their own right. And translation, thanks to its surrounding polemics, turned into a space to wrestle over with arguments and emotions, with room opened up for not only specialists to operate but also the reading audience.[15] This activity granted Barańczak almost a cult status as a poet-translator celebrity in post-1989 Poland. His translations of poetry and interlingual experiments, which were treated as a constituent element of his creative writing, were even put on stage and turned into a theatrical play. Performed for the first time in 2013 in the Poznań New Theatre, the play had a very telling title: *Mister*

Barańczak.[16] As the English form of address "mister" was used in the original Polish, it encapsulated the poet's intercultural standing.

What particularly interests me in this context is why Barańczak resorted to literary translation and nonsense poetry at the moment of a political disruption in 1989 and the urgent need then to redefine the literary landscape in the early 1990s. As he was writing his homophonic multiple "Oratorium Moratorium," he let out a torrent of other translation experiments, conceptual translation books, and thematic anthologies. Compensating for the poet's previous absence from the official publishing scene, this series of translations offered a refreshing boost to the Polish language, reopening it to other influences and integrating it back with the West. His translation books started filling the many literary gaps left after the previously limited circulation of Western writers.[17] In 1990, exactly twenty years after his first manifesto on the vigilant poetry of the 1968 generation, Barańczak published a second manifesto, this time on translation practice.[18] In what he called "A Small, but Maximalist Translatological Manifesto," he waged a campaign against generalizations and reductionist approaches to poetry translation and its artistic role.[19] At the same time, Barańczak started publishing experimental translingual exercises that involved a range of Western languages (principally English, German, Italian, and French) and stretched the Polish language beyond its previously isolated comfort zone. He introduced a range of new experimental genres: these spanned translingual "pseudo-novellas" (texts sounding as if written in another language), "identographs" (texts looking as if written in two different languages at the same time), "phonets" (homophonic translations), and many others[20]—all bringing Polish and other languages together in sound, shape, and image. Calling himself a "radical English leveler and subverter of traditional hierarchies," he argued that equating these different languages means they are all of equal worth to one another and should have an equal status in the international arena.[21] Ostentatious departures from literal senses in his renderings were also attributed to liberating and democratizing properties. As he coined a new term for his free translations of English limericks—"libericks"—he underscored the Latin etymology of *libertas* (freedom). Thanks to this exercise, the translator's hands were finally not tied by the reign of original meanings but could enjoy "the freedom of topics, problems, emotions, and perspectives."[22] In Barańczak's agenda, the recourse to experimental translation was a way of abolishing constraint but also challenging the original's exclusive authority. As he provocatively remarked, homophonic translations "liberate us from the obligation of slavish fidelity toward the original and any senses unlawfully imposed by it."[23] Translation practice for him did not boil down to a blind replication of literary models emanating from major cultures; it rather invited critical discussion about different modes of reading them, and, while opening up a space of integration, should also leave room for emancipation and independent thinking.

This shift to translation and interlingual experiments, however, was hardly seen as a response to the post-1989 reality, just like Barańczak's interest in nonsense writing was largely received by critics with surprise and even slight condescension.[24] Nonetheless, the poet found both these areas of artistic expression of paramount importance in the early 1990s and often combined them with political and satirical topics. This was the case with "Oratorium Moratorium" and other homophonic multiples but also, for instance, with the parodistic and immensely unpopular volume from 1995, *Bóg Trąba i Ojczyzna* (God, Trunk, Fatherland), which mocked the Polish sense of self-importance and the repertoire of national myths.[25] The aesthetics of nonsense became a weapon against the absurd reality and unexpected repercussions of the 1989 events; it was a sort of "double negation," in which the real absurdity could be canceled out by a literary one.[26] In a letter to a friend written after the presidential elections of 1990, in which the Solidarity leader Lech Wałęsa did not win the first round, Barańczak mentioned how he took up writing nonsense poetry for the first time: "Depressed after the Polish elections, I myself saw a pathological routine in the way my days would unfold since then. I would wake up at the crack of dawn and get down to the newest paper. When I was done reading, something would get into me: I was incapable of any intellectual work until I cleansed my brain with pure nonsense."[27] According to Barańczak, this procedure was inevitable, and a sense of humor would very often come in handy in the postcommunist reality; the role of a nonsense poet was similar to that of a metaphysical one except that the nonsense poet had nothing else left but laughter.[28] Though everyone hoped against all hope that the introduction of democracy would automatically solve all human problems, it did not.[29] Individual members of society were still confronted with both new challenges and old dilemmas, whether of a mundane and practical or ethical and metaphysical nature.[30] Before 1989, the Polish lyricist and cabaret performer Jeremi Przybora wrote nonsense verse, which "helped millions of people walk away almost without a scratch from the few decades of heavy nonsense that constituted the Communist reality of the Polish People's Republic."[31] Likewise, Barańczak's own nonsense writing also had its mission to fulfill after 1989.

What exactly were these challenges that Barańczak kept warning against in the early 1990s? He found the answer in Miłosz's poetic formula, "the spirit of generalization," which he made an overarching theme of his critical reflection. In his 1992 talk "Poetry and the Spirit of Generalization" (published in 1996 in an essay collection under the same title), he argued that the spirit of generalization did not disappear after the fall of communism in Eastern Europe. It would still haunt every society, regardless of geographical location and time period, as it had for past centuries. Taking broad ideas and ideological "isms" for granted led interest groups to advocate the notion of the collective and replace the truth of the individual with false generalizations. The mechanism of generalization, as discussed in George Orwell's "Notes on Nationalism" (1945), forces an individual to merge into a bigger group and fall into the trap of tribalism. To illustrate this threat, Barańczak alluded to rising nationalisms in the Balkans, in a sense heralding the ethnic conflicts later to unfold in the Yugoslav wars: what legitimized killing was the situation in which humans no longer saw themselves as individuals; each person was no longer a unique being with a particular name, but a "Serb shooting a Croat, or the other way round."[32] A remedy to this should be poetry that renders the voice of the individual, not a poetry dictated by any of the manipulative umbrella terms. It can perhaps also trespass on the boundaries of nationalisms through translation: the act of transferring a foreign tradition to a local one means that it is possible, if not to share, then at least to situate the experience of a specific individual in relation to someone else's in a different part of the globe regardless of political or national affiliations. At the same time, there are a few practical insights from this lesson: the speaking self has to use language in a way that opposes the mechanism of "totum pro parte," taking a part for a greater whole, and favors "pars pro toto," a poetical synecdoche that zooms into a portion of a panoramic entity.[33] Elsewhere, Barańczak repeated this argument, praising the poetic imagination for "not seeing the forest from behind the trees"; instead, it should focus on certain single species as opposed to overwhelmingly exuberant projects and "what George H. W. Bush called the vision thing."[34] Barańczak's essays were interpreted as a call for polyphonic language and the pluralist diversity of individual stances.[35] The "part for the whole" approach assumed that the whole may break into many different alternatives that reflect various partial readings. These parts, however, should be complementary, not conflicted with one another. As generalized speech—the total—cannot represent plural individuals, each of the puzzle's multiple pieces, rather, should stand for itself, all pieces coexisting in a polyphony of different forms.

Barańczak's own poetry[36] and translation work throughout the 1990s served as a literary annex exemplifying his ethical appeal in practice. In the realm of poetry translation, his campaign against the total was perhaps most visibly reflected in the practice of multiplying translation variants. What was at stake here was the idea that the original is an ostensibly monolithic textual whole (the totum) that should be challenged and split into various dialectical readings (partes). This way, poetry in all its polyphonic richness could be open to different individual approaches performed in translation. In his translatological manifesto, Barańczak invited other translators to challenge his own readings through polemical interpretations, but he also wrote about "the polemics with oneself,"[37] the possibility of producing more than one rendering by the same translator. The idea of Barańczak's polemics with oneself has been recorded in print many times, as he often published his collections of poetry in different reeditions, juggling equally creative alternatives, paraphrasing earlier fragments with synonymic variants, and breaking down the original polysemy into plural possibilities.[38] He also placed translation multiples or "variations on a theme," as he dubbed some of them, in which he adopted multiple interpretative lenses, in his nonsense poetry anthologies. For instance, he translated the same poems by Langston Hughes, Ogden Nash, and Dorothy Parker in different ways. In one case he looked at the original text from the perspective of a parent, and then from that of a child; in another case, he zoomed down to the level of "microbiology" and out to the political landscape of the Middle East, presenting each of the renderings next to one another.[39] A special place in his repertoire belonged to homophonic multiples, in which the "part for the whole" technique could dismantle the original into plural creative mishearings. As these homophonic procedures stretched out the semantic capacity of the original in many ways, they also served as a playful excuse to smuggle various political topics and imagery into some variants. In this way, one of the partial perspectives could also unexpectedly bring to the fore an issue otherwise unheard and unrepresented in the generalized whole.

In a running commentary to another of his homophonic multiples published alongside the reprinted version of "Oratorium Moratorium" in 1995, Barańczak joked about the explosive power of sound. According to him, for example, Chinese lends itself to dangerous mishearings owing to its tonal nature. As he remarked: "[D]eviations from the proper model of intonating a word—nay, one vowel!—can change the sense of a pronounced sentence from an order in a restaurant to a provocatively revolutionary and political exclamation."[40] This seemingly innocent mispronunciation, a mere sound shift, can have serious consequences for the political reality and performative power of language. In his homophonic multiple of the short Italian aria "Dalla sua pace" (On Her Peace of Mind) from Mozart's *Don Giovanni*,[41] he tweaked his mishearings to a similar effect. The piece is originally sung by Don Ottavio, fiancé of the previously seduced Donna Anna, who swears to vindicate her honor: "On her peace mine also depends, what pleases her gives me life." In the first of four columns, Barańczak places the lyrics of the original Italian libretto, which he then homophonically translates into three poems that run in parallel to each other. Nothing is left of the original "sua pace," the heroine's peace of mind, as it undergoes quite brutal treatments in all three variants. Although each culminates in the same grotesque refrain—"w mordę mi da!" (will smash my snout)—all three nonsensical scenarios differ from each other almost entirely: the first scenario introduces drunken slaughterers, the second one catchers of llamas, and the third one—Apaches. The third absurd variant, however, also manages to slip other unexpected threads into the story. Even though attributing violence to "Apaches in Dallas," it also simulates the communist newspeak fueled by both physical and verbal aggression:

Dalla sua pace	W Dallas Apacze	[Apaches in Dallas
la mia dipende	rabina bili prętem	Were hitting a rabbi with a bar
quel ch'a lei piace,	Kwęka i płacze?	He is whining and weeping?
vita mi rende.	Zwyczajny endek!	A mere Endek!]

The antinational character of this invective is somewhat paradoxical. The authorities of the Polish People's Republic would stigmatize their opponents with the label "endeks" (NDs), alluding to members of the ring-wing National Democratic Party of interwar Poland, treating them in effect as enemies of the state. At the same time, citizens of Jewish descent were also persecuted and infamously forced to emigrate during the anti-Zionist and then anti-Jewish campaign of March 1968. The absurdity of calling a rabbi by this name lay in the fact that the National Democratic Party constituted an antisemitic and nationalist political group. Through his homophonic slippages, Barańczak wanted to ridicule these mutually exclusive generalizations. As he fans out three absurd scenarios, he also reiterates different nonsensical mechanisms of justifying aggression. Suffused with the macabre and grotesque, his homophonic multiples dismantle the original aria, teasing out its darker shades. At the same time, some partial readings and creative mishearings could smuggle completely different and unexpected perspectives into the mix.

Oratorium Moratorium

In 1991, the London-based Polish dissident outlet and political quarterly *Puls*, gathering readers with different political views since 1982, released its last few issues. Nestled among essays and debates concerning the political situation after 1989, readers could find a surprising literary bonus: Stanisław Barańczak's homophonic multiple. Written as a poetic commentary on recent political events, it focused on the initial years after the fall of communism in Eastern Europe and on the period of time before the Soviet Union's final collapse. The main title of the work—"Oratorium Moratorium"—already hinted at Barańczak's viewpoint of what he saw as political stalling for time and a temporary prohibition of activity on Western Europe's part. Different opinions on and assessments of the situation were interwoven in the orchestrated conversation of different voices reluctantly welcoming "New Europe." These voices were introduced, in a long, baroque subtitle, as "the balalaika-cantata band of the Western World Harmonia Mundi with soloists and a mixed choir expressing equally mixed feelings."[42] When Barańczak republished his multiple in 1995, he admitted that he had first tried his hand at inventing phonetic equivalents for the French lines of "La Marseillaise," the French anthem, in 1990 during a visit of his friend, Edward Balcerzan. The playful rivalry between the two soon snowballed into a more serious contemplation:

> The intellectual work on what might seem a purely abstract task promptly and quite naturally turned into a more general reflection on the nature of relations between Eastern Europe and the Western World; it was at the same time situated against the background of certain contemporary events. Mind you it was the year 1990, and the speed of the real socialist system falling into a shambles in the countries of the former Eastern Bloc was received by Western Europe not so much with enthusiasm, but rather with great anxiety.[43]

By way of immediate response to this political reality, Barańczak arranged his intricate translation in the form of an oratorio ("oratorium"), a semi-operatic, though rarely staged, musical composition intertwining the voices of soloists, a mixed choir, and an orchestra. The musical genre of oratorio, most prominent in the baroque period, engaged with sacred themes and was used by both the Protestant and Catholic Churches, with the latter allowing for its performance during Lent despite the prohibition of spectacles otherwise in that period. Partly alluding to this backstory, Barańczak also used his oratorio as an outlet for a subversive artistic message. He composed his elaborate work from well-known and slightly clichéd tunes representing different political camps and ideological projects. Most of his "Oratorium Moratorium" employed translation multiples of the same two passages from "La Marseillaise," the voice of the West. The melody of "La Marseillaise" famously became the rallying tune of the French Revolution and was sung at revolutionary public occasions. Though banned by Napoleon, it continued to serve as an unofficial anthem of the international revolutionary movement in the nineteenth century. Rather ironically, the multiples based on "La Marseillaise" were interspersed with self-invented or altered lyrics from a socialist realist song by Isaak Dunayevsky, "The March of Friendship," redolent of the Eastern Bloc. It is no coincidence that Barańczak placed the French revolutionary song next to a Soviet anthem to freedom that praised a collective fight allegedly for the same idea: "Wygramy walkę o trwały pokój, wrogom wolności wzniesiona pięść!" (We will win the fight for permanent peace, the fist is raised against the enemies of freedom!). In his multiple versions of "La Marseillaise" and fragments of the communist song, Barańczak toned down their zealous appeals for action; different renderings dismantled the original great visions into a disillusioned discussion about recent events and concrete viewpoints. What could sound like a forced debate about the elephant in the room resonated with the artificial framing of the performance. Barańczak underscored this impression with grotesque Italianate (and often faulty Italian) stage directions: "tutti frutti senza Speranza" (all fruits without hope), "alla maniera un puoco imbecile" (in a bit of an idiotic manner), and "con sclerosa morose" (with sluggish sclerosis), as well as jingles from *The Merry Widow*'s potpourri. In the final lines, as the stage directions have it, the musical crossover between two political songs segue into a different tune: the whole oratorio is rounded off by the subtle melody of Beethoven's "Ode to Joy," also the anthem of the European Union.

The key idea behind "Oratorium Moratorium" lies in distributing various voices and political arguments among different renderings of the same original fragments. Barańczak translated these fragments by closely imitating in sound the first few lines of respective wholes, then primarily following the lyrics in terms of rhythm and assonants. Besides criticizing the political standstill, Barańczak's homophonic multiples bring forward a mixture of opinions representing, variously, naïve optimism, apprehension, and even some aggression in the enforcing of liberal and federal ideas in the newly welcomed countries. This multithreaded conversation consequently spans two different homophonic translations of the French anthem's introduction ("Allons enfants de la Patrie . . ."), seven different versions of its refrain ("Aux armes, citoyens . . ."), and two passages of the socialist realist song, with altered lyrics. All of these fragments come in a gamut of multiple voices and keep recurring in a different order. For instance, the two variants of the opening of "La Marseillaise" in Polish appear first at the beginning of the oratorio and then again toward its middle, after a sequence of two differently translated refrains and a longer passage from the social realist song. The two variants of the anthem's opening are sung respectively by a choir of tenors and a choir of basses, which also sets the tone for a more diverse vocalization.

While both present rather skeptical stances, each is expressed differently and supported with distinct images and arguments:[44]

Allons enfants de la Patrie, Le jour de gloire est arrivé! Contre nous de la tyrannie L'étendard sanglant est levé L'étendard sanglant est levé.[45]	Tam ląd sam cham Arafat ryje [*Pcha lont nam cham Arafat w ryje] Lecz Wschód i Wschód—to sprawy dwie. Tu co prawda też ciągłe chryje, Byle lud—krok w przód i się drze: Byle lud na wyprzódki się drze! [Arafat the coarse himself is drilling the land there (*Arafat the coarse is pushing the fuse in our snouts); But the East and the East are two separate matters. It is true constant tiffs happen here too, The people have barely made a step forward and yell, The people are barely in the race and yell!]	Zalążek glątw ta klapa kryje, Gdzie żur z jagłami?— któż to wie? Lud jak wprzód tam ni tyra, ni je, Wolność ma, lecz znów czegoś chce: Ma jej w bród, ale znów czegoś chce! [This flop is hiding a seed of hangovers Where is the sour rye soup with millet? Who knows? The people previously neither worked, nor ate, Now have freedom, but want something more, Have freedom galore but want something more!]

In these passages, Barańczak creatively "mishears" the original lyrics into two different renderings.[46] The first variant features the reasoning of those anxious about the dangerous similarities between the Middle East conflicts and the Eastern European situation at that time. Sung only by tenors from the choir, this passage demonstrates the complete chaos in the postcommunist countries after their liberation. Their new political demands were received by the West with surprise as too sudden and premature. The other variant, sung by bass vocalists from the Western choir, warn about potential consequences ("hangovers") of the abrupt political change. It doubts the existence of a potential remedy to the situation, as no one can find Polish sour rye soup with millet, a popular next-day dish, soothing a hangover. According to this other faction, the Eastern European demands are not so much ill timed as completely unjustified. Full of unbridled ambitions, citizens of the postcommunist countries were already dissatisfied with the previous political situation, and so, after 1989, in the light of increasing freedom, they should have consequently approved of the ongoing transition. To question this point, Barańczak invents here an alternative homophonic translation for the French (*la*) *tyrannie* ([the] tyranny). Earlier on, the spoiled Eastern European people only "(ni) tyra, ni je" (neither worked, nor ate), which perhaps in the eyes of the West did not qualify as so terrible a condition. However, this phrase still homophonically echoes the more obvious phonetic equivalent in Polish hidden underneath: "tyranije" (tyrannies). Reading or singing this passage out loud can wittily activate its grimmer undertone. As the original French song permeates the homophonic multiple, the double-edged message exposes the hypocrisy lying behind this dismissive attitude: revolution is welcome and celebrated as long as it takes place in Western Europe, the "civilized" land. The very same senior leaders who once zealously anticipated the unity of Europe are now terrified by the prospect of peaceful revolution and integration. In Larry Wolff's words, "the iron curtain is gone, yet the shadow persists."[47]

In these multiples, Barańczak gives a foretaste of the polyphonic exercise that different soloists and parts of the choir go on to perform in the seven variants of the refrain of "La Marseillaise." Four of these, the "Western" four versions, span similar themes and forms as they map various Eastern European countries while showing complete indifference as to their fate. Performed respectively by a soprano, the entire choir, a tenor, and then all singers, these versions are loosely intertwined with the socialist realist song refrains—two surprisingly similar voices resonating on behalf of the Soviet agenda, represented by the whole choir and then by the choir reinforced by three soloists. The four renderings of the anthem's refrains here seem aligned with the socialist realist song's two alternative refrains: Barańczak makes sure to highlight a clear continuity between the Soviet Union and the West in their disrespect of individual minor nations. He presents a symbolic affinity between the two in a very pessimistic, but also melodramatic, tone. The second social realist refrain, descending into the pan-European "Ode to Joy," is emphatically performed by the widest range of singers in a combined effort. Crowning the entire musical procession is a grand, grotesque finale with a standing ovation, applause by all vocalists and musicians on stage, and a loud exclamation carrying the last words: "Świat tak czy owak toczy się w przód" (The world trundles forward anyway).

Before that, the progression of refrains reveals the somewhat hypocritical position of the West, who only wished to deal with Eastern European affairs if they happened behind closed doors ("przy zamkniętych drzwiach"). These passages[48] quite explicitly comment on the proceedings of the 1989 revolutions as well as the gradual dissolving of the Soviet Union and its federation into independent states. Broadly speaking, the refrains briefly cover Eastern European upheavals and turbulence, revealing instructions and demands toward particular countries, for example, "dość drak / na placach Prag" (enough of rows in the squares of Pragues), "dość bitw / na polach Litw" (enough of battles on the fields of Lithuanias), and "ścisz ryk / ludności Ryg" (lower your scream, people of Rigas). They also openly dismiss the potential repercussions of these revolutions, remaining flippant about events such as the early stage of the Croatian War of Independence in the midst of the Yugoslav wars: "Niech Serb / za herb / ma młot i sierp: Chorwacie-chwacie cierp!" (Let the Serb have the hammer and sickle as their crest; and let you suffer, the brave Croat), and the Nagorno-Karabakh War with its ethnic conflict between Armenians and Azerbaijanis: "Niech krach / i strach / Żre Karabach / Lecz przy zamkniętych drzwiach" (Let the collapse / and fear / eat up Karabakh / Though behind closed doors). In the last refrain of "La Marseillaise," just before it smoothly moves on to the social realist finale, the Western choir ultimately decides to turn a blind eye to what is happening in the former Eastern Bloc. As if the problems could somehow magically solve themselves from behind closed doors ("zza zamkniętych drzwi"), this voice tries to pretend that the days of harmony and peace will soon return ("wnet harmonii i spokoju wrócą dni").

The overarching theme for this sequence, a complete lack of compassion, equally spans the two social realist parts. The respective voices talk of minor peoples such as Uzbeks, Tatars, Balts, Moldavians, Slovenians, Slovaks, and Romanians. They express utter disinterest in these peoples' fate, for example: "Spis krzywd Uzbeka / nas nie urzeka" (The list of the Uzbeki's harms does not impress us), "Strata Tatara / nie wzrusza nas" (Losing the Tatar does not move us). They call this negligent attitude into question by referring to specific conflicts: "Rozpałka gwałtów / Los Bałkan, Bałtów?" (Ignition of violence, The fate of the Balkans, Balts?). They also give a grim diagnosis over the lack of international solidarity and cooperation between countries: "Internacjonał skonał i zgasł" (International solidarity has agonized and waned). As the French-based fragments mingle thematically with the social realist lyrics, they also veer off from the original idea of freedom. Barańczak's rendering offers a bitter reckoning: the

Western-elevated message from "La Marseillaise" applies only selectively to that part of the world. Departures from the original lofty ideals are also reflected in sound—respective homophonic sequences move further and further away from the initial closely matching lines as the whole debate keeps disintegrating.

The remaining three variants of the French refrain starting with "Aux armes, citoyens..." read as follows:[49]

Aux armes, citoyens,	Choć zżarła schizma ją,	Ocalmy choć bon–ton!	O, car! Mocarny pan!
Formez vos bataillons!	Choć rwie debata ją,	Choć żre debata ją, Euro–	On nie dopuszczał zmian!
Marchons!	Euro–	Pa Śro–	Nagan–
Marchons!	Pa Śro–	Dkowa i Wscho–	Nym stan–
Qu'un sang impur	Dkowa i Wscho–	Dnia jednak wie	Dartem jest pan–
Abreuve nos sillons	Dnia zgodnie przegna zło!	gdzie dno!	Demonium: zły to plan!

	[Though eaten up by the schism,	[Let's at least save the good form!	[Oh, tsar! Mighty lord!
	Though being torn by the debate,	Though being eaten up by the debate,	He allowed for no changes!
	Euro–	Euro–	A reprehen–
	Pe, Cen–	Pe, Cen–	Sible stan–
	Tral and East–	Tral and East–	Dard is pan–
	Ern, will together expel the evil]	Ern, still knows where a rock bottom is]	Demonium: it's a bad plan!]

In introducing tonal and prosodic shifts throughout these three versions, Barańczak's creative mishearings again break into distinct semantic messages; they each reveal the internal inconsistency of Harmonia Mundi. As stated in the stage directions, they are to be performed respectively by *tutti* (everyone), all basses from the choir, and, quite tellingly for the last passage's undertone, a ninety-four-year-old bass soloist. These refrains not only reiterate different political stances but also explicitly appeal for a pluralist dialogue through translation variants. The first version represents the most optimistic scenario, commenting favorably on the capacity of Central and Eastern Europe to fight unitedly against "the evil" and overcome the political schism. According to this voice, despite being torn by the debate ("choć źre debata ją"), this part of Europe can peacefully achieve a state of freedom without re-forming their original military battalions. However, the original "bataillons" can still homophonically resonate through the Polish phrase. This effect plays into a tension between, on the one hand, the French military means of striving for freedom (battalions) and, on the other, the Western-downplayed idea of pacifist "debate" in the Polish translation. In his diagnosis of this somewhat naïve optimism, Barańczak alludes to the assumptions of Western commentators, which were informed by the early experience of bloodless coups or nonviolent revolutions taking place in the Warsaw Pact countries from 1989 onward. However, events such as the violent unrest in Romania, wars in the Balkan melting pot, and other conflicts from previously described refrains had to complicate this wishful thinking. Accordingly, the second translation variant is more doubtful, calling on the Western countries to put on a brave face while Eastern Europe again hits rock bottom. This version of the French anthem's refrain comes at a later point in the oratorio, by which time readers have learned other stances. As this voice follows the two social realist refrains, and the Western choir's hypocrisy has been revealed, the only possibility that remains for Harmonia Mundi at that point is at least to save the "bon ton," the good manners, on the surface. Even though he distanced himself from these viewpoints, Barańczak still included each of them in his homophonic multiples. Tracing and reconstructing the debate around the fall of communism in Eastern Europe from different perspectives, he opened this translation forum for multiple dialectical readings of the French combative song.

Himself a columnist writing twice a year on Eastern Europe for an American audience,[50] Barańczak was aware of the existing speculation and political interpretations of the end of communism. In a bitter article for *Salmagundi* in 1990, he discussed these different stances that were in circulation at the time. Opening with a quotation from Philip Larkin's poem "Annus Mirabilis" about reactions to the 1963 sexual revolution—"Then all at once the quarrel sank: / Everyone felt the same"—Barańczak implied a parallel with the more recent miraculous year, 1989. When scanning through the different unfavorable opinions in the West he put on the table, we can find prototypes for Harmonia Mundi's different voices in "Oratorium Moratorium." There, we have both skeptical conservative policymakers and left-wing opinion makers disinterested in how the oppressed people in Eastern Europe actually lived. The article singles out those who believed that the end of communism would be the end of history (it only "opened the can of nationalistic and chauvinistic worms," and "history will continue as long as human evil exists"), that there would be no transformation into a democracy through peaceful evolution (the examples of Poland, Hungary, Czechoslovakia, and others proved otherwise), and that "where no Soviet tanks were involved a bloodbath could always be avoided" (the Romanian case unfortunately complicated that generalization).[51] The panoramic account of the Annus Mirabilis in Eastern Europe as covered in the West, Barańczak argues, could only show the forest without focusing on individual trees. If attentive viewers had zoomed into the celebratory scenes, they would have noticed behind all those national flags proudly carried in the streets of Vilnius and Lviv unpromising details such as the polluted Baltic Sea.[52] Even a quick glimpse of some banners in a Sofia square, for instance, would have informed viewers of other upcoming problems: some Bulgarians on the streets in fact went out not to celebrate, but to protest against the country's Turkish minority.[53] Listening more carefully to the voices of Eastern Europe and identifying in enough time the actual social, economic, and ethnic tensions might have spared unnecessary conflicts and perhaps also saved people's lives.

The same appeal to listen to and acknowledge all points of view is the main premise of Barańczak's translation multiple. However, the dramatic sequence in "Oratorium Moratorium" also explicitly cautions against the opposite scenario. In particular, the polyphony of discussion can be endangered by suppressing other perspectives, including those deemed uncomfortable or unpopular. This manifests itself in the treatment of the last homophonic variant of the "La Marseillaise" refrain. As per stage directions, its performer is an elderly bass soloist, whose part resounds "as a complete surprise and sudden reminiscence from childhood." Though singing with the ostensibly progressive Western choir, he voices a critical and opposing view redolent of the older generation. Openly disapproving of the post-1989 political mayhem, he questions the entire idea of a liberating revolution. The third homophonic variant (the last of the seven in total), dwelling on the era before Poland regained its independence in 1918, draws an unsettling parallel: as long as the Russian tsar controlled the major part of partitioned Poland and, a few decades later, the Soviet Union imposed its hegemony over the region, there was neither structural chaos nor civil unrest. It is only what happened afterward that brought the most lamentable consequences for both time periods. Just as the post-1918 era paved the way for social nationalist and fascist movements, so the post-1989 events resulted in ethnic conflicts, ethnic cleansing, and internal wars in Eastern Europe and beyond. The bass vocalist postulates that history can run its course and, therefore, that the state of regained freedom might not be sustainable. This viewpoint clearly counters the democratic agenda and integrational tendencies of the early 1990s.

In Barańczak's oratorio, however, democracy rather paradoxically transpires to contradict its own assumptions. This translation is more radical in its political interpretation of the post-1989 reality than earlier versions. As the bass voice renders an untimely and inconvenient opinion, it becomes an unwanted burden for the Western choir. A new persona non grata, the elderly singer vocalizing this standpoint, as the stage directions has it, is "quieted by force and escorted arm in arm by security guards."[54] Given that his viewpoint does not fit in with the newly established ideological program, it is forcefully pushed out of the political arena; it undergoes censorship in the same way as would have happened in the communist period. From today's perspective—looking back at all post-1989 transformation failures and violent upheavals in some Eastern European countries, including the Bosnian genocide of 1995—it is easier to understand the weight of this scene. With this experience under their belt, readers may more readily appreciate Barańczak's ethical demand to acknowledge all individual calls and rights of veto. When the poet reprinted "Oratorium Moratorium" in 1995, he admitted that it was precisely because of those tragic events that his "political satire" had perhaps lost some of its original comic quality.[55] Still, in the oratorio's absurd and grotesque atmosphere, the depiction of guards forcefully leading the bass singer off the stage signals a sinister affinity between the Soviet political means of coercion and the post-1989 drive to impose a Western "democratic" agenda.

Barańczak draws a further parallel between the aggressive intervention of the Western choir Harmonia Mundi and the communist apparatus. After the inconvenient voice is ousted from the performance, a moment of confusion ensues. Then, the choir continues to sing a differently rendered refrain of the progressive "La Marseillaise" in order to disguise the politically incorrect blunder. Quite tellingly, just after the glitch, another part of the oratorio does not proceed as planned and has to be interrupted because of the ideologically inadequate message.[56] Instead of continuing with the French anthem, two women soloists accidentally perform the first two lines of the second social realist refrain: "Weź, ludu, dudy / W miech tak jak wprzódy ... !" (People, be humble enough to accept your defeat like you did previously). The democratic faction immediately jumps to conclusions and identifies the passage as ideologically unsuitable. Consequently, it has to be subdued: "It turns out that this fragment was removed during the rehearsals as too didactic and one-sided." To justify its decision, the choir easily scapegoats the women for being former communists; it accuses them of joining forces to create the National Unity Front, a communist front that supervised elections and functioned as a coalition for the dominant party as well as its allies in the Polish People's Republic. In singing along and drowning out the communistically colored passage, Harmonia Mundi also gives away their own strategy as a new kind of censorship: "Bata errata / Poprawi błąd?" (The lash's erratum will correct the error?). In Barańczak's bitter reckoning, this type of interventionist erasure jeopardized the entire of idea of a polyphonic discussion by means of translation multiples. As much as the intricately composed oratorio was intended to serve as a forum for different arguments and critiques introduced through homophonic translations, this pluralism would be nipped in the bud with a heavy dose of irony.

While staying with the aesthetics of nonsense, political satire, and linguistic experiment, Barańczak's "Oratorium Moratorium" also slips into more sinister and apocalyptic undertones. In this respect, his work might have reminded a Polish reader of the interwar satirical poem "Ball at the Opera" (1936)[57] by the Polish Jewish poet Julian Tuwim, which Barańczak had reviewed for a US readership a few years earlier.[58] Tuwim's narrative poem was a desperate response to the worsening political climate on the eve of the Second World War; it ridiculed the fascist agenda and political slogans of the time through nonsense, exoticism, and "linguistic violence,"[59] as Barańczak himself called it. While drawing a parallel between the late 1930s and the post-1989 reality, Barańczak fused a satire on the different political voices with a foreboding of a potential catastrophe. He implied that the only deliverance from such a catastrophe would be found in the multiples. If anything, it is the breaking of a single discourse into plural, smaller narratives that may stop the total, regardless of which side of the political barricades it is on. However inconvenient or unpopular another point of view may be, it should always be heard and freely voiced, and also acknowledged in the debate. This is why Barańczak insisted that his homophonic multiples comment on the original notion of liberating revolution from different angles and engage with it in a dialectical way. In the ideal version of such an open dialogue, these individual perspectives, even if at first appearing as mutually exclusive and difficult to reconcile, might still be negotiated through constructive polemics. The pluralism that Barańczak hankered after and projected through his multithreaded oratorio differed from an externally imposed westernized program. According to the equally totalizing agenda of Harmonia Mundi, there was not much interest in understanding Eastern European nations, with all their doubts and fears; any voices of protest would be ignored or even actively suppressed in the name of democracy. This attitude in turn provoked linguistic violence and aggressive appropriation through homophonic translation. While serving as a hallmark of intercultural integration and emancipation, homophonic multiples could also smuggle in more subversive threads to challenge sweeping statements and simplified visions. Using a democratic platform to undermine any of the narratives, but also being able to critique the shortcomings of the whole project itself, lay at the heart of Barańczak's ethics of the multiple. As it assumed the weighing and testing of all different viewpoints, it could help acknowledge them all but also productively point to the limitations of each.

Mister B., but How to Live?

In 1990, Barańczak formulated different challenges for the postcommunist publishing and literary culture in his article "Goodbye, Samizdat." The big unknowns of the 1989 transformation crystallized around issues such as the place of the poet in society and new modes of writing when there was no longer any need for Aesopian language. As the former paradigm of the total, with its underground counternarrative, dissolved into multiple and less fixed alternatives, Barańczak called for a fundamental redefining of the cultural space:

> Now that Poland is no longer ruled by a communist-military clique, black-and-white ethics no longer applies. To preserve the pluralism won during the long struggle against state censorship, while at the same time doing away with the distinctions between "official" and "unofficial," is the task now facing the Polish culture.[60]

A solution to these binaries that Barańczak seemed to advocate came a year later. In the political quarterly *Puls*, in the 1991 issue preceding his "Oratorium Moratorium," he published a curious review. It was a "double review," its authors apparently a pair of twins who had two completely divergent political views.[61] The title was quite telling: "Like a twin with his twin: The double voice of the Kłapczyński brothers on Janusz Szpotański's oeuvre."[62] The double review adopted two radically different perspectives on the Polish satirical poet, who in the late 1960s was arrested and imprisoned for his dissident literary activity. While this literary hoax—for the twins were entirely fictional—first appeared in prose, Barańczak republished it in his 1995 book, alongside "Oratorium Moratorium,"[63] in the form of a conceptual poem. There, the two voices of twin brothers ran in parallel; they were placed next to each other on the left- and right-hand side of the page, representing respectively the two sides of the political spectrum in post-1989 Poland.

The poem served as an epilogue to the book with Barańczak's translation multiples and other literary experiments. According to Barańczak's tongue-in-cheek commentary added in 1995, readers had demanded from his literary exercises some more practical way of helping them come to terms with the political reality of the early 1990s. They appealed to the poet's active stance and ethical attitude, asking, "All good, but what does this have in common with the questions of Ideology and Politics that preoccupy us every day?," and "Mister B., but HOW TO LIVE?!" ("Panie B., ale JAK ŻYĆ?!").[64] His response to these calls came in the form of this double poem: a dialectical interpretation of the same original read in parallel by identical twins, with the two parts of the whole running next to each other, column to column. In his letter to the editor of *Puls* included as a foreword in both 1991 and 1995, Barańczak claimed that his own readings, informed by his own dissident experience, would have been deprived of a critical distance. "Am I at all able to read Szpotański's poems afresh and judge them soberly?" he asked himself.[65] Instead, the poet invented former students, Karol and Butrym Kłapczyński, identical twins who always "held exactly opposing opinions on every possible topic and in every single situation."[66] As Barańczak's twisted story had it, Karol emigrated to the United States to become professor in comparative literature and one of the leading Marxists and feminists at Montana State University; Butrym, on the other hand, stayed in Poland to become a conservative journalist acting on behalf of the partially made-up Christian National Association ("Chrześcijańska Asocjacja Narodowa").[67] Both having replied to Barańczak's request simultaneously, the imaginary twin brothers then sent their reviews on the same day. This synchronized appearance of readings from two different ends of the political spectrum prompted Barańczak to publish them together in 1991; as he wrote, this work constituted a "critical literary double voice about Szpotański by two such extremely bipolar personalities."[68]

The twins had their rough equivalents in the postcommunist political reality.[69] Barańczak's project coincided with a different artistic take on twins or doubles whose forking paths unfold into completely different life stories. While Krzysztof Kieślowski's three different Witeks from *Blind Chance* were known to a wider audience before 1989, the imagery of twins or doppelgängers recurred in the Polish cultural scene in the early 1990s. In 1991, the same year that Barańczak wrote about his Kłapczyński twin brothers, Kieślowski made his renowned film *The Double Life of Véronique*. It focuses on the lives of two identical-looking women: the Polish Weronika and the French Véronique, both speaking their respective national languages, their fates closely intertwined across reunified Europe. Critics often read the film allegorically as a commentary on the relationship between Poland and Western Europe; some see an analogy between the death of Weronika and the decay of communism in Poland, from whose mistakes Western Europe could learn.[70] Speculating about parallel lives and "what if" scenarios, Kieślowski's film toyed with a tempting idea at the time: it mapped two alternative political directions within Europe and moved between two potentially identical selves dropped onto opposite sides of the dissolving Iron Curtain.

However, while Kieślowski's twins are separated geographically and chronologically, Barańczak's verse makes his twins meet and face each other despite their unreconciled stances. What brings them together textually and spatially in Barańczak's double poem is the very act of reading the same original in different ways. The question Barańczak poses in his twin reviews is of a more practical nature for Polish political life: how to come to terms with different, often mutually exclusive narratives and the postcommunist legacy that continued to polarize the political arena. In other words (Barańczak's own), how to "preserve the pluralism" beyond the black-and-white ethics.

The monochromatic picture emanating from the twin reviews seems far from nuanced. The Kłapczyńskis' readings veer off from each other from the very beginning, starting with their titles. These fiddle with different stereotypical categories: "Under the lash of class hatred" ("Pod szpicrutą klasowej nienawiści") and "On the chessboard of national treason" ("Na szachownicy narodowej zdrady"). The following double verse is constructed to make the unfavorable reviews reflect each other textually in a distorted mirror. On the one hand, they overlap almost entirely in terms of composition, syntactical structure, and fragments selected for analysis; on the other, they radically diverge from each other precisely in the places where the critique of the same original poetry is supported with ideological arguments. Depending on the interpretative variant, the reviewers criticize Szpotański's texts for completely opposite reasons, starting already with the original publication place, London:[71]

gdzieżby indziej, jak nie w tej stolicy reakcyjnego konserwatyzmu, ukrywającego pod nienagannie lśniącym melonikiem imperialnych pozorów pustkę i czczość kolonialistycznej hipokryzji	gdzieżby indziej, jak nie w tej stolicy lewackiego liberalizmu, ukrywającego pod imponująco wydętymi biustonoszami swoich katedralnych kopuł uwiąd i płaskość ateistycznej hipokryzji
[where else than in this capital of reactionary conservatism, hiding a void and emptiness of colonial hypocrisy under the impeccably shining bowler hat of imperial appearances]	[where else than in this capital of leftist liberalism, hiding an atrophy and flatness of atheist hypocrisy under the impressively bloated bras of its cathedral domes]

By the same token, the twin brothers focus on the same images from Szpotański's poetry to argue their own divergent points. For instance, the satirist's depiction of the tsarina simpering in front of a mirror serves as evidence for two possible readings: either it is said to prove the author's "male chauvinism" and his "treating the woman as a sexual object," or it testifies to his "Asian-Soviet taste" and "masochist bewitchment by the power of that daughter of revolution."[72] Another fragment from Szpotański's ballad is diagnosed as either "spreading the plague of blind consumerism" among the "healthy social stratum, the working class," or "breeding the germ of the communist hydra in the nation's womb" and meddling with the "healthy substance" of traditional Polishness.[73] In yet another passage, the adventures of Comrade Szmaciak manifest the author's "class discrimination," identified thanks to poststructuralist philosophies such as the "simplest deconstruction by means of Paul de Man's or at least Derrida's method"; in the alternative scenario, Szpotański's "anti-national prejudice" is revealed owing to the conservative methodology—the "simplest Christian and national reading."[74]

It does not really matter that the twin brothers are separated both geographically and ideologically, each pursuing his own totalizing perspective serving the opposite side of the barricades. Despite all these discrepancies, their voices are still, rather bizarrely, united in a polyphonic, harmonious chord. In fact, as the parallel verses proceed in an almost identical manner, they also conclude with an exclamation of protest to the same end and a call for mobilization. It might come as a surprise that Barańczak responds to the audience's activist demands and pressing questions by simply placing two lines of argumentation next to each other. But this simple exercise is of no lesser ethical relevance than any of his previous poems. In the new political reality, the greatest challenge for society will come down to facing multiple radically divergent, but also equally one-sided, worldviews. Although each Kłapczyński might not realize his own biased way of reading the same text, confronting his brother's reading helps him reflect on the limitations of his own. It is only through Barańczak's projected brotherly reunion that their voices unmask each other's simplified and totalizing visions of the world. While two facets of the same text are each prone to reduction and simplification, when on their own, liberation can come from the dialogue between individual stand-alone perspectives. Owing to the twin metaphor, two feuding brothers can meet and confront their approaches in an open forum. Even though seemingly conflicted, the Kłapczyński brothers, just like all three different Witeks or Weronika and Véronique from Kieślowski's films, are, in the end, cut from the same cloth; accordingly, they should be able to look beyond partisan lines. Only when acting together can each of these separate parts of the whole illuminate and verify the other's assumptions, and collaboratively create a new dialectical quality.

This is also a lesson to be learned from Barańczak's translation multiples. Different partial readings put in a dialectical conversation work against the spirit of generalization and totalizing language discourse. In the newly transformed political reality after 1989, similar projects could address the pressing question of how to come to terms with the multiplicity of different perspectives and how to reconcile them in a constructive dialogue. Besides the postulate of a critical debate over different possibilities, Barańczak also reinforced the idea of reciprocal acknowledgment and acceptance. His polyphonic orchestra in "Oratorium Moratorium," while introducing plural voices, does not entirely appreciate the perspective of the other. The Western choir opens the forum of translation multiples to different political interpretations but still objects to listening to Eastern Europe itself; it particularly wants to suppress those opinions that cast doubt on the pace of the political transformation and on the unfair rules of the game. When looking at the local polarized scene after 1989, Barańczak saw a similar danger: falling prey to the spirit of generalization and enforcing a single, totalizing reading could too easily lead to ideological blinkers and political tribalism. Instead, the metaphor of the twin-mirror suggests that it is still possible to reconcile the multiples. Though ostensibly different, the twins share much more than it seems. Their partial readings can illuminate the limitations of their respective biases only thanks to a mutual support. Reflected in Barańczak's artistic creed, this dialectical and polyphonic solution is the only way out of the impasse of the total. In this spirit, in 1994 Barańczak ended one of his poems:

> Więc to prawda, bracie w zwierciadlanym szkle?
> Mam jakiegoś ciebie, masz jakiegoś mnie?
> [So, brother in the mirror glass, is it true
> That you have some sort of me,
> and I have some sort of you?][75]

4

Winding the Clockwork Orange Three Times

Like ... old Bog himself ... turning and turning and turning a vonny grazhny orange in his gigantic rookers.
—ALEX IN *A CLOCKWORK ORANGE* BY ANTHONY BURGESS[1]

The "2 in 1" in the Making

In a 1989 Polish review of *A Clockwork Orange* by Anthony Burgess, the reviewer commented on the novel's uncanny absence in Polish translation at that time: "In our country, with two or three book circulations, nothing should surprise us, though this book has not appeared in any of them. It has never appeared for one reason: it cannot do so. Even if it were translated, it would not be the same novel anyway."[2] On the eve of Poland's political transition, this reviewer did not know what history already lay behind the book's translation. Likewise, he could not possibly tell what twisted life was still ahead of it. Despite all updates possible from today's perspective, one point in that statement still captures the novel's actual adventures in Polish: it could never be, and indeed has never been, "the same novel." The Polish translation did come to fruition, but no one could really predict the follow-up. The original *Clockwork Orange* with its Russianized futuristic language would break into two or even almost three—by no means the "same"—novels, to be read in parallel.

This translation multiple gained cult status in Poland because all the variants were created, one after another, by the same translator, Robert Stiller. He first introduced two renderings to the market in 1999 as full-length book versions "R" and "A" ("R" for Russianized, "A" for Anglicized). Presented as two different sides of the same coin, these separate variants corresponded to two distinct sociopolitical realities in Poland: the communist era with Poland as a satellite country under Russian hegemony, and the postcommunist, US-inspired capitalist system under strong Anglo-American cultural influence. They also had two different, but compatible, titles: *Mechaniczna pomarańcza* (A Mechanical Orange) and *Nakręcana pomarańcza* (A Wind-Up Orange). The rendering's double format was underscored by other tie-ins such as the publisher's corresponding blurbs, the covers' graphical layouts (see fig. 4.1), and the translator's afterwords. I treat this simultaneous release of the two versions in 1999 as an anchor for Stiller's experimental project, even though the first variant, "R," was in fact prepared much earlier. The multiple was also projected by Stiller himself as "a double pleasure"[3] of reading and comparing these two texts with each other. He also worked, on and off, on a third variant—version "N" ("N" for the Polish *niemiecki*, Germanized). Though only partially completed, this last variant opened up the discussion to even more hypothetical scenarios. By bringing different ideological readings together within translation, Stiller's multiples served as a simultaneous forum for political critique, commenting on three alternative realities.

It is not surprising that the idea of multiplying *Clockwork Orange*s in Polish and treating them as subversive textual commentaries came from none other than Robert Stiller. A Polish Jewish polyglot, he claimed knowledge of a few dozen languages (including European languages but also Malay, Chinese, Hebrew, and Sanskrit) and translated literary works from around twenty of them.[4] At the same time, he was a very controversial literary figure in Polish cultural life who will most probably go down in history as a difficult and confrontational man and a rather wayward *homo politicus*.[5] His sharp tongue and fervent tone in biting polemics earned him the title "enfant terrible" in the domain of literary translation; from the 1970s onward, his provocative texts could be read in the liberal magazine *Literatura na świecie* (Literature in the World), which he coshaped at that time.[6] In 1999, when his double translation of *A Clockwork Orange* was published, it immediately became one of Poland's most celebrated literary experiments in its own right. Appealing to readers of different genres, and with a considerable sci-fi fandom,[7] the translation multiple has reverberated throughout the past two decades; it yielded seven reprintings for version R and four for version A, and culminated in a combined special edition of the two in 2017 (see fig. 4.2).[8] Stiller also promised the third version N on different occasions, so readers and critics were kept on tenterhooks waiting for its release.[9] Considering Stiller's knack for subverting literary norms and provoking his audience, I read

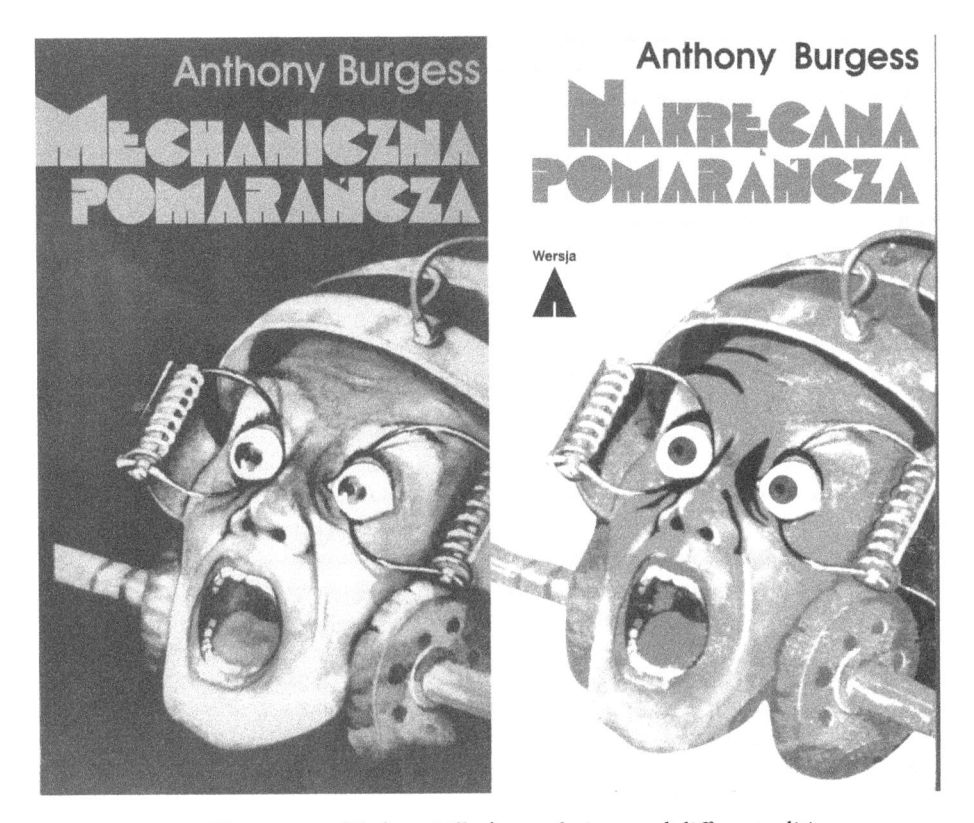

FIGURE 4.1. The covers of Robert Stiller's translations and different editions of Anthony Burgess's *A Clockwork Orange*: the so-called version R (Russian) and version A (American), published simultaneously in 1999 as *A Mechanical Orange* and *A Wind-Up Orange*. Courtesy of Nina Stiller (the Foundation for Robert Stiller) and Grzegorz Cieply (Vis-à-Vis Etiuda Press).

his translation multiple of *A Clockwork Orange* as an act of pluralist resistance. It took the novel with its original orange metaphor well beyond its original locus, becoming a platform for protest against different political agendas and sources of moral decay. In this respect, Stiller's orange on its own is by no means clockwork, mechanical, or wind-up: it becomes a very self-aware process of negotiating between various sociopolitical realities. While his translation multiple recorded the postcommunist zeitgeist, it also testified to Stiller's own skepticism and reluctance to take at face value any of the political narratives available at the time. His Mechanical, Wind-Up, and all other Oranges turned into a dialectical confrontation of different readings of oppressive political systems.

FIGURE 4.2. The special double edition of both versions (Russian and American) of *A Clockwork Orange* combined into one volume in 2017. Courtesy of Nina Stiller (the Foundation for Robert Stiller) and Grzegorz Cieply (Vis-à-Vis Etiuda Press).

The history of literary translation has included translations of the same novel published independently at roughly the same time by different translators and publishing houses. This is technically possible in the context of a decentralized system and free-market publishing. Launching alternative translation variants into circulation almost simultaneously, however, usually leads to competition between them. But when in 1999 the same Polish publishing house, Etiuda, released these two book-length translation variants by the same translator, the situation was quite different. They were visually and textually introduced as tie-in books rather than as competitive products. Stiller explicitly labeled them as two different versions of the original: "wersja R" (version R) and "wersja A" (version A). Their titles—"A Mechanical Orange" and "A Wind-Up Orange"—were also similar, with the first variant coined after the existing translated title of Stanley Kubrick's film adaptation.[10] To highlight the kinship between the two books more explicitly, the publisher presented them as visually mirroring each other. Both front covers feature the same gray-shaded image, futuristic font, and graphical layout. The protagonist's head is set tight in the machine used for the novel's fictional psychiatric technique, with his pried-open eyes, screaming mouth, and face contorting in pain and horror. The only difference between the covers is the background color: black for the R version and white for the A. On the back, the publisher's blurbs overlap in greater part; they both suggest that the novel's plot finds relevance in the reader's surrounding reality, either the past or the current one. "We had first-hand experience of this," reads the blurb for the Russianized version;[11] the Anglicized one says: "Sounds familiar. [...] We are currently experiencing this first-hand."[12] The two different scenarios are tied together as Stiller's alternative projections of two political developments in postcommunist Poland.

This unusual twin constellation and double-edged reading of the original novel was primarily endorsed by the translator himself. Stiller included three texts[13] to this end, all of which explained the project's unique format and revealed the meandering story behind it. In the afterword to version A, he appealed to readers to stock up on both Oranges and enjoy this unique experiment. He also argued:

> One Orange cannot replace the other in anything but the plot. In all other respects, a parallel reading and comparison of the two can become a double pleasure; and there is neither a similar case nor satisfaction comparable with that, nor such fun and joy, in world literature.[14]

Beyond this, the project unpacked the explosive potential of the novel's peculiar language as it got filtered through Stiller's own understanding of the original's sociopolitical implications. It was then reiterated in its Polish translation double as alternative running commentaries. Readers of the two translations, even if grounded in two historical visions, were encouraged to think of both approaches on equal terms and to try to see them in a broader perspective.

I need to make a small caveat about the timing of Stiller's publication, however. As already mentioned, his version R was created much earlier, in the 1970s, and had existed in provisional distribution since 1989.[15] In contrast, version A was developed in the late 1980s and early 1990s, partly capitalizing on the wave of political transformation. Since this chronology is documented in Stiller's texts, this could raise further questions: Should the first translation be taken as the default up to 1989 and then give way to the more valid version A? This question, however, does not really match the final framing of Stiller's translation multiple. When he put version R again into circulation in 1999, he made sure it appeared in a new double format with another version released on the side. In other words, he did not wish to discard the previous version as outdated; the dual release of two *Clockwork Orange*s in 1999 challenged this intuition. Though the versions' successive creation was acknowledged, the synchronized publication of the translation double projected a different mode of reading. It allowed readers to look back at both variants from a distance and assess the relevant political systems in retrospect. After the 1989 transition and his creation of version A, Stiller himself did almost everything humanly possible to assert the rendering's double status. According to his claims, he had intended to create his "dualistic translation" from the very beginning anyway.[16] The translations were originally meant to test two linguistic hypotheses about the potential development of the Polish language. Regardless of the timing of this mastermind's plan, he clung to this idea during his negotiations with publishing houses throughout the 1990s. As he admitted later, he turned down an offer from one press to separate his translation double and release just one version in 1994.[17] Since he had actively shaped the novel's twin image from 1989, it was the full-fledged double translation that was eventually popularized among the readership. The chronological sequence and turn of events, therefore, mainly helps in signposting the intellectual process that led to the final double format.

Stiller found a pretext for his double reading in Burgess's original English language with its strong interference of Russian, which itself has a long history. Published in 1962, the novel is narrated in the first person by the protagonist, Alex, a teenager from somewhere in near-future England who leads his gang on all-night orgies of random, as he calls it, "ultra-violence." Together with his companions, he uses a specific slang distorting regular English sentences with random Russian words; these are often twisted or adapted to English pronunciation, inflection, or vocabulary: for example, "baboochka" (Russian "бабушка": grandmother), "gulliver" ("голова": head), "horrorshow" ("хорошо": well), "rooker" ("рука": hand), and "chelloveck" ("человек": man). Burgess named his linguistic invention "Nadsat," which is a transliteration of the Russian suffix "-надцать" (teen), depicting it as an element of a youth subculture. Although Burgess borrowed the idea of a literary youth subculture from British groups of the 1960s such as the Mods and the Rockers, he preferred to use an artificial English-Russian construction rather than any contemporary British slang. He had been worried that a youth idiom would become outdated even before publication, so he looked for alternatives. As the story has it, he saw some teenage gangs in the Soviet Union during a holiday in Leningrad and allegedly decided to combine their language with English.[18] The way Nadsat was itself constructed already hinted at the problem of hegemony and violence. The protagonist's idea of "ultra-violence" also translated into the language he used and brutally distorted. A linguistic aggression was manifest in the expansion of barbarisms, the violence of one language upon another. The original readership was aware of this politically colored allegory. In the 1970s, to the Anglo-American reader, the first connotations of any Slavic words were communist dictatorship and moral decay.[19] In his Polish translation, Stiller pushed his reading of Nadsat along these lines to the extreme. Dwelling on this sense of linguistic oppression, he identified Nadsat's resonance with the Polish communist context even before 1989.

According to Stiller's later accounts, he had prepared two chapters of his first version of *A Mechanical Orange* (version R) for publication as far back as 1974.[20] In that year, those chapters in Polish were meant to appear in the magazine *Literatura na świecie* along with his text critiquing Burgess's invented language.[21] Unfortunately, we will never have access to Stiller's proto-Orange, as his translation did not appear in print at that time. According to Stiller (and often repeated by him), his version R was allegedly withdrawn from print at the very last minute, leaving the critique on its own.[22] After that, the communist censorship authorities prevented him from publishing the translation with any state publishing house. Even though Stiller received some distribution offers from the underground press, he preferred the official media because "the case was too serious" for the limited impact of publication in the underground circulation.[23] In the wake of 1989, the situation changed and version R provisionally appeared in print, although only as a supplement to the science fiction magazine *Fantastyka*. This booklet was then illegally reprinted by an independent press in the same year and again in 1990, before Stiller was able to release a properly authorized version in 1991.

Stiller was ostensibly surprised by the censor's inference. He claimed that the novel did not contain, "formally speaking," any message targeted against Poland, its political system, Russia, or the Soviet Union and its allies.[24] But if the first two chapters of Stiller's *A Mechanical Orange* were at all similar to the full-length R version that later appeared in print, it is quite easy to guess why the censors would not have approved it. Polish Alex narrates the story of his crimes using a language strongly tainted with Russian interpolations and extensive stylizations. The original frequency and density of these neologisms—there were around three hundred entries in the glossary that Burgess attached at the end of his novel—were more than tripled by Stiller.[25] This device was meant to enhance the sense of oppression and linguistic "ultra-violence." As critics speculated later, the censors must have feared that the degenerates' use of Russian vocabulary threatened the prestige of the Soviet state.[26] On top of that, Stiller's Russianized idiom sounded familiar, as it compromised the "newspeak" used by communist officials and Soviet infiltrators. It also anticipated dissident novels published later in the second circulation. For instance, Tadeusz Konwicki's novel *A Minor Apocalypse* (1979) featured an analogously distorted language that denoted betrayal and corruption in the society of the time. In the novel, the Polish and Russian words for "Poland" ironically merge in the formula shouted by the crowd: "Polska, Polsza, Polska, Polsza!" The mix represents a state of cultural decay in which the communist apparatchiks blend in with the people's voice to smuggle in pro-Soviet ideas.[27] In the context of Alex's banditry in *A Clockwork Orange*, a similarly symbolic amalgam could have alarmed the vigilance of censors.

The novel's broader antisystemic undertone could have also been at stake. Burgess's works had not existed in Poland before the 1989 transition, even in underground publishing, due to his antitotalitarian message.[28] Even so, there was potential for dissidence and controversy. In 1988, a second-circulation Polish magazine published a fragment of *1985*, Burgess's polemics with George Orwell, lampooning British society for its expanding syndicalism. On this occasion, Burgess's Polish translator decidedly linked the chaos and tyranny described in the *1985* passage to contemporary Russia and "the reality it imposed on its neighboring countries."[29] Similar anti-regime sentiments in *A Clockwork Orange* might be why the novel had been swept under the rug back in the 1960s and 1970s. Stiller, in his 1974 critique, signaled a politically subversive reading: he argued that the novel's final dilemma meant "the end of democracy and throwing ourselves in the pit of totalism."[30] Perhaps this was why the editor of *Literatura na świecie* needed to tack an official critical "gloss" onto Stiller's text, toning down its message and framing it as slightly paranoid.[31] But the novel's potential gravity and resonance still loomed large. In a readers' survey carried out in 1989 by *Fantastyka*, some of the respondents picked up on the clear parallel with Poland's political oppression. One of them praised the novel's "realism" as analogous to George Orwell, whose works had been strictly banned from print for the best part of the communist era. This reader added: "Try going out after 10:00 p.m. to check. Good riddance! In *Nineteen Eighty-Four*, the hope lay in proles; in Burgess's world there is no hope."[32]

Stiller was probably aware of the potential consequences at the time. Nonetheless, his individual crusade for the novel's publication helped mythologize

A Clockwork Orange in Poland. In the 1990s, he kept advertising it as a forbidden fruit, claiming that "legend still revolved around the book and its translation."[33] The most suggestive records of this legend-in-the-making were his insinuations about the censorship. As he claimed, "rumor had it" that his translation of the first two chapters had been withdrawn in 1974 on the recommendation of Zenon Kliszko. This politburo member allegedly saw Kubrick's movie at an exclusive screening sometime in the early 1970s, shrugged in disgust, and shouted: "There will be no Clockwork Orange in Poland!"[34] Stiller's anecdote quite smartly identified an already stigmatized communist politician as an evil bully, thanks to a similar, and infamous, earlier intervention by Kliszko. In 1968 he had been responsible for the party's taking down of Kazimierz Dejmek's production of Adam Mickiewicz's Romantic play *Forefathers' Eve* at Warsaw's Polish Theatre on the grounds of its Russophobic references. A great scandal, this event was followed by repercussions of significant grandeur: nationwide student protests, and the political crisis of March 1968. As soon as Stiller's word-of-mouth story was associated with the political persona of Kliszko, it struck the right chord in a myth-making narrative.

This lore also found its way into the publisher's blurbs: "someone shouted that there should be no Clockwork Orange in Poland! And the censorship was waging a war against it for 15 years."[35] It also caused outrage among the novel's first readers participating in the *Fantastyka* survey. One insisted: "How can this novel be received? With pity and fury toward the bandits who once brutally robbed us of this and so many other works. Death to censorship!!!" (original punctuation).[36] All this culminated in granting the novel almost a cult status toward the end of communism and after 1989. The Polish Foundation of the Centre for Documenting Acts for Independence listed the first two editions in book form of version R from 1989 and 1990 as publications demonstrating how Poles had fought for independence over centuries.[37] This reputation was definitely fueled by Stiller's personal obsession with the fate of his translation before 1989, which escalated into a fierce campaign against censorship, editors, and the previous political system.[38] It did not exactly come to an end with the 1989 transition despite all expectations, either. "Now that democracy, collective wisdom, and justice have triumphed, there should be no obstacles for his books to become available for every mother's son," a critic ironized about Burgess's reception in postcommunist Poland.[39] Stiller first made some unsuccessful attempts to release two translations of the novel simultaneously, which left him equally disenchanted about the postcommunist reality. The new system of free-market publishing did eventually create technical possibilities for his two Oranges to appear, crowning years of struggle, and Stiller's initial disappointments with new publishers, incompetent editors, and piracy found an outlet in his double-edged critique of both political systems in his translation double.

Exactly how and when Stiller developed the idea of producing two alternative translation variants gets lost in the shuffle. In 1999, he stated: "Intended from the very beginning, the A version was created after many years,"[40] a claim that still leaves a lot of unknowns. For instance, it is difficult to tell for sure which scenario was true: Did Stiller originally plan to produce both renderings already in the 1970s and formally put them in writing? Or did he hesitate between two translation solutions and possible language combinations, which then found relevance and took their final shape on the wave of Poland's political transition? What can be said with a high degree of certainty is that he toyed with the idea of creating version A even before the fall of communism. The early 1989 publication in the sci-fi magazine was already classified as "version R," and Stiller announced the upcoming alternative Orange in a brief introduction attached to it.[41] He then admitted in a 1991 interview that he was preparing the second version,[42] which in time led to its first publication alongside version R in 1999.

At first, his "dualistic translation" aimed to confront two possible directions in which the Polish language could have developed under the influence of either Russian or English. While the cultural impact of Russian was self-evident at that time, Stiller insisted on noticing the other, opposite influence—English—in Polish. Despite the political pressure, he argued, young people were largely attracted to the English language.[43] From today's perspective, that linguistic trend in the 1970s could sound like post-factum wishful thinking. However, it was definitely at stake in Stiller's project toward the end of communism. In the face of ongoing political developments, he considered which cultural dominance would tip the balance in Poland, a political conundrum that sparked two potential scenarios at the turn of 1989.[44] In 1991, Stiller continued to weigh up whether Soviet cultural dominance would persist, or "quite the opposite situation," whether Polish would gradually transform along the lines of English.[45] He acknowledged the greater historical stakes of version A in his 1999 publication, although to him "the result of this game still remained undetermined."[46] In Stiller's translation double, Nadsat served as a linguistic touchstone that probed two plausible if not actual trends. It also put forward the question of cultural hegemony over a minor language, which fed into a broader diagnosis of Poland's political condition.

To demonstrate the gravity of his experiment, Stiller schooled his readers on different degrees of understanding its depth. To rephrase his special stratification system,[47] level absolute zero would be adequate for those who degraded his double rendering to the status of "yet another of his, ha ha!, eccentric pranks," and to those, Stiller had "nothing to say." The first level was about recognizing in his "dualistic translation" at least a sophisticated literary play and stylistic translation experiment. Level two required reflecting on alarming linguistic forecasts about how minor languages like Polish might become extinct under prevailing economic and cultural powers. Finally, the most advanced level, which Stiller encouraged, was to reach deeper into the areas where politics, sociology, ethics, and history were inseparable from language. Accordingly, he appealed for a more in-depth reading of the languages he invented for his Mechanical and Wind-Up Oranges in order to unmask two different Polish realities. He also saw the roots of Burgess's grim depiction in a mixture of cultural contexts: the lifestyle of American hippies and beatniks, the crimes of the Charles Manson group, and the French civil unrest of 1968—all filtered through the language of British tabloids and combined with the image of bolshevism.[48] The Western negative associations probably found their way into his 1974 text to tick the boxes of the ideological profile required of publications in the official press. Still, they shed some light on Stiller's line of thinking. As the Nadsat used by a group of criminals was ingrained in broader trends, so the Polish translations should also go beyond a mechanical code switching. For this reason, Stiller was unhappy with Burgess's own proposition regarding how to translate *A Clockwork Orange* into Polish. In a correspondence with Stiller, the British author apparently advised him to replace the original Russianized language straightaway with an Anglicized Polish. Back then, Stiller only commented that Burgess was unaware of Poland's specific history and the linguistic and cultural implications of its geopolitical location. He added that Burgess "would have never guessed how serious this problem was and how unique in the global perspective."[49] In this respect, Stiller was probably not very far from the truth.

That the translation's "duality had a deeper validation"[50] manifested itself in how the double-edged languages of the Mechanical and Wind-Up Oranges worked together. Stiller's version A would not have been read in the same way without, first, the preceding version R with all its baggage of experience and recounted misadventures, and second, the 1989 transition, which revaluated its political timbre in the postcommunist context. The idea of the translation double equally left an imprint on version R. When it was contrasted with its Anglo-American counterpart in 1999, the communist undercurrents became even clearer. To this end, Stiller singled out a particular fragment as the interpretative key to the novel, situating the notion of "subliminal penetration" in the thick of the plot.[51] The message of his translation double was sharpened by Burgess's scene in which two doctors comment on Alex's language as follows:

"Quaint," said Dr. Brodsky, like smiling, "the dialect of the tribe. Do you know anything of its provenance, Branom?"

"Odd bits of old rhyming slang," said Dr. Branom. "A bit of gipsy talk, too. But most of the roots are Slav. Propaganda. Subliminal penetration."[52]

Stiller primed readers to see this passage as pivotal to his double reading of the novel. Anchored in the ideological machinery of propaganda and subliminal penetration, the Russianness of Nadsat in the novel was not accidental. As Stiller argued, it would be therefore "sheer stupidity to replace this shadow of destruction with an empty linguistic puzzle."[53] Taking the shadow of destruction up a notch, Stiller's readings of the passage pointed the finger at the culprits very precisely. When Dr. Branom examines Alex in Stiller's translation double, he identifies two different sources of moral decline in the criminal's slang, depending on the version:

Version R:
Coś niecoś ze szwargotu przestępczego. Ale po większej części rdzenie lub zapożyczenia *rosyjskie*. Propaganda. Infiltracja subliminalna.[54]
[A bit of criminal jabbering. But most of the roots and borrowings are *Russian*. Propaganda. Subliminal penetration.]

Version A:
Coś niecoś rdzeni rosyjskich i szwargotu przestępczego. Ale po większej części *amerykańskie*. Propaganda. Infiltracja subliminalna.[55]
[A bit of Russian roots and criminal jabbering. But most of them are *American*. Propaganda. Subliminal penetration.]

According to studies on Burgess's invented argot, this passage did not exactly capture the principle behind his Nadsat, especially when it comes to the "gipsy talk."[56] In contrast, Stiller's renderings of this scene almost worked as an explanatory gloss embedded within the text. To sharpen the political contrast even further, the language identified by the doctor in version A is precisely of American provenance, rather than English more generally. When so clearly contrasted with its counterpart, the Russian propaganda and subliminal penetration from version R enters the Cold War–inspired fight over the Polish language. This time, its fate hinges on the balance between two political realities, which back in the early 1990s could be considered as two equally plausible political projects. While the novel's plot stays unchanged in terms of the sequence of events, the translator fiddles with his Russianized and Americanized Nadsats to signal different factors and occurrences that led to the events. As I will suggest later in this chapter, the repetition of the entire scenario is key to understanding Stiller's assessment of Poland's 1989 transition between two seemingly different political systems.

The Mechanical and the Wind-Up Languages

How did Stiller construct his two distinct Nadsats, the Mechanical and the Wind-Up ones? He approached these two completely different cases from both a linguistic and a historical perspective. Aware of affinities between Polish and Russian as Slavic languages as well as discrepancies between Polish and English, Stiller had to look for two distinct pathways into his interlingual idioms.[57] To make the Russian interference more palpable in the thick of Polish, he first boosted the number of Russianized words and phrases, the three hundred or so entries in Burgess's neologism glossary swelling to over a thousand instances in Stiller's R version. Although version A later built on this material to some extent, Stiller kept the number of neologisms at roughly the same enlarged count. He envisioned the linguistic experiment on a completely different scale compared to the original, hence the intensification in his Nadsats. In this experimental fervor, his invented languages absorbed other cultural influences and unfolded somewhat differently from Nadsat in the original novel.

Besides ubiquitous Russian-modeled neologisms, Burgess's Nadsat derived its playful vocabulary from teenage slang, infantilisms, Cockney dialect,[58] and other forms of English patois. Stiller invented his two languages with the same premise of multilingual and dialectal diversity in mind. For instance, he patterned some of his language on the Warsaw dialect as well as on *grypsera*, a sociolect used among recidivist prison inmates. In the self-referential scene with two doctors quoted earlier, Stiller explicitly revealed the latter source of influence. In Polish versions, Branom does not speculate about Alex's argot as adapting some "gipsy talk" but rather labels it specifically as "criminal jabbering" ("przestępcze szwargotanie").[59] Developed during the nineteenth-century Russian partition, the Polish prison cant grypsera has traditionally had multilingual influences: Russian, Ukrainian, Yiddish, and German.[60] It is also partly through this linguistic conduit that Stiller's Nadsats smuggled in borrowings from more languages. He discovered that this multilingual heritage lay dormant in Polish, with some made-up barbarisms already existing in regional jargons or sociolects. In addition to these hybrid forms, Stiller beefed up his artistic idioms with newly coined borrowings from other languages. More specifically, he derived his inventions from those languages that Polish historically has had most contact with, such as German, "Czech, Jewish, and Ukrainian here and there."[61]

Critics of Stiller's double translation have primarily disparaged these multilingual ventures. They have largely viewed it as a mixed bag that deprives "subliminal penetration" of a single coherent agent.[62] While Stiller could simply have followed the original Nadsat's broader sphere of sources, which spanned German, French, Dutch, and Malay,[63] his project reached somewhat further. First, his technique of weaving German, Yiddish, and other loanwords into the Nadsat of the R version equally applied, as Stiller had it, "*mutatis mutandis*, to the A version."[64] In other words, both narratives—the Russianized and the Anglicized ones—unfolded against the background of other linguistic influences. Second, Stiller did not mechanically replace respective loanwords from Russian to English with each other across his two versions. Returning to the dialogue between the two doctors, we find Stiller's subtle hint at his actual strategy. Dr. Branom from version R classifies Alex's language as "A bit of criminal jabbering. But most of the roots and borrowings are *Russian*."[65] In comparison, his doppelgänger from version A takes a clear step further than his predecessor: "A bit of *Russian roots* and criminal talk. But most of them are *American*" (my emphasis).[66] Russianisms from version R therefore do not disappear altogether but are accumulated in version A in a recursive chain. To give an example of this idea, for the original "Who you getten, bratty?,"[67] Russianized Alex would ask: "Ty *szczo* [что; what] dostał, brat?"[68] In turn, his Americanized alter ego would say: "Ty *szczo did get*, brat?" (my emphasis),[69] displaying both the Russian and American barbarisms side by side.

Why did Stiller opt for such a strange smorgasbord of different linguistic forces in his translation multiple? His projection of two hypothetical linguistic scenarios onto the format of his double experiment offers a good explanation. The Mechanical and Wind-Up Oranges aimed to capture two moments in the hyperbolized development of Polish. On the one hand, they foregrounded its linguistic surveillance to two great cultural powers; on the other, these symbolic hierarchies were still set against the background of other multilingual influences at play such as German, Yiddish, and Ukrainian. Even though the experiment oscillated between two hypothetical alternatives, it was still embedded in the political status quo. In other words, even if American dominance tipped the balance in version A, it still could not erase the previously prevalent Russian oppression throughout communism. Likewise, occasional Anglicisms were smuggled into version R; these Anglicisms allegedly followed the strong inclination toward English among Polish teenagers of that time. The key question was not which influence would eliminate the other after 1989.[70] Instead, the postcommunist power game continued within language: Which of the two equally important players would slightly tip the balance on the wave of the transition? Would the English language have a considerable impact, with a much smaller, but still visible, influence of Russian, or the other way around?

In envisioning and mapping out these political processes, Stiller resorted to various linguistic and literary models at hand. The reservoir of existing idioms in the mix was quite rich—ranging from Russian calques still present in the public media (version R), to the "Ponglish" of Polish immigrants in the United States and teenagers in Polish bilingual schools (version A), to prison slang, to the Warsaw dialect, among others.[71] As regards literary inspirations, Stiller knew the celebrated 1973 Polish translation of the chapter "Anna Livia Plurabelle" from James Joyce's *Finnegans Wake*. He could have modeled his inventive idiom after this rendering, stretching the monolingual borders of Polish by means of English, among other languages.[72] When it comes to Russianisms of phrase in Polish, this mixture has a much longer lineage in Polish prose. One of the offshoots revolves around the eastern Polish regions now called the Borderlands (*kresy*), which were lost with the westward shift of borders after the Second World War. These lands were often mythologized in literature, for example in Czesław Miłosz's *The Issa Valley* (1955), Tadeusz Konwicki's *Bohin Manor* (1987), and Andrzej Stasiuk's *Tales of Galicia* (1995). The Borderlands nostalgia alongside stylizations with Ruthenian and eastern Slavic mixtures surely do not evoke the sense of Nadsat's ultra-violence. Nonetheless, it could still serve Stiller as a repository of regional variations and oral forms from which to paint a diverse literary landscape. Analogously to the inclusion of Yiddish (discussed later), this interlingual repertoire helped him pursue a side project in his translation multiples—that of salvaging traces of Poland's multicultural past.

The Mechanical language is perhaps more radical in its political resonance, in bringing back the trauma of "Russified" Polish. The Russification of language, as a symbol of the imperial conqueror's political and cultural oppression, was strongly resisted in the nineteenth century under the Russian partition. A host of pejorative features were associated with Russian and Russified characters in the literature of that period.[73] Some expressions restored by Stiller for his version R are redolent of that strand and are actual relics of a different political era. For instance, in the Russianized rendering, Alex's favorite Korova Milkbar is said not to be subordinate to any "ukaz" that prohibits mixing alcohol into their milk cocktails. This politically symbolic word was used to denote a decree or edict announced specifically by the Russian tsar, as opposed to the standard Polish "prawo" (law) in version A,[74] for the original "law."[75] Similarly, Alex in this version is dragged by policemen to their "cyrkuł," the police office that existed in Poland under the Russian partition. This has a different bent than the standard "biuro" (office) in the Anglicized rendering[76] and the original Nadsat equivalent of "cantora" (Russian контора).[77] Stiller revivified this linguistic network of institutional constraints (decree; police office) to link together different periods of Russian hegemony in Poland. While the main focus of his experimental Nadsat would be on the twentieth-century political setting, Stiller's Mechanical idiom dug into the historical texture of Polish for other hotspots of ultra-violent cruelty in different forms. For instance, one reviewer of version R associated its explosive mix of languages with the Red Army traveling toward the West at the time of the Polish-Soviet War of 1919–1921 and then again during the Second World War.[78] In this sense, different grammars, traditions, and perceptions of Russianisms in Stiller's rendering served as a literary seismograph of Russia's political hegemony in Poland. The Mechanical language definitely aimed to touch this sore spot in the Polish national consciousness.

Stiller viewed the Soviet political and cultural influence in the late twentieth century as a return to the same aggressive agenda of Russification, though continued in a premeditated and tacit manner.[79] Stigmas of cultural coercion come to the fore as version R reimagines the surrounding reality of that time. In this translation, Alex sees a poster of a movie produced not by "Statefilm"[80] but precisely by "Gosfilm." This name has its roots in the USSR State Committee for Cinematography—Goskino (Gosfilm until 1963)—and is contrasted with "Film Ojczysty" (Fatherland's Film) in version A.[81] Alex also finds his way not to a "cottage"[82] but to a "dacza," a summer house that was often state owned and given to Communist Party members. This Russian-modeled term is in contrast to the phonetically Anglicized "kantry haus" (country house) in version A.[83] The protagonist and his gang constantly confront "milicyjniaki" or "poli milicyjniaki."[84] This neologism—coined after the Polish People's Republic's military police, the *milicja* (militia)—reappears in various places in version R and extends its politically situated imagery.

Quite tellingly, in this rendering's prison scenes, Alex also uses the name "zek"[85] pointedly for his fellow inmate, whom he later beats to death. In version A, the inmate is phonetically Anglicized as a "pryzner" (prisoner), while the original Alex calls him simply a "plenny" (пленный: captive). "Zek," however, is a very specific term for a prisoner of Soviet labor camps, a term that was spread in English mostly through Aleksandr Solzhenitsyn's accounts of Stalinist repression.[86] In communist Poland, the traumatic testimonies of zeks in labor camps circulated in different forms. Even though Solzhenitsyn's writing was banned from print, readings of the Polish translation of his *Gulag Archipelago*, published in 1983 in Paris, were transmitted by the Polish Radio Free Europe before its official release in 1988. The Polish strand of gulag literature had also started coming to the surface. The most renowned account was Gustaw Herling-Grudziński's *A World Apart* (1951), with its first Polish edition released in London in 1953 and read in émigré circles before entering the Polish underground press in 1980; another one was Barbara Skarga's 1985 memoir *Po wyzwoleniu* (After Liberation). After the end of censorship, the first few years of postcommunist Polish prose abounded with similar late-coming memoirs from prisons and labor camps in the USSR.[87] On the wave of this strand of publications, Stiller's political label of "zek" immediately fueled negative sentiments about the figure of the perpetrator.

Though placed among other zeks in version R, Alex is invested in the corrupted system of coercion and violence he represents and internalizes. As a result, he manages to escape the consequences of killing his fellow camp prisoner. The Russianized context of his narrative hints at the institutional culprit of similar crimes upon zeks. It also fleshes out the violence dormant in language as Alex's brutality and vulgar talk are imbued with Russianisms. In the camp prison scenes in particular, they become a reminder of the specific gulag jargon from Polish gulag prose.[88] This argot was often described as a combination of the so-called *poligramota* (political grammar) and the most atrocious vulgarities coming from Russian.[89] It functioned as a multinational vehicular language whose swear words and curses also had cognates in Polish and whose shared etymologies would be discovered by Polish-speaking prisoners.[90] As Stiller balances different strands of prison cants, including the gulag jargon full of Russian swear words, he is suggesting that moral decay starts with the roots of the language. This also feeds into a different belief: that Polish culture has for decades cast Russian in the role of an abusive and vulgar language.[91] In Stiller's take, the Russianized language of ultra-violence used by Alex and his aggressive gang finds correspondents in existing Polish swear words. Stiller used a wide range of abusive expressions, which are mostly absent from the original. These include adjectives deriving from *jebać* (Russian ебать: fuck), *suka* (сука: bitch), *sukinsyn* (сукин сын: son of a bitch), *gnój* (гной: dirtbag), and *chujnia* (хуйня: clusterfuck), as well as, among other things, a palette of the derogatory *ryło* and *morda* (рыло, морда: snout). As this interlingual affinity is reestablished, Russian vulgarisms take us back to the origins of the Polish abusive language. It is in the zone of coercion and violence where Polish and Russian have found a point of contact and can now rub against each other. In the novel, this amalgam resonates even more because the characters often wear masks. Their violent language metaphorically becomes a source of disguised and anonymous aggression—in particular, aggression carried out by the communist political apparatus but also seen in many other instances in history.

Stiller indulged in making his Russianized Nadsat sound even more vulgar, which has often been put down to his sarcastic attitude toward the former oppressor.[92] Deforming Russian and downgrading it to the role of a vulgar or barbaric language intruding on Polish culture was a strategy to overcome the postcolonial complex. Early postcommunist works were often underpinned by a sense of moral and cultural superiority toward the "Eastern" barbarians.[93] The flagship piece of this strand, Dorota Masłowska's international bestseller *Snow White and Russian Red* (2002, translated by Benjamin Paloff), can in fact be seen as a later incarnation of Stiller's version R. The novel's aggressive protagonist, the tracksuited bully Nails ("Silny"), uses an equally distorted vulgar language to express his hatred for "the Russkies." At the same time, his mindset is grounded in the new post-1989 westernized world, since "the Russkies don't really lead the way on the world markets."[94]

Earlier instances of repressed Poles identifying themselves with "Western" values as opposed to "Eastern" barbarism had been recorded in the gulag testimonies[95] and the nineteenth-century literature under the Russian partition.[96] But it was with the political transition, and Eastern Europe being reclaimed by the Western sphere of influence, that this narrative came back into force. A lot was written around that time about the specific place of Poland or, more broadly, central Europe or post-Soviet states on the postcolonial map in relation to Russia.[97] While similar debates focused on whether this could be seen in postcolonial terms at all, the trajectory in these considerations usually led eastward. Seeing Poland's postcolonial condition beyond the Russian-Polish equation is the most remarkable import of Stiller's translation double. His intervention offers a much more complex perspective as it locates Poland as torn equally between the East and the West. This aspect of the postcommunist identity adds a whole new dimension to the Eastern European scenario, whose politics has more recently evolved in more alarming directions.

When Stiller announced his upcoming Americanized translation of *A Clockwork Orange* in the early 1990s, one reviewer treated this idea exactly as a touchstone of Polish society's colonial mentality regardless of the imperial source. "Well, Poles are the model proletariat," she insisted ferociously, and then compared them hyperbolically to contemporary slaves.[98] As Stiller's project was about to fork into two different linguistic paths, it was clear what the political stakes of his translation double were. "Western" and "Eastern" values would be compared with each other against the backdrop of Polish postcolonial memory. With an eye to this ambivalent consciousness, Stiller's translation double represented two bipolar voices. His Wind-Up language in version A illuminated the other side of the coin from that in version R. This second reading, according to Stiller, could allow for ridiculing the language of local teenagers "snobbing it up in American style."[99] Similar cultural aspirations under the Anglo-American world's dominance went neck and neck with the pursuit of the Western lifestyle and drive for consumerism throughout the 1990s. These rapid social and political developments were often reflected in postcommunist Polish prose as it started revolving around predatory capitalism, shady business, street life, and tabloid sensationalism.[100] The reality presented in Stiller's Wind-Up Orange worked as a barometer of this fast-changing landscape. In version A, Alex and his gang turn into children of American mass culture, whose worship of physical aggression is modeled on lurid violence in pulp movies and video games.

It was along these lines that the Wind-Up language fiddled with the protagonist's concept of ultra-violence. Whereas the Russianized version kept the original prefix "ultra" in both its translated variants ("ultra gwałt" and the more playful "ultra kuku"), the Americanized one changed them into "super" ("super gwałt" and "super kuku"). The "super-violence" embedded in this rendering's Americanized world sounds like an ironic variation on the idea of superpowers taken from a superhero blockbuster. When Alex watches a series of brutal movies as part of the Ludovico technique, he realizes that his gang's shenanigans extend the chain of violence that has been carried out at different moments of human history. In Burgess's original, Alex calls on the doctor's assistants, asking them to switch off "all this dratsing [драть: tear] and ultra-violence." In his Russianized version, Stiller renders this phrase as "całe to zrażanie się [сражение: fight] i ultra gwałt." In the Americanized version, however, Polish Alex identifies the movie as "cały ten *fajting* [phonetic: fighting] i *super gwałt* [super-violence]" (my emphasis). When read in the American context, this image resonates with brutality neutralized by popular action cinema.

As Alex and his gang often indulge in the said "fajting" or "big fajting," this activity becomes an Anglicized name for a constant element of their lifestyle. Stiller also coined another neologism, "grabing" (*grabować*: plunder), for their routine of robbing random victims. Although completely made up, Stiller's coinages echo analogous borrowings from English with the -ing suffix that emerged in Polish over the 1990s such as clubbing (*klabing*), zapping, lobbing, and sponsoring.[101] These language fashions, similar to the spreading usage of "super,"[102] found their way into Stiller's Americanized idiom to mock Western copycatting. Only a few years later, critics felt that this hypothetical Ponglish from the Wind-Up Orange had in fact come true. As everyday Polish got flooded with Anglicized jargon hybrids on the wave of Anglo-American cultural dominance, some believed that Stiller's invention was becoming the default speech of young Poles.[103] However, Stiller's usage of these terms is very carefully orchestrated. The Anglicized prefixes and distinctive gerund forms refer primarily to Alex's criminal activities, which suggest a rather ironic diagnosis of the teenage Americanized lifestyle. However prevalent and in vogue, the superficial promotion of "super-violence" with all its *fajting* and *grabing* did not bode well, promising nothing better than its Russianized counterpart.

The linguistic texture of the Wind-Up Orange managed to capture yet another aspect of the postcommunist world. The 1989 political transition in Poland was followed by the so-called Balcerowicz Plan, an economic "shock therapy" under the lead of Jeffrey Sachs. It fostered a rapid transition from the state-governed economy to a US-modeled free-market economy. This was also reflected in the surge of neologisms imported to Polish to give new names to the flood of new goods and other aspects of the capitalist world.[104] As if going with this tide, Stiller's Americanized language re-created the literary world of things by multiplying borrowings and neologisms associated with the new reality—cars, shops, economic products. In particular, this applied to the phonetic imitations of English words in places where both the original and version R used standard words: "kastomer" (customer), "szopy" (shops), "kar" (car), "brejksy" (breaks), "trafik" (traffic), and "hajwej" (highway), among many others. For instance, Stiller stuffs the description of one of the gang's many all-night orgies with newfangled Anglicisms. These insertions make the scene more scattered and dynamic, playing on the effect of an adrenaline boost:

> A później szosą na *west*. *Trafik* [traffic] nie był duży, więc *aj did pusz* [I did push] girę normalnie w dechę prawie że na wylot [...]. To jest dopiero *eksjating* [exciting], to jest coś! do śmiechu i do łomotu w *super gwałt* [super-violence]. Wreszcie dotarliśmy do takiego osiedla i *dżast after det* [just after that] był jakby taki mały osobny *kantry haus* [country house] z kawałkiem ogrodu. [...] [O]dpuściłem gaz i po *brejksach* [breaks], a ci trzej chichrali się jak *med* [mad], i widzieliśmy *inskrypszyn* [inscription] na *gejcie* [gate]. (my emphasis)[105]

This Americanized Nadsat toys with the idea of teenagers pretentiously imitating a cool language but also hints at broader social trends in the 1990s. Stiller's ironic take on Western values counteracts the post-1989 optimism among younger generations of Poles. Stiller mimics their shallow fascination with the stereotypical speed of life in the United States channeled through Hollywood cinema, TV, and video games. This rendering is also peppered with allusions to the newly promulgated lifestyle model, with Stiller repeatedly adding the phrase "haj feszn" (or "top feszn")[106] (phonetic: high/top fashion) to the narrative. In this way, he captures the West-patterned high-life aspirations across the proto-capitalist Polish classes.

This diagnosis of an aspirational and consumerist drive in society came through even more strongly in the popular 2005 stage production of the novel's version A. Adapted by the well-known Polish director Jan Klata for the Contemporary Theatre in Wrocław, the play kept the novel's title, *Nakręcana pomarańcza* (A Wind-Up Orange); its Ponglish hybrid language; and its Americanized setting.[107] This adaptation counterbalanced an earlier one based on version R entitled *Mechaniczna pomarańcza* (A Mechanical Orange) and staged in the Stefan Jaracz Theatre in Łódź in 1991 (see fig. 4.3). While the earlier play used Stiller's Russianized language and imagery, Klata followed Stiller's critique of society's McDonaldization. For instance, in a self-referential scene key to the novel, Alex reads a fragment from a manuscript entitled *A Clockwork Orange*, written by F. Alexander, one of his victims, about imposing laws and conditions on "a mechanical creation." In the 2005 theater production, as the passage unfolds in Ponglish, Alex's companion Georgie is gobbling up a large, juicy chicken leg in the foreground. While Alex's reading and Georgie's dinner were two separate scenes in the novel, the director synchronized the sequence on stage to make them comment on each other. His adaptation of the "Wind-Up Orange"—made in the USA—exposed the rules of the newly established consumerist system with its vapid "hej feszn" pursuit and consumption craze.

In debunking the myth of a flawless capitalist democracy, Stiller's Wind-Up Orange was not the only voice of disappointment. A social and economic exclusion post-1989 as well as a crisis of moral and aesthetic norms led other writers to give vent to their frustrations through disintegrated narratives about freedom and historical memory; the influx of foreign capital and products also fueled the suspicion that the country was still oppressed by foreign economic powers.[108] In this context, the bipolar politics of Stiller's double rendering also records these deeper ruptures in a coherent narrative after the fall of communism. Placing version A's capitalist reality on a par with the corrupted system in version R shows how a new utopian world turns into yet another dystopia. Here, the two systems of governance become different manifestations of the same political servitude. While the Russianized language unmasks the former apparatus of violent repression and ideological constraints, the Americanized one points to a different type of conformism. In the latter, it is about internalizing imported lifestyles and replicating the ready-made mindsets imposed by powerful systems of economic and cultural persuasion. According to Stiller, this is the inescapable fate of minor

FIGURE 4.3. Posters of two theater plays based on Robert Stiller's translation double of *A Clockwork Orange*: *A Mechanical Orange* (1991, directed by Feliks Falk) in the Stefan Jaracz Theatre in Łódź (designed by Zbigniew Koszałkowski) and *A Wind-Up Orange* (2005, directed by Jan Klata) in the Contemporary Theatre in Wrocław (designed by Aleksandra Kochan). Courtesy of the Stefan Jaracz Theatre in Łódź, Zbigniew Koszałkowski, and the Contemporary Theatre in Wrocław.

cultures and minor economies engulfed by more powerful forces in the globalized world. The orange may be "mechanical" as a product of a totalitarian system and straitjacket of censorship; it may also be "wind-up" when blinded by economic incentives and commercially promoted models. Either way, it can never be left to its own devices and always ends up being a cog in a larger wheel.

Multiples Going Round in Circles

Stiller's translation double hinges on reiteration and repetition. This technique finds its roots in the original plot, which is also propelled by repetitive patterns and recurring images.[109] For instance, the same question, "What's it going to be then, eh?," recurs in the opening of each of the novel's three parts.[110] Burgess himself called it the composition's "arithmology"[111] in his introduction to the American edition of his book entitled "A Clockwork Orange Resucked." Stiller incorporated this text into his version A as an interpretative key to his own translation project.[112] The original's reiterative structure is counterbalanced by the linear progression of twenty-one chapters standing for the age of majority and suggesting the protagonist's coming of age. The Polish translation double complicates this scenario by introducing an extra element of circularity. Toward Burgess's last chapter, Alex tentatively undergoes a conversion, hinting at a happy ending to the script. However, its Polish counterpart is not exactly finished at this point, as the translation double invites a different mode of reading. The two versions can be read one after another or in parallel. This narrative compound either makes one rendering break straightway into the next one or concur with the other scenario's culmination. This lets the story be told anew over and over again, as if the tape were rewound and replayed in two scenarios, always leading to the same repercussions. What happens in this process of retelling and coiling the original plot into a loop?

Just before what he promises to be his last act of ultra-violence, Alex claims that tomorrow is another day. From then on, he will move to leading a good life and "all that cal [кал: crap]."[113] We are left with a cliffhanger with these reassuring words and can choose either to believe in Alex's resocialization or distrust his intentions. In the Polish translation multiple, believing the protagonist's promise is even trickier, as there is a risk of being fooled twice. Since history tends to repeat itself, we have to suspend our disbelief first at the end of version R and then again in version A. Caught up in the cycle of recurring scenarios, the Russianized Alex and the Americanized Alex relive the same adventures in two realities on the brink of political transformation. Playing both these film reels through

Poland's successive moments in time casts a shadow over Alex's repeated declarations about his future conversion. Even the protagonist himself is well aware of the inescapable cyclical fate: he fears that a son of his might end up repeating the same mistakes. Stiller's translation double adds another dimension to the vicious circle of history: the generation of Russianized Alexes can usher in the generation of the equally corrupt Americanized Alexes, who do not learn from the mistakes of their own forefathers.

Stiller's publication of his translation double in 1999 hit right in the middle of this generational overlap in Poland. And he saw his work as a unique case, the same novel being translated twice in a completely different way "for the older and the younger."[114] In this respect, Stiller's translation combo partly drew on the prominent strand of generational conflict in postcommunist prose.[115] Yet, the lives of the Russianized and Americanized generations in the translation double were governed by the same narrative and so also challenged the idea of their conflicted stories. As two different horizons merged, they revealed grotesque twin realities underpinned by curiously similar principles. In this way, Stiller turned the apparent untranslatability of experiences between generations into their perfect translatability. This compares to Jorge Luis Borges's thought experiment in which his twentieth-century character Pierre Menard creates a translation of *Don Quixote*. In order to go beyond the letter of the original, Menard paradoxically ends up re-creating Cervantes's seventeenth-century text as it was, word by word, without formally changing anything. This little treatise on unstable meanings across time can shed light on Stiller's translation double. Like Menard, Stiller translated by making the same words resonate in two different contexts, both for the younger and for the older. Each time Stiller matched up echoing threads between the two variants, he also assumed a range of internally translatable experiences corresponding to both realities. In the moment he put a translation mirror between them, they started lending themselves to unsettling comparisons.

This little trick helps us evaluate the post-1989 worlds through a series of parallels in the genre scenes, escalating violence, and abuse of power that equate the communist and the new democratic governments. Despite the alleged improvement in economic conditions, not much seems to change otherwise. Political slogans remain unaltered regardless of the media outlet. In version R, they appear in a "gazeta" (newspaper), "dziennik" (daily), and "żurnał" (журнал: magazine); in version A, the same slogans reside in "njusy" (phonetic: news) and a "magazyn" (magazine).[116] In one of the final chapters, Alex is forced to jump out of a window by the antigovernment lobbyists who intend to use his case as a political tool. To this end, they sneakily plant a "broszura" (brochure) in version

R and a "buklet" (phonetic: booklet) in version A. Both of these, however, read "Death to the government" and entice the protagonist to "[o]pen the window to fresh air, fresh ideas, a new way of living." Read against two political backdrops, the phrases must relate to two different governments and opposition movements with their destructive ideas and newly promoted lifestyles.

This mirroring of political mechanisms extends to many other instances in Stiller's translation double. When the character of F. Alexander, a writer, calls Alex a "victim of the modern age" twice, in the different contexts of versions R and A, readers have to wonder what the referents for each "modern age" might be. The writer blames people for selling their liberty to the government in return for a quieter life.[117] Again, that can mean different things in each respective version. Depending on the political context, securing a peaceful or comfortable life might require denouncing neighbors to the communist authorities or accepting the government-endorsed intervention of international businesses in citizens' choices. For this reason, when the Ludovico technique enforced by the ruling party is praised in a "żurnał" and "newsy," the propaganda anticipating "a nice crime-free era"[118] forks into two ironic promises. The Russianized version offers a "*przewsochodna* [превосхóдная: superb] i wolna od zbrodni epoka," while the Americanized version guarantees a "fajna git *gordżes* [phonetic: gorgeous] i wolna od zbrodni epoka" (my emphasis).[119] The promised epoch is claimed to be superb or gorgeous, depending on whether it is the Soviet-led or US-dominated world. Irrespective of ideological camps, these and other slogans across the two versions lead society to blindly follow their premises in an equally manipulative way. By establishing a parallel between the communist and postcommunist orders, Stiller's experiment discredits divisions between the two feuding generations. In his take, their conflict is heated up artificially and stems from the same delusions that both groups keep cherishing.

This reckoning also puts a spotlight on the myth of the posttransition miracle. To this end, Stiller extends the circularity ingrained in the original novel to his cyclical interpretation of history. His translation double plays on this notion in various ways, each time foregrounding continuity between the two political periods. For instance, the back cover of version R asks rhetorically about the group of Alexes who were still active after 1989: "How many others of such people in charge have kept their lash and dull knife until now?"[120] This finds its justification in the novel's timeline as, in the course of the plot, the young offenders transform from bandits into policemen. The same group who would previously have destroyed the social order go on to constitute and shape it. Stiller translated this into real events: "[T]he same monstrous teenagers from 1962 are now, as of 2005, in their fifties and they govern, exercise power, and have their say in the matters of our country and society."[121] This has its roots in a later part of the novel, when vulnerable Alex meets his previous companions who are now wearing police uniforms. As they come to arrest him, they take advantage of their position and beat him up. Ironically, these are the same people who had once "wanted to have things more democratic like."[122] That pro-democratic intervention in version A sounds even more ironic as Pete opposes Alex in his additionally Americanized language: "A nie że ty *ołdy tajm* [phonetic: all the time] gadasz, co machnąć a czego nie. *Only* bez urazy" (And not that you are saying all the time what to twack and what not. Only no offence) (my emphasis).[123] But later, the highest spoke in fortune's wheel turns to the lowest: one of Alex's comrades, Dim, a freshly recruited policeman, becomes the one who dictates the rules in the new order along with another thug, Billyboy. Though assuring "Not no more, droogie,"[124] Dim demonstrates a greater violence than previously. In Stiller's translations, Dim's language is tainted respectively with Russianized and Americanized influences. We no longer take his words at face value when he makes promises as the novel progresses: "Było i już nie jest, mój *drużku* [друг: friend]" (version R), and "Było i już nie jest, mój *budku* [buddy]" (version A) (my emphasis).[125] Even if, with this, he claims that "what happened in the past, stays in the past," the generational change within the group of shady characters occurs before readers' eyes.

This generational succession helps us better understand the postcommunist transition, with the year 1989 as an overturning milestone in European history. In particular, Stiller resets the clock and puts the story in motion twice to complicate the memory of the Solidarity movement. In 1991, he had considered attaching to his version R the entire thirty-two-page brochure by Gershon Legman entitled *The Fake Revolt*.[126] In this text, Legman famously decried the "fake" countercultural and sexual revolutions of the 1960s in Western countries, setting them against the "real" student revolts in Paris. To Stiller, political dissidence in Eastern Europe culminating in the fall of communism in 1989 was another example of a "fake" revolt. It did not put an end to the destructive influence of the ruling establishment in Poland; even more, in Stiller's own words, "that fuss with Wałęsa on display" led to unfortunate repercussions, which filled him with disgust over time.[127] His criticism probably extended to the Roundtable Talks, often seen as politically makeshift and discarded for their superficial dealings with the past. More specifically, the infamous so-called thick line policy was an explicit proposition by the first post-1989 prime minister, Tadeusz Mazowiecki, to leave the past behind, separating it from the ongoing transformation. This strategy was frequently lambasted for its disregard of the unpunished crimes of the communist regime.

The thick line policy in Stiller's translation double works the same: since no official condemnation or penalty has been inflicted on the Alexes from version R, they could have easily transformed into the new group of Alexes in version A. The sins of "the older" cohort are inherited by "the younger," leaving an indelible legacy to loom large in society. In the novel's final paragraphs, Alex speculates about "a new like chapter beginning."[128] There, Stiller creates a gray area around Alex's instant conversion. The repetition of Alex's promise reenacted in both versions becomes a magical formula that captures the novel's plot in the loop. Toward the final passages of the Russianized narrative, starting a new "chapter" might mean rereading the same story from chapter 1. This time, however, a new story can unfold in its Americanized reincarnation, and then over and over again in any other Oranges to arrive in future.

Here, the cyclical nature of history offers no hope for getting out of the clockwork impasse. While constant returns to the starting point imply the lack of progress, Stiller sees this mechanism in darker colors. To him, repeating one's mistakes and playing the same scenario anew is in fact a backlash, a qualitative regress that he plays out in a quantitative way in his translation double. One example of this regress is his accumulation of more barbarisms in version A. As the remnant Russianisms from the previous version could not be entirely eradicated, they still shine through the newly superimposed Americanized language. This burgeoning intrusion extends to other destructive phenomena. For instance, Stiller across the two versions enlarges the group capable of speaking the corrupted language. Even though Nadsat is exclusive to the degenerate teenagers in Burgess's original, Stiller includes some adults among its speakers. The critics were not particularly fond of this approach,[129] whereas Klata kept it in his influential stage adaptation of *A Wind-Up Orange*. In Stiller's take, Nadsat spreads to characters such as the prison chaplain and the elderly women at the bar, and an accusatory finger is pointed at these extra culprits for their complicity in the gang's atrocities. According to Stiller, the question of responsibility for society's decay is more complex. It equally concerns, as he would have it, "these nice elderly women, always ready for perjury for the benefit of criminals" and "these decent people, completely blinded by [...] preaching."[130] In other words, guilt resides not only with the perpetrators but also with all those who turn a blind eye to their crimes and allow them to thrive.

The prison chaplain speaks more and more Nadsat across the two versions when trying to appeal to the prisoners.[131] For instance, he condemns the criminals for their urge "to live easy," using the prison slang in version R ("za frajer") and, in version A, a phonetic Anglicism ("za fri," for "free").[132] In some instances in version A, he also curiously synchronizes his language with Alex's phrases. First, the chaplain speaks: "*Rajt* [right] ferajna! Więc na *end* zaśpiewamy hymn 435 ze śpiewniczka" (Right, you lot. We'll end with Hymn number 435 in the Prisoners' Hymnal). Right afterward, Alex seconds him, echoing the vocabulary: "Ja płytę, ma się rozumieć, już *rajt end* redy [ready] miałem na stereo" (Of course I had the disc ready on the stereo) (my emphasis).[133] As Alex and the chaplain converge in their Americanized languages, we see the priest's fallible face: in giving the inmates incentives to snitch and toady, he is ready to corrupt them to his advantage. The chaplain also knows Alex's gang's idiosyncratic expression of approval—"fajno fajn" (finah-fine)—invented by Stiller in both versions with no equivalent in the original. This catchphrase is used by the chaplain at the moment when Alex agrees to conspire with him; information provided by Alex about other prisoners will help the chaplain ingratiate himself with the governor.[134] This phrase shared between the characters signals their tacit conspiracy. Like many other instances of a symbolically marked lexicon in Stiller's translation double, it starts working as a shibboleth that confirms the speaker's group identity with its representative set of values.

Why did Stiller decide to single out the chaplain in his two Oranges? This most likely has to do with his own judgment of the Polish clergy and the position of the Catholic Church in Poland. The novel's prison chaplain is a careerist who gives the same automatized sermon to rounds of prisoners and uses Alex as an informant to climb the institutional ladder. By stigmatizing the priest with the tainted Nadsat in his translation double, Stiller points the finger at the clergy for their participation in systemic hypocrisy and moral decline. Although the activity of the Catholic Church in Poland before 1989 was considerably constrained and mostly oppositionist in its attitude, there were also cases of priests collaborating with communist secret services and serving as whistleblowers.[135] Since the fall of communism, the Catholic Church has significantly strengthened its position in legal, political, and even interventionist terms.[136] Its influence on democratic elections, government policies, and public life has been considerable, all of which Stiller disapproved of.[137] He quite openly expressed his negative attitude in journalistic opinion pieces and in his translations of anti-Catholic and anticlerical writings that he promulgated throughout the 1990s.[138] This can also be seen in his depicting the chaplain in a worse light, in both versions, by means of vulgar or pejorative augmentatives often absent from the original. These include variations on the invented neologism "świętojebliwy" (fucked holier-than-thou) for the original "holy chelloveck" (holy man); "kaznodziejstwo i wzniosły bałach" (sermonizing and lofty bullshit) for "preachy gooveriting" (preachy talk);

and many others of the kind.[139] The chaplain acts here as the focal figure of the corrupt clergy, who neither set a good example for the younger generation nor try to rectify their faults. As a result, Stiller deems the priest and the whole church accountable for perpetuating the same corrupt dynamic.

Contrary to the chaplain, the old women at the bar speak the tainted Wind-Up language exclusively in version A. In several scenes early in the novel, the women make clumsy efforts to pick up the Americanized lingo and copycat the phonetic Ponglish phrases such as "God bles ju" (God bless you) or "Tenk ju" (Thank you).[140] While this may simply mean that the older generation is also keeping up with the linguistic fad, the women in fact articulate the Americanized words only when agreeing to cover for Alex and his friends in front of the police. Again, as the women accept the gang's generous tips to keep quiet, the Wind-Up language comes to denote bribery and a tacit collusion to abuse the system. Here, the women's corruption reflects Stiller's criticism of capitalism with its money-driven morality conditioned by lucrative incentives. In the age of "soft power," society's decay stems not so much from an authoritarian political force as from ethical laziness and comfort too easily bought with blood money.

The spread of Nadsat among more people in the Americanized version makes this diagnosis even grimmer vis-à-vis its Russianized predecessor. In comparing the two, readers can decide which one has been the lesser of the two evils. According to Stiller, while Poles had firsthand experience of similar degeneration in communism, the post-1989 "diseased system of lawlessness, hypocrisy, and incompetence" comes with the same consequences, "if not even much worse ones."[141] As these two worlds come together in Stiller's translation double, the common binary and Manichean opposition between the two historical periods erodes. The later one even seems to take a turn for the worse, with Nadsat revealing more areas of decadence and depravity among new groups of interest. The eventual backlash can take place regardless of the time, political system, and currently ruling government, as long as there is a group of ordinary citizens thoughtlessly permitting the ongoing corruption.

As if in an epilogue to this story, Stiller's Clockwork Orange has made yet another rotation. Since 1991, Stiller repeatedly promised to create a third version of *A Clockwork Orange*, this time with a Germanized language,[142] to "make his own *Love for Three Oranges* come true."[143] The third rendering, the so-called version N, was meant to appear under the title *Sprężynowa pomarańcza* (A Spring-Assisted Orange). The idea came from Stiller's observations of the years leading to Poland's accession to the European Union in 2004, which he saw as Poland's "entering the political orbit of the unified Germany." That time saw many political developments that potentially fed into Stiller's Germanized version. As France and Germany formed a stronger alliance, arguments over the European Constitution and Treaty of Nice unfolded; Polish-German relations during that time were overshadowed by debates around the planned Centre against Expulsions in Germany as well as Germany's disapproval of Poland supporting the Iraq War.[144] In addition to those political trends, a Germanized language in Stiller's Spring-Assisted Orange could have renewed another westward trajectory of Polish postcolonial discourse. It could draw from a rich reservoir of cultural and political oppression: the nineteenth-century Germanizing practice in the Prussian partition, the German orientalizing discourse around its "Wild East" leading to the Second World War,[145] and the trauma of the war itself. The Spring-Assisted Orange, however, has never appeared in print.

In April 2016, I contacted Robert Stiller about his translation triple and version N, which was still missing from the equation. In response, he sent me a sample chapter of his unpublished manuscript. He also promised to return to working at the full-length book "in the near future" due to this unexpected revival of interest in his triple project.[146] In December that year Stiller passed away, leaving his *Love for Three Oranges* unfulfilled. The excerpt he left behind (see fig 4.4) by no means covers the whole range of possibilities. However, it still lifts a veil on the potential directions in which a Germanized Alex could further go. In the excerpt, we can see how Stiller fiddled with the tensions between different tints of Germanness.[147] He included some German words and expressions that have been enrooted in Polish for decades or centuries. Elsewhere, readers could recognize the aggressive language of Nazi officers, especially in Alex's frantic exclamations "raus raus raus" (outta there!) and in the insult he uses: "ferflucht" (*verflucht*: damned). Following the Second World War strand, it would have been particularly interesting to see Stiller's further take on the novel's prison scenes. The infamous Ludovico technique that forced Alex to watch movies about Nazi killings could also pose interpretative challenges. Other places in the version N excerpt reveal that, in his Spring-Assisted language, Stiller was undoubtedly continuing his salvaging mission. In trying to retrieve the prewar multicultural imprint on the Polish language, Stiller assimilated some Germanized forms via Yiddish, one of the languages from which he independently translated. Such hybrids were "cwancyk" (צוואנציק: *zwanzig*, twenty) and "fertyk" (פארטיק: *fertig*, ready), among many others. In the crucial scene at the bar, the women also thank the boys by saying "danke szejn" (*danke schön*, thank you very much) with its characteristic sound shift in Yiddish: "sheyn" (שיין). Whether Stiller wanted to comment ironically on a cultural stereotype here or imply anything about these characters is difficult to guess without having the

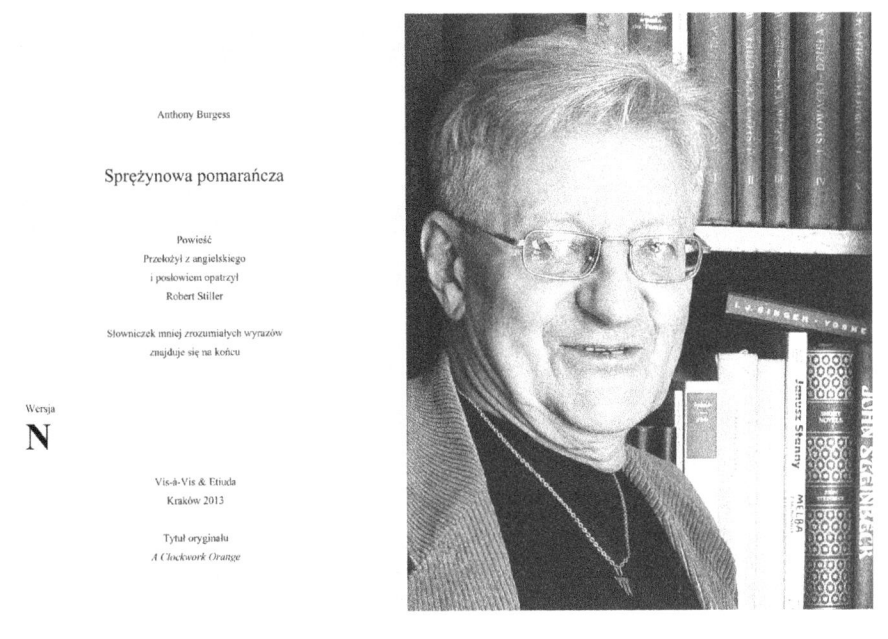

FIGURE 4.4. Left: The first page of Robert Stiller's unfinished manuscript of version N (German) of *A Clockwork Orange*: "A Spring-Assisted Orange." Right: Robert Stiller (1928–2016). Courtesy of Nina Stiller (the Foundation for Robert Stiller).

whole text. But even in its fragmentary format, version N still offers a promising insight into how the same story would have unfolded for the third time thanks to Stiller's imagination. I would still postulate that "A Spring-Assisted Orange" should be treated as a constitutive part of Stiller's translation multiple, even if only on the conceptual level. And it has often been seen as such by readers and critics who, prior to Stiller's death, patiently awaited its publication for years.

The Germanized version N could have opened up a discussion around many contemporary issues, even though it risked treading on controversial ground. Revisiting the experience of occupation could rub salt into war wounds and ignite anti-German sentiments still lurking under the surface. In 2015, the Polish government objected to the quota of Syrian refugees allotted to Poland under the EU's relocation scheme. This was discussed by some commentators in terms of a new Europe-wide fear of Germany's rising hegemony as well as Poland's historically motivated resistance to the past annihilator.[148] The Polish people also sensed a political ambush in Germany, following the EU's inertia in the Ukrainian crisis and agreements on the Nord Stream pipeline that were made without

Poland's participation. More recently, populist right-wing political movements have managed to capitalize on similar fears and traumas in other central and eastern European countries. Polish society's mindset has been easily teased and tricked into conspiracy theories in which dark international forces secretly plot behind Poland's back. Poland's respective governments have successfully piggybacked onto such attitudes, and the Spring-Assisted Orange could have offered an ironic pronunciation on this condition.

The existence of Stiller's unfinished triplet helps the Polish Clockwork Orange spin at least one turn further. Beyond the Cold War binary, it lets readers imagine even more vividly how its inner clockwork mechanism perpetuates the same scenario. This can take place any time a minor culture serves as the whipping boy in a political reshuffle between different spheres of influence. Again, the cyclical course of history can be seen in the novel itself. In the final passages, Alex predicts that the Orange's mechanism will go on "to like the end of the world, round and round and round." It will continue as if someone "like old Bog [God] Himself (by courtesy of Korova Milk Bar)" kept "turning and turning and turning a vonny grazhny [smelly, dirty] orange in his gigantic rookers [hands]."[149] Owing to this enigmatic higher power, Stiller's translation triple can set the Clockwork Orange in motion at least three times: first in "mołocznia Krowa Bar," then in "mleczarnia Cow Bar,"[150] and eventually in "mlekodajnia Kuh Bar" in version N.[151] And so the vicious circle will keep going "round and round and round" as long as there are more political hegemonies and subversive critiques to come.

Stiller was happy to extend the clockwork metaphor to other hypothetical projects and discursive comparisons. In 2005, he responded to jokers teasing him about a forthcoming Chinese version, an idea that he discredited.[152] Perhaps he would now need to revise his opinion in light of China's position as a global economic, military, and political power. At that time, instead, he announced a different fourth version to be published. It was to have the tongue-in-cheek title of "A Pesky Orange" (*Upierdliwa pomarańcza*) and use impeccable Polish. According to Stiller, the flawless language should paradoxically feel unnatural and Nadsat-like for his readers, since their point of reference for linguistic standards in everyday life was the prevalent rhetoric of Polish journalists, TV presenters, and public intellectuals.[153] His Pesky Orange was therefore meant to demonstrate how the persuasive force of media twists things round. Due to the media's low standards, Alex and his gang could become the actual voice of authority that shapes the language of political debate and forms public opinion.

In this way, Stiller's "Clockwork Orange" could become a capacious metaphor for a range of social trends. It is also not surprising that it inspired others to follow suit. In 2002, two leading music groups, the hip-hop group Paktofonika and rock band Myslovitz, recorded pieces under the titles of "A Mechanical Orange" and "Korova Milk Bar," respectively. These revolved around the themes of creative process, algorithms of music production, repetitive life, and escape in addiction. Likewise, when Jan Klata's stage adaptation of 2005 coincided with pivotal parliamentary elections, critics saw Alex's enforced resocialization as a key to understanding a different political context. In particular, they compared it to the instrumental treatment of morality and the postulate of the "moral renewal" employed by campaigning right-wing politicians, who later took over from the previously dominant social democratic party.[154] In all these instances, Stiller's translation multiples activated the clockwork mechanism to make bigger and bigger turns. Its triple spin could spark reactions to further forms of oppression any time that an automatized lifestyle and system of norms is imposed on the individual by a group of decision makers or a higher power.

In the previous chapter, Stanisław Barańczak's homophonic translations celebrated the coexistence of more than one reading and poetic voice in a very affirmative way. In contrast, the translation multiple of *A Clockwork Orange* may appear to be a more critical than constructive or inclusive project. However, Stiller's subversive critique still offers pluralist leeway for commenting on different political projects that are—perhaps only seemingly—mutually exclusive. Revealing different mindsets and values becomes a playground for testing various languages with their sociocultural implications. At the same time, it leads to an open discussion around several possible identities in a newly transformed world. If there is any positive lesson to be learned from Stiller's poignant experiment, it would be exactly this gesture of presenting all options on equal terms against any constraining publishing norms and political expectations. Embracing the criticism of different agendas assumes a forum for more than one possible reading, more than one translation, and more than one political viewpoint. And this perhaps could be that one step forward that Stiller did not want to recognize in his vision of historical regress. When the mode of translation multiples became available, it also brought the possibility of a more critical perspective and of reevaluating the plural narratives in circulation. As a result, a cog could for once step out of the larger wheel and observe it spinning over and over again from a sufficiently safe distance.

5

Doing Brecht in Different Voices

> *Remember*
> *When you speak of our failings*
> *The dark time too*
> *Which you have escaped.*
>
> —BERTOLT BRECHT, "AN DIE NACHGEBORENEN /
> TO THOSE BORN LATER," TEAM TRANSLATION

Translation beyond the Barricade

After almost a quarter century of silence, Bertolt Brecht the poet reappeared in the Polish postcommunist literary scene rather unexpectedly. The volume entitled *Ten cały Brecht* (All That Brecht), published in 2012, was the first collection of his poetry since the milestone of the political transition. Its release could finally put a symbolic end to the German poet's long, rocky road during the communist years. Brecht's life in Polish translation at that time was not the easiest. Manipulated in publication, censored and tailored for different audiences, Brecht—depending on the context—would come across as either a procommunist or an anti-regime author. His poetry served the purpose of, on the one hand, state propaganda and official circulation and, on the other, the dissident intellectuals and Solidarity activists in the underground press. As a result, Brecht became a peculiar fighting arena for opposing interest groups and their ideological viewpoints. His ambivalent and constantly biased image seemed to have left no room for revision. Always locked into the binary of "us vs. them," Brecht's poetry was bound to face an uncertain future in its postcommunist afterlife. Following 1989, how can we read Brecht's poetry anew? What language can we use when discussing and translating it? How can we let go of the past's conflicted agendas and open it to more readings and viewpoints?

A response to these pressing questions came finally, after more than two decades, from an ensemble of four poet-translators affiliated with the literary magazine *Literatura na świecie* (Literature in the World), or *LnŚ*. In the poetry collection revealing "All That Brecht," Jacek St. Buras, Jakub Ekier, Andrzej Kopacki, and Piotr Sommer each presented their own selection of Brecht's poetry and variations on individual poems. They manifested their plural approaches to Brecht's poetry in the book in many ways. The title, *Ten cały Brecht*, which literally means "this whole Brecht," has an ironic tone to it: a limited selection of eighty-one of his poems could hardly represent Brecht's oeuvre of over two thousand. But the phrase also reads as the offhand "all that Brecht" (analogous to "all that jazz"). In this sense, the volume is laying out for consideration the poet's fixed image and his reception, which pose so many challenges from today's perspective. The difficulty of revisiting Brecht's legacy has mainly lain in its political resonance overshadowing any aesthetic qualities.[1] The formerly instrumentalist uses of his persona by opposing factions has left twenty-first-century readers facing the question of whether they "wanted the Brecht he was or the Brecht they wanted."[2] As a remedy to the latter option and to complicate the answer to the former, the translator quartet suggested a different mode of approaching Brecht's writing. Discarding the rules governing the circulation of Brecht in communist Poland, Buras, Ekier, Kopacki, and Sommer projected a quadruple reading of his poetry, with some of the same poems appearing in different textual shapes in translation. This translation multiple invited a more distant and metacritical approach to Brecht's slightly problematic poetic output. It finally let the Polish Brecht speak in plural voices.

The creators of this new mosaic of different Brechts see the volume very much as a collaborative endeavor. In a telling gesture, they, the translators, are the ones named on the front cover as the book's authors (see fig 5.1), rather than the poet himself, the original author. Bertolt Brecht's name—or just his surname, which functions like a motto or brand labeling what his poetry stands for—is shifted into the book's title, and the emphasis is on the quartet of translators inviting readers to their workshop around Brecht in Polish. Naming the translators as authors on the cover also goes against the grain of publishing and reading norms, and it is notable that no major library catalog followed this authorial classification.[3] In the lead editor's own words: "[T]he image of the poet emerges from the crossroads of four readings, [four] interpretative and creative perspectives, and this, more conspicuously than usual, alters or at least revises the author's status."[4] As the volume turns into a literary story about reading Brecht told through a

FIGURE 5.1. The cover of *Ten cały Brecht* (2012) with Brecht's name in the title and the four poet-translators listed as the book's authors. Courtesy of Artur Burszta.

series of subjective accounts, the four translators act as the book's real authors. The microphone for voicing these narratives is shared among these multiple translators, each putting his own variant on the table on a par with the others. In this way, the volume serves as a pluralist and inclusive theater stage, allowing for more actors to enter the literary scene and recognizing more than one legitimate scenario of the Brechtian performance.

This chapter discusses the translation multiples of the *LnŚ* poet-translators at the intersection of different political and cultural developments. First, the polyphonic format of the book openly dissents from the ideologically driven reception of Brecht in communist Poland with all its nuances and peculiarities. His poetry had been particularly susceptible to political manipulation due to its socially engaged lyricism, which could cut both ways. On the one hand, Brecht's support of communism as a weapon against fascism and an instrument of social justice went down well with communist officials; on the other hand, the antisystemic potential of his poetry resonated with many dissident intellectuals. This had resulted in the author's ambivalent position in the literary scene of the time, which the 2012 translation multiple set out to revise. Second, the collaborative enterprise by the *LnŚ*-affiliated translators of "doing Brecht in different voices" should be read against the backdrop of *LnŚ*'s fundamental role as a liberal platform for circulating world literature in translation. This monthly journal, first published in May 1971, constituted the most influential official forum at that time for exchanging views on different interpretations and translations of literary texts. On occasion it promoted multiplied translation and other experimental formats, with a long-standing practice of publishing more than one translation variant and illuminating original authors from multiple angles. Even before 1989, this subversive practice was nourished by discussions on translation ethics led by the magazine's editors and translators. With these two contexts in mind, it will be easier to understand the pluralist gesture of the Brechtian translation multiples for its twenty-first-century audience.

Brecht's first steps into the Polish postwar landscape left no room for doubt as to his political mission. Poland in the Stalinist period, before the Poznań antiregime protests of 1956, brought forth an ideologically one-dimensional Brecht. The author was praised for putting socialist realism into theatrical practice, while critics of his plays were considered "enemies of the revolution," solidifying the order based on exploitation.[5] Only one collection of Brecht's translated poetry was at that time published by the State Publishing Institute (PIW). That 1954 book explicitly introduced Brecht as a eulogist of "the new, developing, just world, whose symbol is the Soviet Union."[6] The tendentious selection was a product of a broader ideological agenda pursued in the publishing and other cultural politics of the Polish People's Republic. Brecht's visit to Poland in 1952 was also discussed in politicized categories; attitudes toward Brecht among the Polish readership on that occasion served as a "litmus test" probing broader political trends in society.[7] In general, this heavily tainted reception of Brecht was not an isolated case in the Eastern Bloc. For example, the Soviet state's policy of canonizing some foreign authors aimed to render Brecht as an "ideologically appropriate author" among the citizens of the Soviet Union; this in turn led to a loss of interest in his works among many readers and a rather poor reception as late as the 1970s.[8] However, following Brecht's introduction to the Polish official circulation in the 1950s, a somewhat different scenario unfolded there on the wave of rising tensions between the government and dissident groups. Being somehow in the thick of it, Brecht's poetry became subject to political polarization along partisan lines and across the official and underground circulations. The poet was simultaneously seen as a communist by the regime's supporters and as an antidote to communism by its opponents. On the one hand, the official introduction to his plays in 1976 marketed Brecht as "one of the greatest hopes of the left-wing literary movement," which could have a positive impact on the ideological and artistic aspects of Polish theater.[9] On the other hand, Brecht became the unlikely hero of Generation 1968 (New Wave) intellectuals, whose works were distributed in the underground press. Polish dissident poets often either translated his works or positioned themselves toward his writing. As they rechanneled his attacks on the previous system of oppression, they could voice their own resistance and intellectual protest against the current regime.

The key poet and translator who helped introduce Brecht's poetry through the underground press was Ryszard Krynicki. He was not exactly a favorable reader of Brecht's works, and he was vocally critical of Brecht's support of communism. In 1981, he admitted that he could not understand why Brecht started serving "the deceitful utopia," in the name of which crimes were committed and nations resettled.[10] For this reason, he initially translated Brecht's poetry "a bit too much in his own way."[11] These first translation attempts in Krynicki's "own way" were already available in 1974 thanks to Galeria O. N., an independent niche graphical gallery run by artists. This ushered in a long struggle to publish the unpublishable in the official zone, additionally fueled by the 1976–1980 official ban on publishing Krynicki's own works. However, he finally managed to introduce Brecht's poetry to a broader audience through the second circulation established in Poland in the late 1970s. A collection of Brecht's translated poems titled *Elegie bukowskie i inne wiersze* (The Buckow Elegies and Other Poems) appeared first in 1979, and then again in 1980, and made quite a splash in dissident circles. These poems were circulated as political *bibuła* (prohibited materials released by the Polish underground press), and the collection was seen as "one of the most anticommunist books," impossible to get published in any official publishing house.[12] However, Krynicki managed to smuggle his translations of twelve of Brecht's poems into *Organizm zbiorowy* (The Collective Organism), a collection of Krynicki's poetry officially released in 1975. Krynicki's Polish translations of Brecht could therefore be a more powerful weapon than his own authored poems—working as camouflage for forbidden subjects and antiregime sentiments in the same way as many other literary translations published in the Soviet Union.[13] In hiding behind Brecht's disguise, the poet-translator could take advantage of the Aesopian language and play polyphonically with the censors' vigilance.

Similar artistic gestures escalated into even more politically engaged forms of resistance with Brecht's mediation. Krynicki was the first to translate into Polish Brecht's "The Solution" ("Die Lösung"), a poem with an explicitly anti-regime message. He first dedicated his own poem "Our Special Correspondent" to Brecht's "The Solution"; however, Krynicki's poem was consequently banned from print in the years 1969 and 1972, and appeared only in 1973 in a small underground chapbook.[14] He then published a Polish translation of "The Solution" in the official circulation even before 1989, making it "a little sensation" and a unique case in the Eastern Bloc.[15] Brecht's iconic lyrical manifesto lambasted the East German government's violent actions in suppressing the workers' uprising of 1953. It ended with a perverted suggestion that it would be easier if "the government dissolved the people and elected another" ("die Regierung löste das Volk auf und wählte ein anderes").[16] With this symbolic motto on the banners, Krynicki's Polish translation of the poem, "Rozwiązanie" (Solution), helped the Solidarity opposition to man the barricades. The Polish version was placed on the front page of the Solidarity trade union bulletin for the central and eastern region in 1981,[17] published above an article on the twenty-fifth anniversary of the 1956 Poznań protests by Polish workers, which were violently suppressed and afterward hushed up by the People's Republic of Poland government (see fig 5.2). Such a framing of the Polish translation established a parallel between the East German demonstrations described by Brecht and the Polish uprising three years later. It also gave a new lease on life to dissident activity following the more recent protests of that time. These included especially the series of strikes in July 1980 in Lublin, which culminated in the events of August 1980 in Gdańsk, with Lech Wałęsa taking the lead. By refreshing these recent memories with the help of Brecht's words, the paper's editors implied that the Polish scenario for "the solution" might pan out differently—coming true under the auspices of another group of newly "chosen" people, namely the opposition now actually serving its nation.

The circulation of Krynicki's Brecht gathered more pace and impetus. Krynicki recalled how some of his translations were printed on the Solidarity movement's leaflets, with occasional fragments edited or altered for propaganda reasons.[18] For instance, one leaflet featured another of Brecht's poems translated by Krynicki: "What Are You Waiting For?" ("Worauf wartet ihr?"). However, the printed title was now changed to "What Are *We* Waiting For . . ." ("Na co czekamy . . .") and graphically placed in the middle of a photograph of oppositionists (see fig. 5.3). The red and white coloring alluding to the Polish national flag and the visual

FIGURE 5.2. Ryszard Krynicki's translation of Brecht's poem "The Solution" ("Die Lösung") in a regional bulletin of the Solidarity union, Lublin, 1981. *Source:* Bertolt Brecht, "Rozwiązanie," translated by Ryszard Krynicki, the Archives of Europejskie Centrum Solidarności. Courtesy of the European Solidarity Centre.

positioning of Brecht's text, as Arkadiusz Luboń argues, highlighted the poet's alleged engagement in the Polish cause.[19] The poet's role implicitly shifted from independent commentator to insider and zealous ally of the Solidarity movement. The first lines of the poem reverberate with a promise of change: "When things remain as they are, you are lost. Change is your best friend." In 1981, historian Timothy Garton Ash spotted this poster copied and distributed by Solidarity activists in the Mazowsze region among many other tokens of political identity.[20] The union's mobilization was often manifest in their use of national symbols and slogans on armbands, badges, and posters. With his protest songs and lyrical manifestos in Krynicki's translation on the banners, Brecht unwittingly reinforced Solidarity's political agenda, jumping on its anticommunist wagon.

In the worlds of publishing and performance, Brecht's poetry was released in different forms, leading to a slightly schizophrenic Polish readership. Toward the end of the 1970s, Brecht's translated works were placed in anthologies of both East and West German authors.[21] Locked into this Cold War impasse, Brecht's poetry

FIGURE 5.3. A Solidarity poster with Brecht's title "What Are You Waiting For?" ("Worauf wartet ihr"; "Na co czekacie") changed into "What Are We Waiting For..." ("Na co czekamy..."); Gdańsk 1980. *Source:* author unknown, the Archives of Europejskie Centrum Solidarności. Courtesy of the European Solidarity Centre.

often had to serve on both sides of the barricades and represent two, usually mutually exclusive, political agendas. The more the poet became a battlefield for clashing factions, the more the context in which his translations appeared and were read became a sensitive issue. According to Julian Kornhauser, another New Wave poet, the reading always depended on the publication place, the way of distributing books or leaflets, the person of translator, and the relevant contextual framing.[22] The 1980s were particularly tricky for the official authorities, who sometimes had to backtrack on their own staging initiatives. For instance, in 1982

Teatr Ateneum in Warsaw was to have staged an official evening of poetry featuring Brecht's cantos, songs, and poems titled Heaven of the Disillusioned (Niebo zawiedzionych)—a carefully procured selection based on heavily censored versions in Robert Stiller's translations.[23] However, the performance was eventually prohibited, only coming to the stage in 1989. When the same poetry evening was about to be staged in Szczecin in 1983, officials canceled it immediately on hearing that the sold tickets were accompanied by leaflets advertising a local meeting of Solidarity members.[24] This frantic back-and-forth happened between the two politicized spheres, with Brecht right in the middle of it. Both the state presses and official cultural production on the one hand, and the clandestine publishing and underground dissident activity on the other, claimed a license for their own Brecht.

Due to these bipolar and instrumentalist readings of Brecht's writing, the political transition of 1989 left his works devoid of their past force. Since there seemed no political or ethical mission to be completed anymore, Brecht's works no longer raised any meaningful emotions in the postcommunist world.[25] Throughout the 1990s, Polish critics puzzled over how to read the author, who carried such specific historical luggage. To many, Brecht only seemed relevant either as a verbal weapon to be used in a fight with a totalitarian regime or as a tainted "travel comrade" from communist times.[26] The Polish audience therefore could not take him seriously as an artist.[27] In 1998, on the centenary of Brecht's birthday, a panel of writers, critics, and readers met to discuss Brecht's absence in the postcommunist literary scene. One of them lamented that Brecht's plays in the translations existing before 1989 were absolutely unsuitable for the stage; they had most often been directed by people whose main concern was "whether Brecht was a party or nonparty writer or whether he was an orthodox party writer or a revisionist one."[28] The lack of suitable translations of Brecht's works since the fall of communism meant that he was completely unknown as a writer and poet, despite his previous resonant appearance. There was no adequate language or literary form in which Brecht could speak to contemporary Polish readers beyond the opposing sides of the barricade. This led some years later to the moment when the mode of translation multiples came to the rescue. The quartet of poet-translators could only complicate Brecht's bipolar image by exposing various Brechts existing simultaneously within one polyphonic book. Given that they also explained their rationale, translation choices, and editorial solutions, the period of the ideologically driven manipulations of Brecht's texts was able to come to a symbolic closure. The volume *All That Brecht* turned into a public literary forum in which many other viewpoints and readings of Brecht's poetry could be confronted and acknowledged equally.

The format of translation multiples to which the Brechtian project resorted came from familiar territory. The poet-translators, as already mentioned, were all affiliated with the magazine *LnŚ*, which truly had shaped publishing practices even during the communist era. Not only did the magazine promulgate new trends in international literature, but it was also a relatively liberal realm for testing ideas around collaborative translation, innovative forms, and multiplied viewings of individual works. The literary monthly was a highly popular enterprise; its print run reached as many as thirty to thirty-five thousand copies for most of the 1970s and 1980s. Issues featured dispersed finds from around the world as well as focused studies of individual writers and the literatures of specific regions.[29] The magazine's title, *Literatura na świecie*, in its literal translation "Literature in the World" rather than "World Literature," alluded to the magazine's agenda of breaking up the monolith of one universal literature that is easily translatable across countries into major languages, particularly into the globally dominant English.[30] Instead, the notion of "literature in the world" promoted a dispersion of viewpoints and readings, which was reflected in the different forms featured in the magazine. It published translation polemics regarding different ideas and textual solutions. These were often accompanied by gripping analyses that read like "sensation novels."[31] The heated-up debates over translations were joined by critics, translators, academics, regular readers, and even politicians,[32] who sometimes suggested alternative translations in support of their arguments. In this respect, the magazine was open to various critical voices and translation strategies. It also managed to reach out to a relatively wide audience and attract readers from outside the profession to the arcana of literary translation. This manifested itself in frequently published letters to the editors commenting on individual renderings and the translators' specific arguments.

The magazine also developed an editorial practice of presenting different renderings of the same work in parallel within one issue. This format invited readers to compare variants and recognize the different readings and views on translation. The prototype multiples placed together by the *LnŚ* editors spanned different genres and publishing formats. In some cases, longer excerpts of texts in prose ran alongside each other on even and uneven pages or in half-page columns to be read in parallel and instantly compared.[33] Claude Simon's *Lesson in Things* (*Leçon de choses*), presented in two alternative variants in 1986, exemplified the magazine's rationale behind translation multiples. The editor, Wacław Sadkowski, added an explicatory gloss to the double publishing format, arguing that this purposeful confrontation would help readers better understand and compare differences, which are ingrained in the practice of translation.[34] Letters from readers expressed distress at this tactic; according to one reader, the magazine was implicitly imposing rivalry between translators and trying to show one of the translators in a bad light.[35] Sadkowski took this opportunity to flesh out the magazine's ethical agenda: a simultaneous publication of this kind was not aimed at any competition or any "either/or" binary, with one version surpassing the other; instead, as he said, the comparative release served as an opportunity to celebrate and acknowledge both of them as "perfect, fully mature, and consequent" readings.[36] The belief that two or more translations could be equally legitimate visions would be consequently endorsed in the magazine's publishing agenda afterward.

The editor's little manifesto also rounded off a series of feuds over translation ethics that had taken place in the magazine the year before. They revolved around the implications of singling out an individual artistic take while flying under the author's flag. The discussion started with the curious notion of "merged" translations, which stirred up some controversy and drew very mixed reactions. The provocative idea had been tentatively tossed around in 1977 by Robert Stiller, who considered cherry-picking the most appealing excerpts from Polish renderings of Heinrich Heine's poems to blend them into one ingenious amalgam.[37] As this was before the era of translation copyright and its regulation in Poland, which began in 1994, Stiller worked on the premise that these renderings served as "communal property."[38] In 1985, his edgy approach was eventually put into practice by Maria Leśniewska, who in the magazine published such a merged translation as a form of experiment. As she blended existing translations of Baudelaire into what she saw as a modernist "montage," she named only herself as the translator; this was supposed to test whether the text would read well without there being any trace of the original translators and come across as sufficiently homogeneous.[39] She justified the experiment in almost Machiavellian terms: as long as the translation product was good, the method was irrelevant, even if it involved "conscious plagiarism" and "stolen verses" from other translators' readings. In response, *LnŚ* commentators tore apart the idea of merged translation voices. One of them made the point that different Polish Baudelaires reflected the translators' plural personalities and individual ways of experiencing the original—it was imperative that these perspectives "for ethical and aesthetic reasons" not be melded into one.[40] Another used more explicit politicized metaphors when comparing the figure of the unified Baudelairean translator to "a one-man institution (established by whom? subject to which top-down decrees?)." In warning against the totalizing force of similar ideas, he twice appealed to the readers: "[D]o take risks, search for individual styles, do not drown in the regular grayness."[41] Blending all individual readings into one unified voice was therefore something that the *LnŚ* circle openly opposed on both the artistic and ethical levels. Their agenda of multiplying interpretative perspectives and claiming a right to each of them separately lay at the heart of the magazine's debates and approach to international literature.

Informed by similar discussions, *LnŚ* openly promoted multiple translation in poetry by placing plural renderings of single poems next to each other for didactic purposes, "so that readers can themselves draw conclusions" about the translators' distinct approaches.[42] This editorial solution was used in several issues throughout the 1980s. In 1995, the magazine organized a roundtable around a concept of translation multiples based on plural versions of Dante's *Inferno*.[43] The issue featured seven variants of "Canto II,"[44] and more recent translators were invited to explain their perspective in conversation with the editors. The new *LnŚ* editor (and later one of the Brechtian quartet's poet-translators), Piotr Sommer, discussed with Stanisław Barańczak the analogous Anglophone projects of that time, which were published as artistic books with translation variations: Michael Hofmann and James Lasdun's *After Ovid: New Metamorphoses*, published in the United Kingdom in 1994, and Daniel Halpern's *Dante's Inferno: Translations by Twenty Contemporary Poets*, released in 1993 in the United States. While *LnŚ* had developed its own editorial tradition from the 1970s onward, the affiliated translators still carefully followed other polyphonic projects in Western publishing contexts. Their finds could later have inspired the Brechtian volume as it developed into a more conceptual book.

More directly, the *All That Brecht* volume was born out of the magazine's special issues devoted to single authors, with larger selections of their poetry presented by plural translators.[45] These selections were often grouped into translators' special features and followed their respective reading lines. At the same time, they allowed for the possibility of the same poem to be repeated in different textual shapes within one issue. These issues were also accompanied by the translators' commentaries, giving insight into their individual reasoning and translation philosophy. For example, the 1980 translation double on T. S. Eliot's "Animula" included one version by a poet-translator affiliated with the New Wave, Krzysztof Karasek. In his accompanying commentary, he argued that translation should be seen in terms of an "essay" in support of one's subjective take on the original. Similar ideas recurred in many other author-focused issues of *LnŚ*.[46] They culminated in variations on several German authors by the four poet-translators who later formed the Brechtian ensemble.[47] An issue in 2006 included a teaser of their multiplied volume in the form of a quadruple selection of Brecht's poetry. All these translation concepts and preliminary steps in editorial multiplications fed into the 2012 publication of *Ten cały Brecht*. The authors of the Brechtian multiple shared the same intuition about different readings, which inevitably belong to individual translation visions. They also continued the magazine's long-standing agenda and translation philosophy, which favored plural readings over unified or merged voices. This ethical stance, together with the meandering story of the Polish reception of Brecht, would help the translation quartet coin all these ideas into one polyphonic book.

Brecht in Translation Slams

Building on the *LnŚ* lineage, the Brechtian quartet explain the rules of their collaborative artistic revision of the poet's image in a couple of ways. They lead readers through the volume step by step, gradually coming up with a makeshift user's manual to their newly born Polish Brecht. Each quarter of the book features a lead motto or leitmotif that shines a light on the poet from a different angle and sets the stage for an individual performance. The poetry selections are followed by corresponding essays, in which each member of the translation troupe gives directions for reading his own personal Brecht. As the poet-translators justify their strategies and idiosyncratic takes, they also reveal which Brechtian clichés they aim to debunk. Each of the reading approaches offers a different solution to problems with "all that Brecht"; altogether, the volume points to at least four possible ways of redefining Brecht's poetry for readers in postcommunist times. While following individual trajectories, these interpretative paths also meet at a few crossroads, in particular when the same Brecht poem finds its way into the selection of more than one translator. These "overlapping" renderings rework *LnŚ* editorial practices for the new format of a translation book. At the same time, they delineate a ground for comparison between the distinct reading approaches, which lead to a visible divergence within the translated texts. Such points of contact between the book's Brechtian interpreters explicitly mark the difference between their individual imaginative worlds. In order to better explain their differentiating role, let me first outline the poetic universes that emerge from the volume. As the four translators perform their own parts, each becomes intertwined with his specific experience with Brecht and reluctance to follow earlier run-of-the-mill readings.

The first voice belongs to Jacek St. Buras, who had previously translated Brecht's early plays and protest songs. In his essay "Under the Rebel's Spell" ("Pod urokiem buntownika"), he explains his attraction to Brecht's rebellious inclinations, especially in their more apolitical dimension. Communist reviewers had always pushed for pedestrian interpretations of Brecht's texts as criticizing the bourgeois world and exploitation of labor.[48] In contrast, Buras sets out to focus on Brecht's recalcitrant attempts to demystify the more universal rules of interpersonal relations, choosing the phrase "on the uncertainty of human relationships" from the first finale of *The Threepenny Opera* for his selection's title. To stress that line of reading, he also translates the song's refrain "The world is poor, man is bad" ("Die Welt ist arm, der Mensch ist schlecht") as "The world is poor, and men are bad" ("Świat biedny jest, a ludzie źli"), placing the lyrical "I" from the song against many others. This suggests that there will always be a rebellious individual bold enough to confront the corrupt majority, regardless of the times. The Brechtian lesson in protest against injustice and compassion for the disadvantaged can be one common denominator of the past and the present. Instead of negating the poet's communist baggage completely, Buras proposes to look for possible relevant threads and redefine Brecht's pro-social agenda for contemporary society. As a result, Brecht in this take resonates as a "lyrical rebel, born do-gooder"[49] known for his spontaneous empathy rather than his later didacticism.

The next rendering, by Jakub Ekier, opposes fixed ways of reading Brecht's poems in the context of his biography and political views. For him, the poet's symbolic signature "I, Bertolt Brecht" (from "Of Poor B. B.") invites readers to examine Brecht as an artist who took on different identities. As Brecht often switched tone of voice, wrote in all three persons, and played with diverse language and styles,[50] he deserves to escape simplistic appropriations. Ekier's strategy of reclaiming Brecht beyond the barricades lies in demonstrating how the poet is "Neither someone's, nor oneself's, nor one only" ("Ani czyjś, ani swój, ani jeden"), as his essay's title has it. In the grand scheme of things, this reading also justifies the main tenet of the whole volume. In order to discover Brecht's true colors, one has to look at the widest possible range of faces and poetic dictions. Likewise, Ekier's selection from Brecht's output is very spread out and wide ranging, and its motto, "Bad Time for Poetry," is the title of a poem from Brecht's *Svendborger Gedichte*, written in exile. Both the poem's title and text ironically comment on the reductionist approach to Brecht's poetry. The poem's narrator, a poet, admits that inside him there contends both "delight at the blossoming apple tree" and "horror at the house-painter's speeches."[51] In other words, the poet's inspiration is shared between a natural poetic beauty and a historically driven mission: even though experiencing all aesthetic and metaphysical dimensions, the poet must decry the propaganda of the unfulfilled student of fine arts, Adolf Hitler, belittled there as a house decorator ("Anstreicher"). Because of this clash of obligations in demanding times, the narrator's poetry is doomed to be read as engaged journalism—just as Brecht's poetry was read by different groups in communist Poland. However, since it is now imperative to foreground multiple spheres of artistic interest and tensions in Brecht's poetry and weigh them against each other, the main hero of Ekier's translation is this conflicted and diverse Brecht who is not easy to pin down.

The third answer to all this Brecht comes from Andrzej Kopacki, the initiator and lead editor of the volume, who in turn focuses on a very narrow selection from only two poetry books: *Hauspostille* (1927) and *Svendborger Gedichte* (1939). Kopacki postulates the discarding of any rhetoric of memory and political readings of Brecht's writing in favor of a maximum emphasis on his self-referential lyricism.[52] For him, the way out of the ideological impasse leads through a precise close-up of the texture of Brecht's poetic language instead of having it speak from distant banners. Kopacki's essay title, "Śliwa pod okiem"—literally "a plum [tree] under the eye" and also a Polish idiom for "a black eye"—playfully alludes to this: Brecht's politically tainted writing made Brecht "come under Kopacki's eye" in the 1970s, and it "immediately started hurting";[53] and yet this moral hangover, the Brechtian black eye, can only heal under a close examination of his poetry, which is represented by the leitmotif of a plum or a plum tree. Brecht's poems such as "Remembering Marie A." ("Erinnerung an die Marie A.") and "The Plum Tree" ("Der Pflaumenbaum") feature plum trees as sensuous imagery symbolizing fertility. At the same time, on a more self-reflexive level, the plum tree stands for the poet's prolific writing and creative abundance, a trait recently absent from the Polish reception of his works.

Post-1989 Brecht was for many years like the plum tree from "Der Pflaumenbaum," as it could no longer bear any fruit. In his rendering, Kopacki reads this key poem in his selection metatextually. In the original, despite the tree's miserable state, it is still possible to tell it is a plum tree "by the leaf" ("an dem Blatt").[54] Kopacki unpacks the expression's double meaning: the German word "Blatt" might mean the plum tree's leaf; it might also mean a page or a sheet of paper, on which the tree from the poem can literally reach its readers. As the Polish "tree leaf"—"liść"—contains no ambiguity, Kopacki decides to render the original phrase in a different way.[55] His plum tree can be recognized "by the little leaves" ("po listkach"), which derive from the Polish "fig leaf" ("listek figowy"),[56] idiomatically, a cover to keep something secret and invisible to the eye. Here, Kopacki follows another association in German: "kein Blatt vor den Mund nehmen," literally, to speak without a "leaf" on one's mouth, to speak openly. In his rendering, the plum tree is constantly covered behind the "fig leaves" of language, just like Brecht is doomed to be obscured by the screen of translation. In 1986, Robert Stiller said that only new translations could help readers discover Brecht afresh and hear him speak in his own voice "without any fig leaves."[57] From Kopacki's perspective, uncovering Brecht can happen when reading his poetic language closely, namely, the surface of the fig leaves. While Brecht still might not speak openly and remain hidden behind them, readers can at least tell "by the fig leaves," by examining the poetry's texture from different angles, that it is indeed one of his possible lyrical voices.

The final part was put together by the *LnŚ* editor in chief Piotr Sommer, also a poet and translator of modern poetry in English. Sommer wished to escape from the clichéd poetic idiom in which Polish Brecht had spoken to the previous generation of readers from underground publishing houses. This fixed language, according to him, came from the anticommunist works of New Wave poets[58] and subsequently some Solidarity activists. In order to free Brecht from this biased perspective, Sommer resorts to indirect translation, which he elsewhere calls "a sin difficult to resist."[59] He sets English[60] as a language mediating between German and Polish, and there are a few reasons for this. First, Sommer's Brecht can finally be displaced from the local reading context with its burden of political connotations. Owing to the mediation of English, Brecht can also enter an international dialogue with Anglophone poets as well as those accessible in English translation. In this sense, Sommer's source Brecht is in fact Global Brecht, a German poet read through the medium of global English alongside other poets in international circulation. Second, Sommer aims to establish a linguistic relationship between Brecht and authors whose poetic language he finds similar in terms of syntactic structures and objectivist narratives—authors such as Charles Reznikoff, C. P. Cavafy, Miroslav Holub, and Aleksander Wat. In Sommer's reading, Brecht is primarily "the poet of sentence,"[61] and so his text's seductive power and rhetoric are better understood when examined on the level of syntax. Sommer's renderings therefore closely reconstruct sentence arrangements following their performative heft, which is also how he had previously approached translating Reznikoff's miniatures.[62] Accordingly, his selection is titled after the Brechtian line "And so I built sentences" ("Und ich stellte die Sätze so"). This is from Brecht's poem "On Speaking the Sentences" ("Über das Sprechen der Sätze"), in which these arrangements are explicitly said to have "visible effects."

Sommer saw Brecht's poetry's lack of ethical mission after the fall of communism as part of a more general trend in Polish culture after 1989. On the wave of political transition, writers often moved on from ethically engaged dissident writing to the poetry of everyday life, and Brecht's absence was a natural consequence of this development. He had become an "old rejected concept," but one to which one can return[63]—an idea from Aleksander Wat's poem that Sommer paraphrased in his accompanying essay.[64] Wat's poem muses on the real meanings of things by examining words such as "exists" and "return" as anchors in language. The concept of "returns," for instance, was well known by *The Odyssey*'s Penelope, who knew its secret: "that one must weave and unweave. And again weave and unweave."[65] In Sommer's view, the "weave and unweave" procedure is the natural course of things in all historical and literary processes, including the current condition of Polish poetry.[66] Old, rejected poets such as Brecht get woven and unwoven into these processes, only to be woven back when needed again to a different end. If so, writers and readers would have to "wait out" the previous Brecht; the poet had already completed his service to what Sommer saw as the totalizing power of "Value" in poetry before 1989.[67] Back in November 1980, following the first actions of Solidarity, Sommer had written a poetic commentary on this paradoxically difficult moment for both Polish literature and Brecht's reception, which was later published in an underground pamphlet:[68]

Według Brechta	*After Brecht*
Przypuszczam, że niektórzy poeci przestali ostatnio rozsyłać swoje wiersze do gazet	I suppose that some poets recently stopped sending their poems out to newspapers
Myślą sobie pewnie: poczekamy aż się to wszystko uspokoi i minie im (gazetom i innym poetom) ta dziecięca choroba obywatelstwa, czy jak to tam nazwać.	They are perhaps thinking: we'll wait until this all calms down and they (newspapers and other poets) get over this childhood illness of citizenship or whatever you call it
Bo minie.	Because they will.
Czytelnicy będą mieli tego dosyć, redaktorom też się znudzi i w końcu zwrócą się do nas.	The readers will have enough of it The editors will get tired of it too and finally they will come to us.
A my otworzymy szuflady i wyjmiemy z nich nasze Wartości Ponadczasowe które, właśnie dlatego że są ponadczasowe, mogą sobie teraz spokojnie poczekać.	And we will open the drawers and take out of them our Timeless Values which are timeless exactly because they can now calmly wait.

Sommer ironizes the urgency of Timeless Values, namely, the ethical principles that governed anticommunist dissident writing and dragged Brecht into an ideological battlefield. After waiting for the "childhood illness of citizenship" to pass, the quartet of poet-translators could finally return to Brecht outside of the political turmoil. His image can appeal to contemporary concerns and the poetry of the everyday when read in individual and intimate acts of unpacking his poetic narratives. Sommer's personal experience of "arranging sentences" involves salvaging the actual timeless qualities and "visible effects" in Brecht's poetry. These can be any lyrical anchors and meanings that one can return to—even those previously manipulated or falsified.

Through these four reading lenses, "all that Brecht" arrives at the crossroads of four different Brechts. Each translator has a different idea of how to reclaim the poet's image and rescue it from the former duopoly. Interpretative keys outside partisan lines range from Buras's focus on demystifying rules of human relations and empathy, to Ekier's postulate of diversity and demonstrating Brecht's shape-shifting nature, to Kopacki's close readings of lyrical conventions and self-referential texture, to Sommer's syntactic approach to the tangible effects of Brecht's narratives. Although these propositions do not overlap in their premises, the volume explicitly promotes a dialectical confrontation between the translators, leaving any further judgment to readers. In fact, we can see that the four spokesmen of Brecht disagree with one another in quite a few matters. For instance, Ekier questions the category of "fragility of human relations" employed by Buras in his reading.[69] Buras admits that he was never fond of Brecht's later literary output, which both Ekier and Kopacki present.[70] Kopacki in turn criticizes the monotonous tone of the socially engaged Brecht,[71] which can be found in Buras's part. Elsewhere, the translators argue in their commentaries over the degree of authenticity in Brecht's flagship poem "To Those Born After" ("An die Nachgeborenen").[72] At the same time, however, the translators agree to disagree. They refer to one another's solutions and redirect readers to each other's renderings of the same poems.[73] In addition to cross-referencing and other little markers of mutual recognition, some of them (in particular Ekier) explicitly acknowledge divergent readings as "equally probable."[74] This open dialogue with alternative translations puts them in an intertextual network of different, and sometimes mutually exclusive, perspectives. Nevertheless, all of the translators agree on the parallel publication of their parts and accept it as a multivocal venture.

These different images of the poet belong to subjectively procured selections, and so it is the same poems in their distinct textual shapes according to translator that are the most interesting places of intersection. The translations of the same original differ precisely because their translators differ in opinion as to how to render them. As their viewpoints rub against each other, these moments of confrontation give us true insight into the potential frictions between their distinct voices. The volume acknowledges a plural presence that is groundbreaking in light of Brecht's legacy. In the past, the same poems in different translations would not have been presented together and would have been placed in two bipolar contexts—and in each mode of circulation, only one translation represented Brecht's writing. Here, open confrontations between translators within the volume move the conversation around Brecht to a public stage. I see these moments as little translation "slams," in which all poet-translators are allowed the same airtime and public presence. Their way of presenting Brecht is no longer about arguing solely either pro or con or tailoring his image to a particular political group or mode of circulation. Instead, the book's creators keep passing the microphone and voicing different ideas about Brecht to a larger forum. The idea of translation slams is particularly compelling in this context. Slams are embedded in the tradition of poetry performance and open mic sessions, an artistic practice that would likely be after Brecht's own heart. In a sense, the whole volume works along these lines, though it is the three "overlapping" doubles that stand out in this respect. These duels, enabling more than one translator to enter the stage in a direct confrontation, completely redefine Brecht's postcommunist afterlife, as more than one persona of the poet can share the spotlight. In the zone of a slam performance, translation multiples turn into a public forum for negotiation and pluralist dialogue with readers, who act as the ultimate judges.

The "overlapping" pieces let readers see how the translators' postulated readings work in practice and diverge in the matter of poetry. Buras and Kopacki face each other over the poem "On the Drowned Girl" ("Vom ertrunkenen Mädchen"), while Ekier's and Sommer's strategies are contrasted in two different poems: "Solely Because of the Increasing Disorder" ("Ausschließlich wegen der zunehmenden Unordnung") and "When in My White Room at the Charité" ("Als ich in weissem Krankenzimmer der Charité"). The first poem, about the body of a drowned girl floating down a river, forks down two separate routes.[75] In his rendering of the dead girl's travel, Buras emphasizes compassion and empathy as values that made Brecht oppose the unfair system in favor of the poor and defenseless. His is a universal version, whether the poem's heroine represents Rosa Luxemburg, whose body was thrown into Berlin's Landwehrkanal, or any other miserable female victim.[76] In contrast, Kopacki's drowned girl joins the literary current of other drowned heroines to underscore the conventional nature of Brecht's poetic language. His original was already a reservoir of leitmotifs recycled in German "water corpse" poetry ("Wasserleichenpoesie") such as

Shakespeare's Ophelia.[77] To stress the self-referential texture of Brecht's lyric, Kopacki refers to the girl in Polish as "topielica." In so doing, he conjures up the spirit of a drowned girl from Slavic mythology, a recurrent theme in Polish Romanticism and the ballad tradition. This way, the original poem refracts into two different readings. But as these remain in accordance with what Buras and Kopacki explicate in their commentaries, the translators practice as they preach. Exposing two different hands-on approaches to Brecht helps lift the veil on the translator's craft.

A similar confrontation takes place in translation slams between Ekier and Sommer, whose double renderings also belong to two separate translation realms. Brecht appears here as two different persons. In Ekier's take, he comes across as a versatile poet who has escaped biographical pigeonholes in favor of the individualist mission of the artist; Sommer's rendering makes him sound more like an orator who is constantly aware of the performative power of words.

Let us see how one of these translation doubles, at the intersection of two distinct voices, can be read along these lines. "Solely Because of the Increasing Disorder" ("Ausschließlich wegen der zunehmenden Unordnung") is a pivotal work of the Brechtian multiple. The poem echoes the purport of the project as it metacritically comments on art being torn between conflicted interests in a time of disruption. This theme also fits squarely within Ekier's section, which diagnoses a "bad time for poetry." At the same time, as Brecht composed the poem into one intricately arranged sentence (finding it impossible to write in traditional rhymed form during his exile years[78]), this "small masterpiece of construction"[79] could easily find its way into Sommer's syntax-oriented translation realm. In their translation double, Ekier and Sommer bring out different shades in the tension between poetry's divergent roles during a time of disorder. On the one hand, Brecht's poem postulates the writing of "one-sided" ("einseitig") poetry in inauspicious political circumstances, with "dry" ("trocken") and "reduced" ("dürr") poetic categories, which were considered adequate during "disorder," whether the fascist prelude to war or capitalism run amok. On the other hand, the poem itself avoids the postulated one-sidedness by its ironic understatement and rhetorical construction.[80] This translation double has to resolve such an inherent contradiction in Brecht's poem in the same way as the whole volume has to come to terms with the biased practice of reading his poetry. Even though Brecht's poetry would often lend itself to one-sided readings, readers still had to take a step back to look at it from a distance and from different angles. A change of perspective sheds new light on how the same words can resonate, depending on who uses them and how they are framed.

Ausschließlich wegen der zunehmenden Unordnung BERTOLT BRECHT[81]	*Solely because of the increasing disorder* TRANSLATED BY FRANK JELLINEK[82]
Ausschließlich wegen der zunehmenden Unordnung	Solely because of the increasing disorder
In unseren Städten des Klassenkampfs	In our cities of class struggle
Haben etliche von uns in diesen Jahren beschlossen	Some of us have now decided
Nicht mehr zu reden von Hafenstädten, Schnee auf den Dächern, Frauen	To speak no more of cities by the sea, snow on roofs, women
Geruch reifer Äpfel im Keller, Empfindungen des Fleisches	The smell of ripe apples in cellars, the senses of the flesh, all
All dem, was den Menschen rund macht und menschlich	That makes a man round and human
Sondern zu reden nur mehr von der Unordnung	But to speak in future only about the disorder
Also einseitig zu werden, dürr, verstrickt in die Geschäfte	And so become one-sided, reduced, enmeshed in the business
Der Politik und das trockene "unwürdige" Vokabular	Of politics and the dry, indecorous vocabulary
Der dialektischen Ökonomie	Of dialectical economics
Damit nicht dieses furchtbare gedrängte Zusammensein	So that this awful cramped coexistence
Von Schneefällen (sie sind nicht nur kalt, wir wissen's)	Of snowfalls (they're not merely cold, we know)
Ausbeutung, verlocktem Fleisch und Klassenjustiz eine Billigung	Exploitation, the lured flesh, class justice, should not engender
So vielseitiger Welt in uns erzeuge, Lust an	Approval of a world so many-sided; delight in
Den Widersprüchen solch blutigen Lebens	The contradictions of so bloodstained a life
Ihr versteht.	You understand.

Wyłącznie przez ten zamęt

TRANSLATED BY JAKUB EKIER[83]

Wyłącznie przez ten zamęt
Rosnący w naszych miastach
   objętych walką klasową
Niektórzy z nas ostatnimi laty
   postanowili
Mówić już nie, że miasto portowe,
   że śnieg na dachu, kobieta
Zapach dojrzałych jabłek w piwnicy
   ani że ciało coś czuje
Mówić nie o tym, co człowieka
   dopełnia i uczłowiecza
Ale jedynie o tamtym zamęcie
Czyli wybrali jednostronność,
   suchość, i uwikłanie
W polityczne zajęcia i w jałowe
   "niegodne" słownictwo
Ekonomii dialektycznej
Po to, by owo straszne stłoczenie
Śnieżnych odpadów (my wiemy,
   nie tylko ziębiących), wyzysku
I ciał wiedzionych pokusą, i
   klasowego prawa nie zrodziło
Zgody w nas na tak wielostronny
   świat, radości
Z tego co sprzeczne w równie
   krwawym życiu—
Rozumiecie.

Wyłącznie z powodu narastającego nieporządku

TRANSLATED BY PIOTR SOMMER[84]

Wyłącznie z powodu narastającego
   nieporządku
W naszych miastach owładniętych
   walką klasową
Niektórzy z nas postanowili nie mówić
   więcej
O portach, o śniegu leżącym na dachu,
   o kobietach
Zapachu dojrzałych jabłek w piwnicy,
   o tym co czuje ciało
O wszystkim, dzięki czemu człowiek
   jest taki krągły i ludzki
A mówić już tylko o nieporządku
A więc stać się kimś jednostronnym i
   jałowym, uwikłanym
W sprawy polityki i w suchy
   "niegodny" język
Ekonomii dialektycznej
Ażeby to koszmarne ciasne
   współistnienie
Padającego śniegu (jest nie tylko
   zimny, wiemy o tym)
Wyzysku, skuszonego ciała,
   sprawiedliwości klasowej,
nie wytworzyło w nas
Aprobaty dla świata o tylu twarzach,
   apetytu
Na sprzeczności tego krwawego życia
Sami rozumiecie.

This happens on stage as the translation slam continues. Already at first glance, the flow of Ekier's rendering has a completely different dynamic to that of Sommer. The construction introducing the ideas and images that "some of us" have decided to pursue is changed by Ekier into the colloquial and not entirely correct "speak no longer that a port city... that the snow on the roof... a woman..." ("mówić już nie, że miasto portowe, że śnieg na dachu, kobieta..."). As opposed to Brecht's "speak no more of" ("reden nur mehr von"), Ekier's list gives a sense of unfinished clauses, of snapshots from life, or fragments taken out of conversations.[85] Ekier writes about his fascination with Brecht's spontaneity in mixing styles and writing as if he were thinking out loud and making up lines on the spot.[86] Such rattle talk here stands for the diverse world with its dispersed voices. However, it is obliged to give way to the new uniform type of "vocabulary," the fixed formulas that urgently respond to current disturbances. As the poem unfolds, the style transforms. The original attributes ("einseitig," "dürr," "verstrickt") turn into "heavy" categories: "one-sidedness" ("jednostronność"), "dryness" ("suchość"), and "entanglement" ("uwikłanie"). As Ekier comments, this aims to make the lines feel nominal, dense, and difficult to embrace.[87] This is also how uniform ideas and political biases divert people and poets from "what completes and humanizes a man" ("co człowieka dopełnia i uczłowiecza"),[88] distracting them from all the different stories that in fact constitute each of them and make them fulfilled as individual beings.

In turn, the constant practice of speaking about the actual disruption ("this disruption—about that disruption" ["ten zamęt—o tamtym zamęcie"]) monopolizes the intellectual discourse. The tension in Ekier's rendering hinges on the artist's positioning somewhere between two easy binary oppositions: the one-sided, homogeneous collectivism promulgated by the "some of us" versus diversified individualism within the equally risky many-sided world of contradictions. According to this reading, it is not entirely clear if poetry can escape entanglement in the partisan mindset and the totalizing "futile" ("jałowy") language. If poetry's varied tone, tribute to many voices "speaking that...," and dialectical reasoning do not come to the rescue, the blame here should lie with external factors. In his version, Ekier has in mind a specific type of social "disorder," a particular occurrence happening in a specific place. As he switches the words, he situates the disorder precisely in the cities: "due to this disruption increasing in our cities" ("przez ten zamęt rosnący w naszych miastach"). Through the phrase "przez ten zamęt" (due to this disruption), he also implies negative effects. It is the ongoing disruption or confusion ("zamęt") located specifically in our cities that hinders artistic creation, with poets now forced to rechannel their energy and writing into other concerns.

In his reading of the poem, Sommer strays from this interpretation. He keeps the euphemism "nieporządek"[89] (disorder, untidiness) in the title and, unlike Ekier, suggests a more general disorder or disarrangement. This version religiously follows Brecht's syntactic structures, modeled after both the original and its closely related English translation. The reason for this meticulous reconstruction is Sommer's belief that this poem's syntax undercuts its ostensibly communicated message, making the poem say something other than it declares.[90] Sommer brings out this quality by delimiting verse lines at ambiguous points with what he later called "calculated retardations."[91] For instance, he breaks the third crucial line at "Some of us decided to speak no more" ("Niektórzy z nas postanowili nie mówić więcej"), leaving this statement as a cliffhanger. Only in the ensuing passage does it become clear that this phrase is just part of a longer train of thought in which particular topics stop being referred to. The cliffhanger, however, makes the first line suggest that these "some of us" stopped speaking altogether and chose silence. By comparison, Ekier's translation at this point considers the alternative of "speak not that ... but speak about that disruption" ("Mówić już nie, że ... ale mówić o tamtym zamęcie") as a choice between two different modes of speaking (better or worse ones). Sommer is suggesting a more radical stand. According to him, "speaking only about disorder" ("mówić już tylko o nieporządku") in fact equates to not speaking at all, "speaking no more." This type of mute poetry, referring back to his ideas about speech performativity, produces no visible effects, no tangible results.

Another, similar cliffhanger gives us more clues as to the source of this muteness in Sommer's reading. First, he transforms the original "vocabulary" ("Vokabular") into the general realm of "language" and tellingly leaves it just before the line break. Even though the following line reveals that it is actually the language of dialectical economics, ambiguity has already been created. Speaking exclusively about disorder traps the speakers not only in politics but also in language as such. In Sommer's line of reading, the one-sidedness of expression becomes a sort of speech disorder, a disarrangement playing havoc with the usual evocative resources. It manifests itself in their reduced performativity: homogeneous and biased language is too futile or barren ("jałowy") to produce concrete effects. Sommer's translation shows how to counterbalance this tendency and restore the right "order." He gives a new lease on life to Brecht's seemingly "dry" ("dürr") poetic language by prompting more bodily images. In Sommer's rendering, the cramped coexistence whets the "appetite" ("apetyt") for contradictions rather than sparking "joy" ("radość"), in Ekier, or even the original "delight" ("Lust"). Sommer's multisided world ("vielseitige Welt") becomes a "world with so many faces" ("świat o tylu twarzach"). It encompasses the appetite, "lured flesh" ("skuszone ciało"), and "what the body feels" ("co czuje ciało"). It allows for speaking about "everything that helps make a man so rotund and human" ("wszystko, dzięki czemu człowiek jest taki krągły i ludzki"), stressing the human's corporal fullness ("krągły") rather than any "round" shape ("rund") or Ekier's idea of "fulfilling" their humanity. As Sommer enhances the vivid, concrete imagery, he draws a contrast between futile poetic language and language that bears palpable realizations and actually moves the addressee.

Ekier and Sommer put forward different paradoxes in Brecht's poem. Ekier contrasts diverse expressive voices and artistic collectivism as possible reactions to political disruptions. By seeking a language that humanizes a person, he also prevents Brecht's poetry from being reduced to one uniform diction. In Sommer's translation, tension arises between the two types of language—the totalizing abstract idiom and the concrete intimate one—that coexist within poetry and evoke the appetite for contradiction. While Ekier looks for the source of conflict externally, Sommer suggests that this conflict is already inscribed in language itself: it lies dormant in the language of poetry and comes to light as the abstract and the concrete meet halfway to confront each other. As Ekier and Sommer reconcile tensions in Brecht's poetry in a dialectical way, these considerations are replicated in their own translation slam. In a time of disorder in how Brecht is received, their translation double teases out conflicted stories in his poetic world of many faces. Whether through diverse idioms or the concrete language of the everyday, "all that Brecht" may finally sound more human, rotund, and rounder in their double viewing.

The V-Effekt

After the one-sided binaries that appropriated Brecht before 1989, postcommunist translation multiples are teaching the Polish contemporary audience a new lesson. Depending on the translator's perspective, Brecht's works can become part of completely different, though internally consistent, poetic universes. A medley of possibilities is spread out in its full diversity, with no single option prioritized. This gesture of turning the translation book into a pluralist form for discussing Brecht can be interpreted against the backdrop of various tendencies. The wide-ranging purport of the project was probably best summarized by the lead editor, Andrzej Kopacki, in his introduction to the volume in the following inconspicuous sentence:

> *This* Brecht (who, by the way, also liked to multiply versions of his own poems) can be read as one multithreaded poetic score for four voices and eight hands.[92]

The sentence is worth unpacking with an eye to every little piece of the puzzle; altogether, it illuminates the book's historical and conceptual background in at least four different ways. For a start, even the use of italics points to a different modality of speaking of the poet. In the book, *this* particular Brecht actively sets out to complicate the image of "all that Brecht," whose echoes still haunted the Polish literary scene. The newly introduced Brecht signals a new, positive trajectory in the postcommunist editorial culture, putting an end to the previous era of text manipulation through publishing and translation practices and instead pursuing a different mode of literary circulation. Plural reading perspectives liberate Brecht from the Cold War "friend or foe" rhetoric as well as allow his poetry to follow other interpretative lines beyond the barricades. In doing so, they also redefine the previous authoritative role of translation and the publication context in establishing who can lay claim to Brecht and to what purpose. Before 1989, it was far easier to hijack Brecht's image due to the polarization of two differently controlled media. In contrast, the translators of *this* Brecht no longer have to suppress other readings in other to promote their own. Instead, they open up his poetry to a more democratic dialogue, with different alternatives treated on a par with one another. In this sense, *this* Brecht promises to be a more constructive prospect for translation multiples in contemporary society. While Stiller's *Clockwork Orange* translation project multiplied different negative scenarios, the Brechtian quadruple reinvents the discussion around multiples in more reconciliatory terms.

This democratic idea ties in with the second point raised in Kopacki's summary—the artistic collaboration being compared to a "score for four voices and eight hands." Brecht's multiple is inviting more people to join the translation band and contribute with differently pitched voices than appeared in previous, individually orchestrated projects. Here, the collaborative endeavor truly embodies what translation multiples should postulate; it features more than one translatorial voice personally represented in a pluralist forum. Moreover, a comparison to the volume's polyphonic and orchestral format alludes to recurrent ideas around translation as musical performance and improvisation. In *All That Brecht*, the translation book becomes a musical performance in the same way that Brecht's lyrical texts and songs functioned in different media with many versions reenacted on stage. This is reflected in translation slams, with two different renderings on an equal footing, and in them the pair of translators occasionally cross four hands (out of the total eight hands involved in the volume) to play Brechtian duets in different keys. The musical element is also inscribed in Brecht's own approach to his texts, which he often treated as a peculiar kind of sheet music, a material for further processing and performance.[93] Some of his "originals" were derived from secondhand materials and existing literary leitmotifs, which were then reworked and performed by him anew in text. Since the status of these texts is already ambiguous, they should be approached, similarly to their musical namesake, as lyrical "variations on the theme."

Brecht's transformative power is the third crucial context mentioned by Kopacki, this time in passing in brackets: the translation multiple is justified by the poet's own practice of multiplying texts. Brecht juggled different versions of his poems, letting their interpretations vary according to their literary context. This was the case with the drowned girl ballad from Buras and Kopacki's translation slam, which Brecht had himself published in at least two different contexts.[94] Brecht reshuffled in this way many other poems, whose meanings changed and whose characters took on different personas depending on a new story and lyrical framing. This specific aspect of his activity once made the theater critic Eric Bentley warn Brecht's readers: "One has always to ask of a Brecht translation what German text it is based on since Brecht himself was forever changing what he wrote."[95] In this sense, Brecht can act as an intellectual patron of the Polish translation multiple. While his views on translation were rather conservative,[96] he could expose the constantly progressive and infinite nature of literary texts in his capacity as a modernist juggler of ready motifs onto which he built a new aesthetic quality. Brecht multiplied his "originals" to demonstrate that the category of the "original" is unstable from the outset. This notion is transposed onto the Brechtian quadruple, as the translators openly admit how tentative and subjective their versions are; they also multiply some of Brecht's poems in different renderings and textual shapes to question the reader's trust in any one given translation. Thanks to the particular direct confrontations in the translation slams, it is possible for readers to follow different interpretations in a play-by-play mode, seeing also how the difference between variants cuts across the imaginative worlds of individual translators.

This, finally, brings us to the fourth way of going about the editor's statement. Since the translation multiples are informed by Brecht's own poetics—as the comment in brackets suggests—the book's distanced perspective on Brecht may also have its roots in his broader philosophy of performance, in particular in the didactic aspect of approaching a performed text. Brecht has been credited for a transition from a faithful reenactment of a dramatic text to its metacritical viewing. The latter revolves around the notion of Brechtian "epic" or "non-Aristotelian" theater, which favors an explicative and discursive insight into dramatic action. By excluding empathy with characters or events,[97] this kind of performance is supposed to prevent viewers from taking what happens on stage for granted and welcome a more distanced approach to it instead. This aesthetic process is propelled by what Brecht sometimes called the "V-effect" (or

"Verfremdungseffekt," translated as "alienation," "distancing effect," etc.).[98] Loosely basing his artistic technique on Viktor Shklovsky's "defamiliarization" (*ostranenie*), Brecht introduced strangeness in order to "renew our powers of cognition."[99] In other words, he intended to push viewers out of their comfort zone and make them reflect on the very act of reenactment. Employing self-referentiality as a form of pedagogy, this method was seen by critics such as Fredric Jameson as a didactic technique of helping the audience "think."[100] In the case of the Brechtian quadruple, the V-effect lay in bringing together different variants of Brecht's poetry to help readers revise the categories they previously took for granted. The V-effect in translation multiples challenged the audience's practice of reading translations as one-to-one representations of the original. It could therefore distance Polish readers from any passive acceptance of a single fixed image of Brecht on either side of the ideological barricade.

This Brecht from the translation multiples became *these* Brechts. The project demystified the pre-1989 manipulative practices that had claimed to show the only "true" Brecht, while in fact enforcing their "own" Brecht. Such instrumentalist readings squeezed Brecht's world of many faces into binary formulas and dangerously imposed the totalizing optic onto his readers. The postcommunist multiples in turn shredded Brecht's image into a diverse mosaic, setting readers against any monochromatic picture. This is also in accordance with Brecht's theater method. When he defined epic theater in his essay "Theatre for Pleasure or Theatre for Instruction," he referred to Alfred Döblin's observation: "[W]ith an epic work, as opposed to a dramatic, one can as it were take a pair of scissors and cut it into individual pieces, which remain fully capable of life."[101] When confronted with a fragmented drama, audiences cannot completely immerse themselves in the narrative and have to reflect on the modes of representation. The Brechtian translation quadruple hinges on a similar premise. Due to all the "individual pieces" being in confrontation with each other, a complex panorama can oust a more convenient monochromatic image. These individual pieces include the four differently procured presentations of Brecht's poetry as well as the strangely "overlapping" translation doubles. If cut with a pair of scissors, these constituent parts of the Brechtian multiple could easily be published as stand-alone texts and act on their own. When brought together, however, they can no longer reenact Brecht but start telling the story *about* enacting Brecht. Just as Brecht's "stage began to tell a story"[102] in the epic theater, so did the fourfold translation turn into a narrative on Brecht's image in flux.

What is the take-home message from the Brechtian translation multiple for readers, critics, and, more broadly, consumers of culture? While enjoyed as performances in their own right, books composed of translation multiples can have a didactic role similar to Brecht's V-effect. As the Brechtian volume invites a more critical viewing of various ideas about his poetry, it also reveals the rules of this dialectic game to its readers. To this end, the translators explicitly demonstrate how texts are arranged in such a way that "the distinctness of motives, circumstances, selections, viewpoints and means of action" can be easily recognized.[103] At the same time, the four translators still employ quite simple literary and critical tools to flesh out the nuance and unpack more readings of a previously politicized text. This might also define the didactic mission of translators, translation multipliers, and critics in breaking totalizing political discourse into a range of alternatives. Instead of succumbing to an antagonizing rhetoric, they must try to show the other side of the coin and acknowledge the presence of a narrative from outside their comfort zone. This leads further to the question of how to activate readers to be more conscious users of translation and political culture, instead of feeling like invisible observers of translation performed before their eyes. Brecht called this mechanism a "fourth wall" illusion[104] in referring to the norms of European stage in 1936; according to him, it was assumed that spectators were unseen in any theater event that they attended. In the mode of translation multiples, the translator's role is also to dispel the magic spell of the fourth wall. Translation multiples activate readers' "cognitive powers" and teach them how to differentiate between distinct takes on the original from a palette of available options. Owing to similar exercises, passive recipients of single "true" perspectives—be it in translation or political discourse—can remove their blinkers. In this sense, the idiom of translation multiples stretches out a polyphonic forum for different ideas, which readers need only to learn how to assess and choose from. At the same time, it puts many other significant issues on the table: it opens up fixed images to alternative viewpoints and tests distancing methods as a refreshing formula in translation ethics. It is now left to readers to decide whether they wish to join this diverse table, sit patiently through all the propositions at stake, and have their say in the discussion.

Conclusion

TRANSLATION MULTIPLES are an ideal medium for teasing out conflicted identities. The multiples work under the assumption that translation is largely seen as a repetition or a clone of the original. On second glance, however, each of these single copies turns out to be cast differently and displays its own individual touch. A mosaic of identities can be orchestrated in plural ways, each time telling the story of the multiples through diverse forms and media. Since translation multiples perform the same text in different ways, they ultimately demonstrate that no single perspective on the original is the same. But translation multiples also take this consideration one step further. In fanning out multiple versions, their creators insist on the plurality of things that are often taken to be singular. This comes forth most forcefully in multiplied forms that reiterate different reincarnations and images of the same speaking subject. Is it the same feeling of being lost in the middle of one's life that different translators talk about in Caroline Bergvall's "VIA"? Is it really the same *me* who observes the promenade differently depending on the day in Sawako Nakayasu's "Promenade"? While questioning familiar and fixed categories, translation multiples often resort to the figures of repetition and reiteration. These figures become the aesthetic principle of the multiples but also have a critical and philosophical relevance. In particular, they demonstrate that there are no monolithic identities but only their partial and reiterated performances. In the world of translation multiples, no one can trust that one is truly identical with oneself.

The question of shifting identities has taken a curious twist in the postcommunist context. On the wave of the political transition, the multiples teemed with twins, doppelgängers, mirror images, and look-alikes—all related, yet distinct from one another. Such tension between difference and kinship cuts across all the examples I discussed previously. The homophonic multiples in Stanisław Barańczak's case mean to present different ideological facets, even if by resisting the pressure to merge them all into one; uncoincidentally, the multiples are also read alongside Barańczak's double poem on twin brothers with apparently irreconcilable political views. Robert Stiller's translation multiple introduces three different Alexes from respective versions of *A Clockwork Orange*. Readers can experience a strange feeling of déjà vu as consecutive stories unreel one by one with the protagonist's look-alike reappearing in several different settings. Then, a battle over different faces of one literary persona sets the stage for the Brechtian multiple. As the four translators reenact the poet's alter egos in the new scenery, their quadruple act reveals Brecht's shape-shifting identities. There is more to this anxiety around split personality and multiple look-alikes with different political identities. Similar leitmotifs recurred in other art forms created around the end of communism in Eastern Europe, with the most memorable cases coming from cinematography. The aforementioned Krzysztof Kieślowski's *Blind Chance* (1981), with its three different reincarnations of Witek, and his *The Double Life of Véronique* (1991), with two female alter egos, are not isolated cases in this respect. Earlier films such as Roman Polański's *The Tenant* (1976) and Andrzej Żuławski's *Possession* (1981) also feature unsettling doppelgängers and twins. These ostensibly identical characters have often been seen by critics in the context of Cold War geopolitics as representing the two sides of the Iron Curtain.[1] Analogous symbolic matchings between different yet similar persons were later redefined for the format of translation multiples. As the political transition of 1989 brought about shifting narratives, translation multiples opened the forum for distinct identities to coexist next to one another. Though differing in values and viewpoints, all the twins, triplets, and other look-alikes could be reunited within one political realm. While differences helped them retain their individual identities, their apparent similarities and kinship justified their standing side by side.

This coincided with yet another transition, namely, reimagining publishing norms in the postcommunist context. With more than one alternative at hand, one artistic form no longer had to forcibly replace or fight the other; instead, a new mode of circulation assumed the coexistence of plural versions. In this context, translation multiples testified to the changing publishing culture on the wave of political transition in the region. Different cases discussed in this book were all born of the shift between two worlds of artistic expression: the one constrained by censorship and totalizing binaries and the other ushering in a fledgling democracy with free publishing and relative freedom of speech. The backstory of translation multiples often points to clear discrepancies between these two literary orders. The first one, the communist literary order, coalesced bipolar tensions between the official circulation, with its monopoly on truth, and the strong opposition from the underground press. In this order, a state-driven publishing monopoly often favored authoritative canonization and officially anointed translations, which could be only challenged by unofficial publications. The newly restored order, on the other hand, drifted toward a more decentralized system allowing for a larger number of alternatives. Surely, the latter could not escape all limitations, as suggested by the arduous round that some of the post-1989 multiples had to travel. For instance, why did it take so long for Stiller to find a publishing house that would release his two Oranges simultaneously as a double set of novels? Why did most library catalogs classify Bertolt Brecht as the only true author of the Brechtian quadruple, while the volume's four authors were in fact Buras reading Brecht, Ekier reading Brecht, Kopacki reading Brecht, and Sommer reading Brecht? Similar questions imply that restraining norms and micropressures continue to influence translation production in free-market publishing. The postcommunist multiples still had to elbow their way into the literary marketplace, capitalizing on a host of favorable circumstances. After all, it did help that their creators were all well-established artists and translators whose cooperation with independent publishing houses and literary magazines could tip the scales. But despite its own flaws and limitations, the new literary order still paved the way for more innovative and pluralist forms to emerge after communism. This could at least resolve the cultural hierarchy and single authoritative system into a number of different propositions without imposing single aesthetic hierarchies or ideological priorities.

In postcommunist translation multiples, this dimension manifests itself even more tangibly in its form and composition. The multiples become literary platforms for different readings questioning the totalizing idea of monopoly on a single truth, or a single authentic vision of contemporary society. All cases discussed in this book advocate a more open forum for diverse voices while offering a range of responses to the new reality. Barańczak answered his audience's questions about "how to live" by compromising vague and totalizing ideas and instead pursuing the agenda of the concrete and the individual. In his "Oratorium Moratorium" and other multiples, he postulates that single viewpoints ought to acknowledge and support each other dialectically. Only through such compound constellations and confrontations can individual ideas verify each other and recognize their own temporary totalities and limiting monopolies. In Stiller's vision, the multiples can critically reevaluate the past and the present against a repetitive political pattern. The vicious circle of history governing his three Oranges discloses how the corrupted society keeps getting roped into a self-reproducing clockwork mechanism. Alternative historical interpretations can also help diagnose the postcolonial legacy of Polish culture as it has been torn between plural linguistic landscapes, cultural influences, and divergent identities. Then, the new generation of Brecht's interpreters employ the polyphonic potential of translation multiples to reclaim the poet beyond partisan lines. While revising instrumentalist readings and pre-1989 manipulations of his poetry, the Brechtian quadruple promote a more collaborative and pluralist platform for discussion around Brecht. While building on the tradition of acknowledging multiple readings in the pages of the affiliated liberal magazine *Literatura na świecie*, the poet-translators symbolically shared the translation stage among a wider and more inclusive mix of performers. The multiples at this juncture revealed how an innovative form could follow a broader democratic agenda. If there is no fixed reading of the same original, then why should there be one authoritative realization of that reading in translation? And if there is no single "proper" perspective in translation, this can as well imply no monopoly for one point of view, one interpretation of historical and cultural events, and one public discourse.

Such considerations could only take place at the intersection of the two trends, namely the state's democratization and the development of a free literary marketplace. These two factors determined a different mode of circulation, which bore groundbreaking consequences for postcommunist intellectual and translation activity. As different publishing houses started commissioning new translations while also restoring previous renderings, this created the technical possibility for more variants to enter the post-1989 circulation at the same time. Translators have also gradually become aware of other renderings in circulation and started recognizing their parallel lives. In some cases, such as intensively retranslated classics, in particular Shakespeare's plays, many translators have acknowledged the coexistence of plural readings in their own texts.[2] They have often debated over other existing variants as well as consciously placed their own version within an intertextual web of multiple translation production. In other cases, thinking about translation in dialectical and plural terms has opened the way for more collaborative projects. For example, Matthew Kneale's book *English Passengers* (2000), with its twenty-one narrators, was in 2014 translated by twenty-one different translators into Polish. Thanks to this diverse cast, each translating self was meant to speak from a different vantage point and with a unique voice about the conflicting ideas and postcolonial resentments rooted in the characters' linguistic worlds.[3]

Similar gestures help us embrace the plurality of translation activity and solidarity between translators. They also challenge the more mainstream mode of reading and thinking about translations as singular and finite products. As similar polyphonic projects keep emerging, critics have also started rethinking the language they use for translation's multiplicity. In a heated debate in the late 2000s, two Polish critics argued over the metaphor of translation as "a war of the worlds," a battle between rival translations as enemies. The opponent of that phrase, Magda Heydel, postulated a new perspective on relations between translators: translation as "a dialogue of the worlds."[4] She firmly stressed: "Translation and retranslation are created not in order to compete, but to give a possibility of coexisting."[5] This adage extends to the postcommunist translation multiples and the ongoing democratization of translation activity. In its plurality, translation is no longer only about a text's relation to the original but increasingly about the translator establishing themself vis-à-vis other translations and translators. Pluralist translation calls for accepting any other interpreter by coming to terms with their completely different opinion about the same original. Here, the act of acknowledging this difference in interpreting the original goes beyond literary works. It could equally pertain to a historical event, political statement, or anything else subject to individual interpretation.

Such an ethically engaged role of literary translation is not a new phenomenon. The marriage of translation and different ideas about activism, ethics, and resistance has been gradually changing the image of translation as a passive and neutral medium of communicating original senses.[6] Translation multiples also contribute to this task of redefining translation's role in cultural production. The Anglophone cases bring out a subversive edge to interlingual writing and manifest resistance against global monolingualism. As they knock readers of translated literature out of their comfort zones and information bubbles, they challenge the illusion of having direct access to the source text by means of one true and accurate translation. The postcommunist multiples generate plural narratives to take a stand on broader geopolitical and ethical issues such as political hegemony over minor cultures, Western response to the fate of Eastern Europe, the fallacies of totalitarian rhetoric, and the dangers of narrow readings limited by one-sided ideological blinkers, among many others. But in all cases, the multiples extend their relevance beyond their local setting. They put forward a few crucial propositions on how to make sense of multiplicity and difference in translation as well as, more broadly, the crossroads of language and one's coexistence in society. In this respect, they open a symbolic textual platform for presenting and balancing distinct reading perspectives. They facilitate confrontations of unique stories behind individual decisions explaining their entanglements in social, cultural, and political matters. They also offer a critical tool for discussing different viewpoints, allowing their readers to judge how these individual visions complement and falsify each other.

If we continue to promote this textual and visual structuring, the multiples might be a remedy against political tribalism and polarization in our times. This would require stepping out of the totalizing frameworks and confronting their individual interpretative limitations. Casting the multiples in their metacritical role might now be of greater significance than ever. It is increasingly difficult to oppose the rhetoric of conflicted groups, which too often belittles or suppresses the opposite side without fairly presenting and respecting that side's rationale. Confrontations in the spirit of the multiples between different factions at odds are never easy. After the 2016 Brexit referendum, the British artist Grayson Perry created *Divided Britain* (2017), a documentary film following the lives and narratives of both the Brexiteers and the Remainers. The film culminates in an exhibition of two enormous vases, almost identical in size, shape, and color, each including visual materials that represent the "leave" and "remain" votes, respectively. While Perry juxtaposes these two stories and the opposing rationales behind each voting group, he also makes those represented on his pots meet and look at each other's visual materials. This difficult encounter is not only about making the two groups aware of each other, which they surely were anyway. Similarly, there is more to it than just making them shake hands or showing that each is a likeable bunch of people, only with different understandings of what is best for their country. The main heft of Perry's gesture lies elsewhere. He openly acknowledged both sides of the barricades at the same time in an artistic and a public context. Having sculpted both stories into the material of two vases, he exhibited the vases next to each other in a museum for both factions to appreciate. Though personally siding with one camp, Perry still attempted to recognize the humanity of the other group without slipping into antagonizing terms. His piece of art was composed as a visual double that fairly represents the political spectrum and that weighs the two points of view against each other. His Brexit vase double did not aim to give more space to his favored option nor block out the other's perspective.

Since the multiples are structured in a similar way, their form allows for an evenly accentuated presentation of information. Even if implicitly favoring some possibilities over others, translation multiples still give a fair share of airtime to many variants that otherwise would need to fight for exposure in the established order of print. In this respect, they symbolically grant "equal conditions," in Jacques Rancière's terms,[7] to plural readings to be voiced in the public sphere. Rancière's democratizing politics of literature assumes a dismissal of hierarchies among characters, styles, and subject matters in the novel that have been in place since the nineteenth century. As literature has become more egalitarian, it has begun sharing artistic space among more visions of society without prioritizing any single one of them. In the same vein, translation multiples follow suit by at least symbolically granting such equal conditions to the otherwise unrecognized translation variants. These outstanding renderings keep fighting for their place in the hierarchical order of print, scraping through local canons and established authoritative orders. Their expanding plurality may be resolved through multiplied poems, books composed of multiple renderings, or comparative series easily accommodated by the digital format. Through these media and platforms, translation multiples can hijack more textual space for less established propositions that do not tick the boxes of a mainstream production. In pushing the envelope of translation circulation and the publishing industry now, they also fight for more symbolic room for other readings and variants to emerge in the future. This can be slowly achieved in the process of socializing and internalizing the practice of translation in all its plurality into the public discourse.

A potentially promising guarantor and executor of these equal conditions could be digital space and electronic publishing. These platforms might aid translation multiples in redefining information structures as long as they facilitate the pluralist circulation beyond echo chambers and filter bubbles. While the main obstructions to democracy and pluralist discourse in the twentieth century were erected by military dictatorships and totalitarian regimes, present-day totalizing mechanisms have largely moved online. Changes in the media structure of the internet, access to thematic portals, and social media profiled by filtering algorithms have led to the extreme ideological polarization of users, especially on the wave of ongoing bloody conflicts all around the world. These new risks are a byproduct of digitization processes, which in principle have aimed to democratize the way in which information circulates, is mediated, and is accessed. The multiples alert their recipients to this problem by stretching out a pluralist platform governed by a more democratic structure of knowledge. Providing direct access to more than one version of a story, on one screen or one page at the same time, may challenge increasingly one-sided and totalizing processes of arranging information. Here, the multiples become an exemplary weapon in the fight for a more pluralist dissemination of information, as their own composition reflects and embodies such a circulation. In the rising tide of global populism and the tribalist rhetoric of conflicted nations, they signal how to embrace contemporary clashes of totalities, as well as those to come. With their promotion of a more diverse textual and ideological spectrum, the multiples ultimately reflect how different worldviews and ideas can coexist not only in translation but also within one democratic society.

NOTES

Introduction

1. Jerome, "Who Was the First Lying Author?"
2. Jerome, "Who Was the First Lying Author?"
3. Robinson, "Philo Judeus," 13.
4. Bellos, *Is That a Fish in Your Ear?*, 5.
5. For example: Venuti, *The Translator's Invisibility* (1995); Hermans, *The Conference of the Tongues*, 33; and Reynolds, *The Poetry of Translation*, 19.
6. This is according to the Three Percent program and database run by the University of Rochester (http://www.rochester.edu/College/translation/threepercent/) and the most recent report by Literature across Frontiers (2015) on literary translations published in the UK and Ireland in years 1990–2012; see Büchler and Trentacosti, "Publishing Translated Literature," 5. However, more recent Nielsen BookScan reports have shown that the percentage of translated fiction is much higher—amounting to 5.63 percent in 2008 and even 11 percent in 2021–2022 in the UK—when considering book sales rather than the number of published titles in translation. See, e.g., Anderson, "Nielsen Reports"; and Tivnan, "Translated Fiction Enjoys Golden Age."
7. Polish Book Institute, "The Polish Book Market." According to Literature across Frontiers' most recent report, other average percentages of translations among all books (both new and reissued titles) published in other European countries are the following: 19.7 percent in Italy, 15.9 percent in France, and 12.28 percent in Germany. See also Büchler and Trentacosti, "Publishing Translated Literature," 5. Also, some of Poland's own reports tend to give an even higher average figure, counting among new releases exclusively (46 percent) and stressing the special position of literary translation in the publishing market. Cf. Dobrołęcki et al., "Raport o stanie kultury 'Przemysł książki,'" 11; and Paszkiet, *Raport o sytuacji tłumaczy*, 14.
8. Casanova, *The World Republic of Letters*, 179.
9. Deleuze and Guattari, "What Is a Minor Literature?"; and Kronfeld, *On the Margins of Modernism*.
10. Nakayasu, "I Choose to Eat and Sleep."
11. Kalmar, *White but Not Quite*.

1. The Multiples Now

1. Walkowitz, *Born Translated*, 240.

2. Drunken Boat takes its name from the online creative project of translating Arthur Rimbaud's poem "Le bateau ivre" (The Drunken Boat) in different ways by contemporary poets and translators such as Erin Moure, Paul Legault, Esther Allen, and Rachel Galvin. As of August 16, 2022, Drunken Boat's translation database stored eighteen different takes: https://d7.drunkenboat.com/db20/translation. Fleurs du mal is an online repository of all the poems from Charles Baudelaire's *Fleurs du mal* (Flowers of Evil), with multiple English translations presented for each poem: https://fleursdumal.org/ (accessed December 12, 2023).

3. Cheesman, Flanagan, and Thiel, "Version Variation Visualization." See also Cheesman et al., "Multi-Retranslation Corpora"; Reynolds, "Prismatic Jane Eyre"; and Reynolds et al., *Prismatic Jane Eyre*.

4. These more "traditional" studies have otherwise traced multiple translations (or "retranslations") of original works by means of textual and comparative close readings over several decades. For instance, the Göttingen Project led by Armin Paul Frank during the 1980s and 1990s examined, among others, "multiple translations into German of American short stories, Polish plays and British and Swedish novels"; Schulte, "Profile: The Göttingen Approach," 1. Similarly, numerous studies of "retranslations" have also looked at several translation variants of one original; Tahir Gürçağlar, "Retranslation."

5. See Michael Cronin's argument in his *Translation in the Digital Age*, 88–89.

6. Walkowitz, *Born Translated*, 240. A good example of a book of the kind compiled for teaching purposes could be Rainer Schulte's edited volume *Comparative Perspectives: An Anthology of Multiple Translations*, whose aim is to "bring students back to the reading and interpretation of the texts" (xxi).

7. Emmerich, *Literary Translation*.

8. Smith, "Matter in the Margins," 28.

9. I am grateful to Thomas Hare for drawing my attention to this example.

10. Richards, *Mencius on the Mind*, 13.

11. Richards, *Mencius on the Mind*, 86.

12. Hawkes, *A Little Primer of Tu Fu*, 82–83.

13. See Prynne, "Difficulties in the Translation of 'Difficult' Poems," 163. Also, some postcolonial approaches to translation offer mixed accounts on the ethics behind the practice of supplementing works from "minor" or postcolonial cultures with more footnotes and glosses. For instance, Kwame Anthony Appiah advocates the use of "thick translation" in order to give justice to a culture different from one's own (Appiah, "Thick Translation"). On the other hand, Maria Tymoczko argues that the "information load" in the translation of postcolonial and minority literatures could result in compromising a text's literary quality at the expense of enhanced didacticism (Tymoczko, "Post-Colonial Writing and Literary Translation," 28–29).

14. See the discussion of "translation memoirs" offering a platform for the multiplicity of translation in Grass and Robert-Foley, "The Translation Memoir," 2.

15. Daniel Hahn's *Catching Fire* (2022), on translating Diamela Eltit's *Never Did the Fire* (2022), foregrounds the process of going through multiple possible variants as "iterations." This "translation diary" was first developed online as a series of blogposts on the website of Charco

Press, and then both the actual translation and Hahn's translation diary *Catching Fire* were published by the press at the same time, in April 2022; they have been advertised together and feature complementary covers designed by the same artist.

16. Ginczanka and Trzeciak Huss, "Poems Translated from the Polish."

17. Derrida, "What Is a 'Relevant' Translation?," 179.

18. Nabokov, "Problems of Translation," 512.

19. For instance, see Kate Briggs's argument questioning Derrida's "law of quantity" (Briggs, *This Little Art*, 287–88); see also Delphine Grass's discussion of translation as both artistic and practice-based research that is capable of reframing translation theory (Grass, *Translation as Creative-Critical Practice*).

20. Thirlwell, *Multiples: 12 Stories in 18 Languages by 61 Authors*.

21. R. Baker, *Cato Variegatus*, n.p.

22. See Matthew Reynolds's discussion in his *The Poetry of Translation*, 86. Exercises in multiple translation around this time sneaked into the domain of poetry, taking the question of form as its starting point. Similarly, in his 1653 Dutch rendering of Boethius's *The Consolation of Philosophy*, Adrianus de Buck tested different poetic meters in his translation doubles of different poems throughout the book (Boethius, *Troost-medecijne-wynckel der zedighe wysheyt*, 5–8, 4–17, 25–35, 41–43, 47ff.). I would like to thank Theo Hermans for making me aware of the latter example. In the German tradition centuries later, similar exercises in multiple translation styles also appeared in a collection modeled after baroque manuals for poetics entitled *Das Wasserzeichen der Poésie* (The Watermark of Poetry) (1985) written by Hans Magnus Enzensberger under the pseudonym Andreas Thalmayr.

23. Walkowitz, *Born Translated*, 240.

24. Weinberger and Paz, *19 Ways of Looking at Wang Wei* (1987), 1.

25. Weinberger and Paz, *19 Ways of Looking at Wang Wei* (1987), 1.

26. Inspired by Weinberger's multiples, Hilario Fernández Long published a series of analogue exercises in ways of looking at Wang Wei in Spanish in 1996 (Fernández Long, "Lengua y poesía china," 33). Many thanks to Rosario Hubert for drawing my attention to this example. See also Hubert, *Disoriented Disciplines*, 271.

27. As Haun Saussy points out, when counted properly, Weinberger's examples in the book actually amount to twenty-two or twenty-three variants of the poem (Saussy, *Great Walls of Discourse*, 65).

28. Walkowitz, *Born Translated*, 240.

29. Compare the title of the 2016 reissue of the book: *19 Ways of Looking at Wang Wei (with More Ways)*.

30. Visuality and pictoriality have consistently been attributed to Wang Wei's poetry in Chinese thought as well as in general scholarship; see, for example, Hsiao, "Wang Wei's and Su Shi's Conceptions"; and Cai and Wu, "Introduction: Emotion, Patterning, and Visuality," 7.

31. Weinberger and Paz, *19 Ways of Looking at Wang Wei* (1987), 3.

32. Uncoincidentally, the American poet Sidney Wade published a variation of Wang Wei inspired by Weinberger's book with exactly thirteen different translations ("ways of looking"). It includes translations by her students at the University of Florida as well as her own rendering rounding off the series as the final, thirteenth version. Wade, "13 Ways of Looking at Wang Wei."

33. Weinberger and Paz, *19 Ways of Looking at Wang Wei* (1987), 43.

34. Weinberger and Paz, *19 Ways of Looking at Wang Wei (with More Ways)*.

35. Saussy, *Great Walls of Discourse*, 64–65.

36. Weinberger and Paz, *19 Ways of Looking at Wang Wei (with More Ways)*, 56.

37. Weinberger and Paz, *19 Ways of Looking at Wang Wei* (1987), 51; and Weinberger and Paz, *19 Ways of Looking at Wang Wei (with More Ways)*, 88.

38. Hofstadter, *Rhapsody on a Theme by Clément Marot*, xvi.

39. Hofstadter, *Le Ton beau de Marot*, 12.

40. Hofstadter, *Le Ton beau de Marot*, 4.

41. I am grateful to Patrick McGuinness for alerting me to this literary tradition.

42. Hofstadter, *Le Ton beau de Marot*, 13.

43. Hofstadter, *Le Ton beau de Marot*, 345.

44. Hofstadter, *Le Ton beau de Marot*, 352.

45. Dayan, "Different Music, Same Condition," 13.

46. Not forty-eight like Sandra Bermann claims. See Bermann, "Performing Translation," 286. Admittedly, Bergvall did use a forty-eighth English translation for the poem's lesser-known appearance in the journal *Chain* (Dante Alighieri and Bergvall, "VIA [48 Dante Variations]"). However, both her audio recording and the poem's 2005 print version from the authored collection *Fig* (2005) excluded the forty-eighth rendering because, as she herself argued, the addition of one more version "broke the rule of the task"; Bergvall, "VIA: 48 Dante Variations," 65. For the audio recording, see PennSound resources: https://media.sas.upenn.edu/pennsound/authors/Bergvall/Rockdrill-8/Bergvall-Caroline_06_Via_Via_Rockdrill-8_2005.mp3 (accessed April 20, 2020). The recording was first published online in 2000 as "VIA (48 Dante translations) Mix w Fractals" and featured the Irish composer Ciarán Maher. It is now available here: https://soundcloud.com/carolinebergvall/via-48-dante-translations-mix (accessed March 27, 2024). On the other hand, the 2011 version from Craig Dworkin and Kenneth Goldsmith's anthology *Against Expression* entitled "VIA (36 Dante Translations)" contained exactly thirty-six translations, which would again complicate this assumed rule. See Bergvall, "VIA (36 Dante Translations)," 81–86. Perhaps all these different versions of "VIA" (in sound and in written form, each of different length) become yet another way of challenging the singularity of what counts as the "original" poem. Many thanks to Francesca Southerden, who gave me the suggestion that in disseminating the poem's different versions, Bergvall could have also attempted to replicate the original circulation of hundreds of different variants of *La divina commedia*. See her later discussion of this reading: Southerden, "The Voice Astray: Caroline Bergvall's Dante."

47. Bergvall, "VIA: 48 Dante Variations," 64. Compare the remark made by Dworkin and Goldsmith in *Against Expression*: "Caroline Bergvall's collation of the British Library's collection of Dante translations is in itself a kind of translation." Bergvall, "VIA (36 Dante Translations)," 81.

48. Bergvall, "VIA: 48 Dante Variations," 64.

49. Dante Alighieri and Bergvall, "VIA (48 Dante Variations)."

50. Bergvall, "VIA: 48 Dante Variations," 67. Note that the trick of turning Dante's words into translators' personal testimonies works well in a language that does not mark gender in its grammar. For instance, in my Polish translation of Bergvall's poem "VIA: 22 wariacje na temat Dantego" (VIA: 22 Variations on Dante), I faced the problem of female translators doomed to

use the original masculine forms. See the discussion of the Polish version in Cayley, "The Translation of Process," esp. n. 26.

51. In this version of "VIA," Bergvall mistakenly attributed translation 6 to Seamus Heaney, 1993, instead of Thomas William Parsons, 1893, doubling the entries for Heaney (the correct and only one should be number 16). This mistake found its way into the text probably following a typo in the 2003 version, in which number 16 is confused with 6 (Dante Alighieri and Bergvall, "VIA [48 Dante Variations]," 59). Both the audio recording as well as the 2011 shorter version of "VIA" correctly refer to Parsons in this place.

52. Trotman, "Found in Translation," 7.

53. Walkowitz, *Born Translated*, 237–38.

54. In the German tradition, an example of analogous exercises of translating experimental literature from multiple angles could be Fritz Senn's 1989 edition with James Joyce's *Finnegans Wake* in several German renderings. Reichert and Senn, *Finnegans Wake: Gesammelte Annäherungen*.

55. Sato, *One Hundred Frogs*, 151–78; Barwin and Beaulieu, *Frogments from the Frag Pool*; and McCaffery, *The Basho Variations*.

56. Waldrop, editor's note to *Reft and Light*, 8.

57. Jandl, *Reft and Light*, 20–22.

58. Jandl, *Reft and Light*, 39–40, 55, 57.

59. Bashō's haiku from 1952 by R. H. Blyth in Sato, *One Hundred Frogs*, 154.

60. See Wershler, introduction to *Verse and Worse*, xii; and the discussion of multimodality in these versions in Borkent, "At the Limits of Translation?"

61. The idea of multiplication and collective creation inscribed in the form of *renga* in the Anglophone context could have been inspired by an experimental book published in English in 1971 by Octavio Paz and colleagues, *Renga: A Chain of Poems*.

62. Sato, *One Hundred Frogs*, 174.

63. I am grateful to Conor Brendan Dunne (then of Trinity College Dublin) for drawing my attention to this book. The book, alongside Matthew Reynolds's edited volume *Prismatic Translation* (2019), further inspired Conor's multimedia work *Camus through the Translation Prism*, discussed in his book chapter "Prismatic Translation 2.0: A (Potential) Future for Avant-Garde Translation."

64. Loffredo and Perteghella, "The Genesis of the Project," 25.

65. I am indebted to Adriana X. Jacobs for introducing me to this example of translation multiples. For a more detailed discussion of the cycle, see Jacobs, "Extreme Translation," 163–65.

66. Holca, "Sawako Nakayasu Eats Sagawa Chika," 387.

67. Nakayasu, introduction to *The Collected Poems of Chika Sagawa* (2020), xx.

68. Nakayasu, introduction to *The Collected Poems of Chika Sagawa* (2015), ix.

69. Nakayasu, "An Interview with Sawako Nakayasu," by Lindsey Webb.

70. Nakayasu, introduction to *The Collected Poems of Chika Sagawa* (2015), xv.

71. Nakayasu, "An Interview on Sawako Nakayasu and Sagawa Chika's 'Mouth Eats Color,'" by Thomas Fink.

72. Nakayasu with Sagawa, *Mouth: Eats Color*, 55.

73. Chuang Tzu et al., "Come Out of Works," 45–50.

74. Chuang Tzu et al., "Come Out of Works," 50.

75. Cobb and Coleman, translators' note to "Come Out of Works."

76. Robinson, *The Translator's Turn*, 25.

77. Scott, *Literary Translation and the Rediscovery of Reading*; and Scott, *Translating the Perception of Text*.

78. While Carson uses an alternative spelling of the poet's name in her poem, I will refer to him by the variant that is more common in English.

79. Compare the discussion of the antithetical variants in Rose, "Retranslating Ibykos and Li Bai," 88–89.

80. Carson, "Variations on the Right to Remain Silent," 32.

81. Harvey, "On Anne Carson, 'Nay Rather,'" 27.

2. Ethics of the Multiple

1. Nakayasu, "An Interview on Sawako Nakayasu and Sagawa Chika's 'Mouth Eats Color,'" by Thomas Fink.

2. See Lee, *Experimentalism in Translation*; Robinson, *The Experimental Translator*; and Robert-Foley, *Experimental Translation*. See also the idea of "experiential translation" in Campbell and Vidal, *The Experience of Translation*.

3. Perloff, *Unoriginal Genius*, 53.

4. Goldsmith, "Why Conceptual Writing? Why Now?," xvii.

5. Robert-Foley, *Experimental Translation*.

6. For a critique of clichéd and racially biased representations of eastern European and East Asian poets in Anglophone (pseudo)translation, see, for example, Jarniewicz, "After Babel," 96; Szymanska, "Can Mirrors Be Said to Have Memories?"; Hayot, "The Strange Case of Araki Yasusada"; and Hsu, "When White Poets Pretend to Be Asian."

7. Horáček, "Pedantry and Play," 109; and Dembeck, "Oberflächenübersetzung," 9–10.

8. See different theoretical considerations of pseudotranslation: Rambelli, "Pseudotranslation"; Apter, "Translation with No Original," 162–64; and Tahir Gürçağlar, "Pseudotranslation on the Margin of Fact and Fiction," 518.

9. Hawkey, preface to *Ventrakl*, 6–8.

10. Legault, "Who Is Writing Is the Translator."

11. Nakayasu, "I Choose to Eat and Sleep."

12. Jacobs, "The Go-Betweens," 480.

13. Jacobs, "Extreme Translation," 154–70.

14. Draesner and Cheesman, *Twin Spin*. See also Rutgers Radical Translation Collective, "Project Details."

15. Göransson, "Toward a Sensationalistic Theory of Translation."

16. Lukes, *Avant-Garde Translation*.

17. Horáček, "Pedantry and Play," 107.

18. Hawkey, preface to *Ventrakl*, 6.

19. Cameron, *Flowers of Bad*, 211.

20. Nakayasu, "An Interview on Sawako Nakayasu and Sagawa Chika's 'Mouth Eats Color,'" by Thomas Fink.

21. N. Moore, *Spleen*, 7.
22. See, e.g., Hur, "An Interview with Anton Hur," by Jimin Kang.
23. Cooperson, "Note on the Translation," xli.
24. Cooperson, "Note on the Translation," xliii.
25. Cf. the detailed discussion of the poem by Stephen Burt, *The Poem Is You: 60 Contemporary American Poems and How to Read Them*, 356–61. See also Edmond, *Make It the Same*, 201–7.
26. Som, *The Tribute Horse*.
27. Edmond, *Make It the Same*, 137.
28. See the discussion of "Modernist translation models" in Brzostowska-Tereszkiewicz, *Modernist Translation: An Eastern European Perspective*.
29. Hofstadter, *Le Ton beau de Marot*, 13.
30. Perloff, "The Oulipo Factor."
31. In fact, Bök's original *Eunoia* from 2001 was republished in 2009 with several new poems, including an Oulipian translation multiple, "Five Translations of Arthur Rimbaud's 'Voyelles,'" which applies different translation constraints to consecutive versions. This addition eventually placed *Eunoia*'s poetics closer to Bergvall's "VIA" and her Dante variations.
32. Nakayasu, "An Interview on Sawako Nakayasu and Sagawa Chika's 'Mouth Eats Color,'" by Thomas Fink.
33. Nakayasu, "An Interview on Sawako Nakayasu and Sagawa Chika's 'Mouth Eats Color,'" by Thomas Fink.
34. Taylor, *The Facts on File Companion to the French Novel*, 326.
35. Variation as a thematic conceit or framing device has been employed in a range of genres. In poetry, examples include Edwin Muir's collection *Variations on a Time Theme* (1934), Douglas Oliver's *Three Variations on the Theme of Harm: Selected Poetry and Prose* (1991), and David Glen Smith, *Variations on a Theme of Desire* (2015), to name a few. Popular books with short stories have featured "variations" in their titles, for instance: G. M. de Pauligny, *Variations on the Theme of Love* (1994); Robert L. Smith, *Desires of the Heart: Variations on the Theme of Love* (2010); and Simon Forster, *Variations on a Theme* (2007). In drama, analogous cases are Terence Rattigan's *Variation on a Theme* (1958), David Ives's one-act play *Variations on the Death of Trotsky* (1991), and Moisés Kaufman's *33 Variations* (2007).
36. Hiroaki Sato, personal correspondence, May 16, 2018.
37. Hofstadter, *Le Ton beau de Marot*, 246.
38. Hofstadter, *Le Ton beau de Marot*, 353–59.
39. Bazzana, *Wondrous Strange*, 267. For a further discussion of Gould's recording "kits" and multiple translation, see Brammall, "Translation Kits."
40. For instance, there are different versions of Bach's *Cello Suites* and no urtext performing edition, making it impossible to determine what "the original score" would be. I am grateful to Eduardo Simpson for bringing this to my attention. For an analogous discussion about multiple originals, see Emmerich, *Literary Translation*.
41. Cook, *Beyond the Score*, 8.
42. Compare Walkowitz's argument about *19 Ways of Looking at Wang Wei* and the fact that "no original 'way' is presented" throughout the volume. Walkowitz, *Born Translated*, 240.

43. In this respect, my understanding of "literary metatranslation" will stay closer to its metaliterary lineage, even though the term was also used by Efim Etkind ("métatraduction," in "Le problème de la métatraduction") for homophonic translation and by Patrick Zabalbeascoa and Montse Corrius of a work containing a scene or passage about translation ("How Spanish in an American Film Is Rendered in Translation," 268). None of these ideas inform the notion of "literary metatranslation" as discussed in this book. Literary metatranslation stays closer, first, to Theo Hermans's idea of "metatranslation," which focuses on textual markers of the translation's speaking subject and self-reflexivity in translations more discursively; see Hermans, *The Conference of the Tongues*, 41–51; and Hermans, *Metatranslation: Essays on Translation and Translation Studies*. The other corresponding idea of "metatranslation" made its way into Anna Cetera's analyses of retranslations of Shakespeare, which shifted re-created plays to the metadramatic and metatheatrical level (Cetera, "Suit the Word to the Action"). On the procedural level, this notion is analogous to what Barbara Cassin called "metatranslation" when describing the process of explaining translation difficulties in her *Dictionary of Untranslatables* (Cassin and Walkowitz, "Translating the Untranslatable").

44. Tymoczko, *Translation in a Postcolonial Context*, 280.

45. The Outranspo is housed at the website http://www.outranspo.com/. For the group's trilingual foundational act, see Bloomfield, Galvin, and Martín Ruiz, "Acts de fundación de l'Outranspo."

46. See Dennis Duncan's question: "But if translation is already a major activity for the Oulipo then where does that leave the Outranspo?" (Duncan, "Translating Constrained Literature," 125). For more discussion of the prominent role of translation in the Oulipo's literary program, see Duncan, *The Oulipo and Modern Thought*.

47. Bloomfield, Galvin, and Martín Ruiz, "Acts de fundación de l'Outranspo," 985.

48. Bloomfield and Robert-Foley, "Tweetranslating Trump," 474.

49. Bernofsky et al., "The 2023 Manifesto on Literary Translation."

50. Venuti, "Spokesperson, Intellectual, and . . . More?"

51. Collins, introduction to *Into English*, viii. See a more extensive discussion of the anthology in Szymanska, "'Into English': A Collection of World Literature."

52. Willis Barnstone, "Commentary," in Collins and Prufer, *Into English*, 28–31; Carl Phillips, "Commentary," in *Into English*, 14–16; Arthur Sze, "Commentary," in *Into English*, 22–23; Cole Swensen, "The case of:," in *Into English*, 52–55; and Alissa Valles, "Szymborska: Torture(s)," in *Into English*, 150–52.

53. In this strand, see especially Anthony Pym's study of active retranslations that stem from "disagreements over translation strategies" in his *Method in Translation History*, 82–83; Lawrence Venuti's "Retranslations: The Creation of Value," reprinted in his *Translation Changes Everything: Theory and Practice*; and Venuti's "On a Universal Tendency to Debase Retranslations."

54. Deane-Cox, *Retranslation: Translation, Literature and Reinterpretation*, 14–15.

55. Deleuze and Guattari, *A Thousand Plateaus*. Adrienne H. K. Rose enlists the following: media and cultural studies, American literature, postcolonial studies, and pedagogy (Rose, "Retranslating Ibykos and Li Bai," 85).

56. Lawrence Venuti discusses the latter assumption as a result of the long-accepted "instrumentalist" model of approaching translation, which dates to the Romans and has spanned many languages and translation cultures. According to Venuti, instrumentalism assumes the

existence of an invariant contained in the source text that has to be transferred in the process of translation. Venuti, *Contra Instrumentalism*.

57. In this sense, translation multiples also continue a mission similar to a range of practices differently classified in translation studies. These could be placed alongside the following: Jiří Levý's "anti-illusionist" translation techniques in *The Art of Translation*, 19; Lawrence Venuti's "foreignizing" ethical agenda in *The Translator's Invisibility*, 2nd ed. (2008), 18; and Theo Hermans's "representations by *displaying*" (as opposed to *replaying*) in *The Conference of the Tongues*, 33. The aim of all these practices, even though by a range of different means, is to subvert the illusion of translation as a transparent textual medium.

58. For instance, more than one translation of Shakespeare's plays were published in the Soviet Union and Polish People's Republic. Similarly, "six different full versions" of Shakespeare's *Sonnets* were released during the socialist regime in Czechoslovakia (Spišiaková, *Queering Translation History*, 37). Scholarly editions also featured multiple translations, for example poetry selections by the Ossolineum Publishing House in Poland, or a famous Czech edition with sixteen different versions of Edgar Allan Poe's "The Raven" from 1985 (Havel and Bejblík, *Havran: Šestnáct českých překladů*). I am grateful to the late Jim Naughton for drawing my attention to the latter example. Finally, it must be noted that some cases of multiple translations were included in issues of the literary magazine *Literatura na świecie* even before the 1989 watershed; these are discussed in more detail in chapter 5.

59. Paszkiet, *Raport o sytuacji tłumaczy*, 14; and Encyklopedia PWN, "Wydawnictwa polskie."

60. For instance, on Czechoslovakia, see Spišiaková, *Queering Translation History*, 40; and on Slovenia, see Pokorn, *Post-Socialist Translation Practices*. For studies on other countries, see Rundle, Lange, and Monticelli, *Translation under Communism*.

61. Looby, "Underground Fiction Translation in People's Poland," 385.

62. Adamiec and Kołodziejczyk, "Rynek książki w Polsce."

63. Fordoński, "Polski przekład literacki," 134; and Looby, "Underground Fiction Translation in People's Poland," 380.

64. For a discussion of analogous mechanisms in neighboring Czechoslovakia, see Spišiaková, *Queering Translation History*, 40.

65. Cetera-Włodarczyk, "Shakespeare in Purgatory," 24.

66. Baer, "Literary Translation and the Construction of a Soviet Intelligentsia," 155.

67. Cetera-Włodarczyk, "Shakespeare in Purgatory," 24–25.

68. See, e.g., Pożar, "Panowie i państwo na Szekspirze," 115–19, 122; and Cetera-Włodarczyk, "The Gates of the Day."

69. Rudnytska, "Translation and the Formation of the Soviet Canon," 61.

70. Rudnytska, "Translation and the Formation of the Soviet Canon," 58–59.

71. Spišiaková, *Queering Translation History*, 42. See also Baer, "Translating Queer Texts in Soviet Russia," 27.

72. Makaryk, "Russia and the Former Soviet Union."

73. Nicolaescu, "Translations of Shakespeare in Romania."

74. Pożar, "Panowie i państwo na Szekspirze," 114–16, 122–26; and Cetera, *Enter Lear*, 144–77.

75. Cetera, *Enter Lear*, 66. See also Staniewska, "Maciej Słomczyński vs. William Shakespeare," 140.

76. See, e.g., Jędrzejewski, "The Polish Translations of Thomas Hardy," 56.
77. Fordoński, "Polski przekład literacki," 135.
78. Looby, "Underground Fiction Translation in People's Poland," 391.
79. Paszkiet, *Raport o sytuacji tłumaczy*, 14; and Fordoński, "Polski przekład literacki," 146–47.
80. Fordoński, "Polski przekład literacki," 146–47.
81. The number of publishing houses in Poland during this period totals 2,000 (1,500 general publishers and 500 specialist ones). See Encyklopedia PWN, "Wydawnictwa polskie." This number stood at around 1,500 still in 2000, even though, according to Krzysztof Fordoński, the market became increasingly divided among the (roughly) twenty largest publishers, including those with foreign capital (Fordoński, "Polski przekład literacki," 138).
82. Fordoński, "Polski przekład literacki," 136.
83. For a discussion of the post-1989 book market in the Czech Republic and Slovakia, see Spišiaková, *Queering Translation History*, 46–49. For the Slovenian context in the 1990s, see Pokorn, *Post-Socialist Translation Practices*, 31–33.
84. The percentage of translations in total book production in years 1956–1986 oscillated between 11 and 13 percent, while the analogous figures from the late 1980s onward rose to around 25 percent and have stayed at this level. These figures are based on two tables prepared by the Biblioteka Narodowa (National Library of Poland), "Tabela 19: Wydawnictwa" and "Tabela 22: Tłumaczenia," reproduced in Dawidowicz-Chymkowska, "Zestawienia retrospektywne 1944–2017," 76–78, 82. I am grateful to Dr. Olga Dawidowicz-Chymkowska for clarifying some of the inconsistencies in the report's data.
85. See, respectively, Borodo, *Translation, Globalization and Younger Audiences*, 59; and Adamiec and Kołodziejczyk, "Rynek książki w Polsce," 2001.
86. Heilbron and Sapiro, "Translation: Economic and Sociological Perspectives," 379, 383. While French, German, and Russian literature had been influential in Polish culture in different time periods before World War II, the postwar dissemination of English-language literature was suppressed during the communist era.
87. Borodo, *Translation, Globalization and Younger Audiences*, 58.
88. These examples come from the following studies: Borodo, *Translation, Globalization and Younger Audiences*, 58; Moc, "Nowe polskie prawo autorskie"; and Górnikiewicz, "L'image de la rose." See also Dąmbska-Prokop, "Tłumacz-kanibal?," 73.
89. Venuti, *The Scandals of Translation*, 47; and Lee, "Translation and Copyright," 243.
90. Baldwin, *The Copyright Wars*, 36, 389.
91. See, respectively, Weissbort, "His Own Translator: Joseph Brodsky," 103; Baldwin, *The Copyright Wars*, 39; Hiley, *Theatre at Work*, 4–7; and McCullough, "From Brecht to Brechtian," 129.
92. Fordoński, "Polski przekład literacki," 138–39.
93. Borodo, *Translation, Globalization and Younger Audiences*, 59.
94. Moc, "Nowe polskie prawo autorskie," 181–82; Borodo, *Translation, Globalization and Younger Audiences*, 59; and Fordoński, "Polski przekład literacki," 138.
95. Looby, "Underground Fiction Translation in People's Poland," 380.
96. The two primary circulations of publications in the Polish People's Republic were the official "first" circulation and the underground "second" one. While these functioned in

opposition to each other, a minor "third" circulation developed in the years 1980–1989. Subversive, nonpartisan, and antisystemic, the "third" circulation was run by counterculture movements who distributed rock music cassettes as well as textual and visual materials by means of fanzines. See, e.g., Sławiński, "Trzeci obieg," 593.

97. Looby, "Underground Fiction Translation in People's Poland," 388.

98. Looby, "Underground Fiction Translation in People's Poland," 381–99.

99. John M. Bates makes an interesting point that the lack of absolute freedom of speech in the second circulation consolidated partisan lines. According to him, Polish underground publishing had its own blind spots such as women's rights and minority issues, but also, most importantly, it was taboo to criticize Solidarity leaders at the time. Bates, "From a State Monopoly to a Free Market of Ideas?," 152, 163.

100. Haltof, *The Cinema of Krzysztof Kieślowski*, 54.

101. Haltof, *The Cinema of Krzysztof Kieślowski*, 63.

102. Sobolewski, "Poetics of Chance (Krzysztof Kieślowski)," 726–27.

103. Haltof, *The Cinema of Krzysztof Kieślowski*, 64.

3. Inner Pluralism in the Wake of 1989

1. In Cynthia L. Haven's *Czesław Miłosz: Conversations*, 117–18.

2. Unless stated otherwise, all quotations from the Polish are in my translation. Stanisław Barańczak to Czesław Miłosz, April 15, 1986, unpublished. The correspondence between the two poets-translators spans the period 1981–1993 and is stored in Yale's Beinecke Library (GEN MSS 661, files 8.148, 8.149, and 8.150). Many thanks to Magda Heydel for sharing with me the photographs of these holdings, an overview of which can also be found in Heydel, "*Wybacz, że znowu zawracam Ci głowę*."

3. Barańczak, "To Tell It All," 110.

4. Barańczak, "Poezja i duch Uogólnienia [1992]."

5. Barańczak's early poems were published in English translation in the early 1980s. Frank Kujawinski released his translations in two slim pamphlets with limited circulation: *Where Did I Wake Up* (1978) and *Under My Own Roof* (1980). Jan Krynski and Robert A. Maguire published their dispersed renderings in literary magazines such as the *New York Arts Journal* 23 (1981), *TriQuarterly* 57, no. 1 (1983), and *Confrontation* 27–28 (1984); and so did Richard Lourie, for instance in *Dissent* (1984) and *Ploughshares* 11, no. 4 (1985). Poems translated by Barańczak and Reginald Gibbons appeared in *TriQuarterly* (1983) and the *American Poetry Review* (1986); they were later included alongside other renderings in Barańczak's collection *The Weight of the Body* (1989).

6. Miłosz, "Stanisław Barańczak (born 1946)."

7. See, e.g., Rosenthal, "Czesław Miłosz's Polish School of Poetry."

8. I discuss the significance of this collection for Barańczak's American persona in the article "A Second Nature: Barańczak Translates Barańczak for America."

9. Haven, "Shaman and Poet Stanisław Barańczak."

10. "Każde słowo wzywając na fałszywego świadka," in Barańczak's "Och, wszystkie słowa pisane." Barańczak, *Dziennik poranny*, 99.

11. "Słowo w stanie podejrzenia," in Barańczak, "Proszę pokazać język," 85.

12. "Parę przypuszczeń na temat poezji współczesnej," in Barańczak, *Jednym tchem*, 3; later reprinted in Barańczak, *Etyka i poetyka*.

13. Practicing what he preached, Barańczak used these two different terms depending on the language version of his essay "The Confusion of Tongues" ("Pomieszanie języków"). Having written about "multivalent consciousness" in the American edition, he directly instructed the Polish audience in his self-translated variant about the "inner pluralism" ("wewnętrzny pluralizm") as a way of embracing multiple values coexisting in the world. "The Confusion of Tongues," in Barańczak, *Breathing under Water*, 226; and "Pomieszanie języków," in Barańczak, *Tablica z Macondo*, 207.

14. Heydel, "Od Donne'a do Lennona," 73.

15. Heydel, "Od Donne'a do Lennona."

16. The play was directed by Jerzy Satanowski. I am grateful to Poznań New Theatre for giving me access to the video recording.

17. Throughout the 1990s, Barańczak published translated books of various Anglophone poets as part of his series Biblioteczka Poetów Języka Angielskiego (A Little Library of English-Language Poets) as well as thematic anthologies. His translated authors spanned several centuries, ranging from Shakespeare to the metaphysical poets and Romantics, to contemporary British, Irish, and American poets.

18. Arkadiusz Luboń convincingly discusses the affinity between Barańczak's two manifestos in his *Przekraczanie obcości: Problemy przekładu w programach i twórczości poetów Nowej Fali*.

19. Barańczak, "Mały, lecz maksymalistyczny Manifest translatologiczny albo." The English version: Barańczak, "A Small, but Maximalist Translatological Manifesto."

20. Though originally dispersed in different places, most of these experimental genres were later collected in Barańczak's anthology of nonsense verse published in London: *Pegaz zdębiał: Poezja nonsensu a życie codzienne; Wprowadzenie w prywatną teorię gatunków*. Its title, which reads in English as "The Pegasus Fell Dumb: Nonsense Poetry and Everyday Life; Introduction to a Private Theory of Genres," was inspired by the Polish Jewish poet Julian Tuwim's collection of literary curiosities *Pegaz dęba: Czyli panopticum poetyckie* (The Prancing Pegasus: A Poetical Panopticon), collected in 1939 but not published until 1950. Mapping cases of macaronic poetry, translational experiments, interlingual homonymies, and exotic rhyme equivalents, Tuwim's book was a paragon of translingual reflection preceding Barańczak's exercises.

21. Barańczak, *Pegaz zdębiał*, 113.

22. Barańczak, *Pegaz zdębiał*, 137.

23. Barańczak, *Pegaz zdębiał*, 118.

24. Some critics treated Barańczak's nonsense poetry and creative experiments as, in his own words, "poetry of second category" (Barańczak, *Pegaz zdębiał*, 8). Others, however, noticed that it continued themes and techniques from his New Wave period: for instance, Leszek Szaruga, "Idiotyzm doskonałości," 138; and Beata Śniecikowska, "'Niepoważna' twórczość Stanisława Barańczaka," 243. Czesław Karkowski also insisted that "the unserious accomplishments of the serious poet are always serious" (Karkowski, "Niepoważne dokonania poważnego poety," 16).

25. In his satirical collection *Bóg, Trąba i Ojczyzna: Słoń a Sprawa Polska oczami poetów od Reja do Rymkiewicza* (God, Trunk, Fatherland: The Elephant and the Polish Question in

the Eyes of Poets from Rej to Rymkiewicz), Barańczak rewrote highly acclaimed Polish masterpieces using the nonsensical leitmotif of the elephant. This image ridiculed what is often proverbially called "the elephant and the Polish question," an obsession with Polish matters and the tendency to detect them in completely unrelated and least significant domains of life. The book also aimed to debunk some nationalist myths and empty gestures, as the poet playfully rephrased the typical Polish military motto of "God, Honor, Fatherland" in the title. Some critics discredited the book as antipatriotic, disgraceful, and irreverent about Polish cultural heritage, for instance Morawiec, "Paskudna książka Barańczaka"; and Romanowski, "Granice śmiechu." Some of the poems were read in the political context of that time; for instance, Barańczak's rewriting of Juliusz Słowacki's nineteenth-century verse, which anticipated the coming of a "Slavic pope," was read as a scurrilous caricature of John Paul II (Piechowski, "Chichot przed lustrem"; and Zięba, "Zapiski z kruchty"). Very few critics defended Barańczak's absurd humor, which could present a legitimately distorted mirror of the surrounding reality (Stala, "Barańczak w krainie słoni"; and Beylin, "Patriotyczna poprawność," 148–49).

26. Barańczak, *Pegaz zdębiał*, 8.

27. Barańczak's correspondence with Wiktor Woroszylski, 1982–1996, quoted in Szczęsna, "Poeta oburęczny, czyli przypadek Stanisława Barańczaka," 18.

28. "Z trzech stron barykady: Rozmowa z Przemysławem Czaplińskim, Piotrem Śliwińskim i Krzysztofem Trybusiem [1991]," in Barańczak, *Zaufać nieufności*, 111. The comparison was also probably informed by Barańczak's experience of translating metaphysical poets already in the 1980s.

29. "Człowiek, Który Za Dużo Wie [1995]," in Barańczak, *Poezja i duch Uogólnienia*, 367.

30. Barańczak, introduction to *Polish Poetry of the Last Two Decades of Communist Rule*, 3.

31. Barańczak, *Pegaz zdębiał*, 8.

32. Barańczak, "Poezja i duch Uogólnienia [1992]," 256.

33. Barańczak, "Poezja i duch Uogólnienia [1992]," 255–57.

34. "Człowiek, Który Za Dużo Wie [1995]," in Barańczak, *Poezja i duch Uogólnienia*, 360.

35. See, e.g., Trubicka, "Stanisław Barańczak jako krytyk języka," 145.

36. The categories of "whole for the part" and "part for the whole" continue Barańczak's earlier antisystemic essay on the "generalizing" and "concretizing" words ("słowo-powszechnik" and "słowo-konkret"); Barańczak, "Proszę pokazać język," 75–80. Similarly, Barańczak's post-1989 poetry, collected in his last book, *Chirurgiczna precyzja* (Surgical Precision) (1998), was quite often praised for packing multiple meanings into relatively minimalist form. This was attributed to "the imperative of many-sidedness," Barańczak's urge to dismantle what is one-dimensional and unilateral by garnering plural meanings and "truths" within one poem; Kandziora, *Ocalony w gmachu wiersza*, 360. Barańczak himself also commented on his "ability to speak in multiple different voices" in his poetry of the time; Barańczak, "O przyjaciołach," 9. Clare Cavanagh looked for the sources of Barańczak's polyphonic poetry in his intense translation activity in the 1990s: "I can hear the echoes of familiar poets speaking unexpectedly with the Polish accent" (Cavanagh, "O *Chirurgicznej precyzji* Stanisława Barańczaka," 154).

37. Barańczak, "Mały, lecz maksymalistyczny Manifest translatologiczny albo," 31.

38. Treating this strand as a characteristic feature of Barańczak's technique of generating multiple variants, Monika Kaczorowska even argues for a respective editorial solution: "It would be sensible if not only critical editions, but also popular versions presented all existing

variants of Barańczak's translations." Kaczorowska, *Przekład jako kontynuacja twórczości własnej*, 135.

39. I discuss Barańczak's exercises in translation multiples from his anthology *Fioletowa krowa* (1993) in "Stanisław Barańczak: Between Autonomy and Support."

40. Barańczak, *Pegaz zdębiał*, 123.

41. The musical provenance of some originals informed Barańczak's experiments, as they were meant to reside in both the intermedial and the interlingual zone. In fact, Barańczak often explored the potential of sound as an alternative means of translation. Besides bringing into Polish operas such as Mozart's *The Marriage of Figaro* and *Don Giovanni*, and Henry Purcell's *Dido and Aeneas*, he also published the widely commented on *Podróż zimowa* (Winter Journey) (1994), a collection of poems musically inspired by Franz Schubert's song cycle *Winterreise* and deliberately departing from the original Romantic lyrics written by Wilhelm Müller.

42. Barańczak, "Oratorium Moratorium," 38.

43. Barańczak, *Pegaz zdębiał*, 125.

44. Barańczak, "Oratorium Moratorium," 38, 40.

45. Encyclopaedia Britannica, "La Marseillaise: French National Anthem."

46. I am also including an alternative variant of the first homophonic opening suggested by Barańczak in his footnote. Barańczak, "Oratorium Moratorium," 38.

47. Wolff, *Inventing Eastern Europe*, 3.

48. Barańczak, "Oratorium Moratorium," 39–42.

49. Barańczak, "Oratorium Moratorium," 39, 40.

50. Barańczak, "Annus Mirabilis," 6.

51. Barańczak, "Annus Mirabilis," 9–10.

52. Barańczak, "Annus Mirabilis," 7.

53. Barańczak, "Annus Mirabilis," 8.

54. Barańczak, "Oratorium Moratorium," 40.

55. Barańczak, *Pegaz zdębiał*, 125.

56. Barańczak, "Oratorium Moratorium," 41.

57. For the English translation by Madeline G. Levine and Steven I. Levine, see Tuwim, "Ball at the Opera."

58. Barańczak, "Taking Revenge on Language." Though originally written in 1936, the full text of "Ball at the Opera" appeared in Poland only in 1982. Barańczak reviewed the whole apocalyptic satire two years later, underscoring the elements of Tuwim's text that turned out to be crucial to constructing his own homophonic multiples. For instance, he observed that phonetic violence and vulgarity in "Ball at the Opera" saturated the poem's atmosphere with a premonition of catastrophe. In Barańczak's view, Tuwim's vengeful language of mutilation and punishment was also enhanced by linguistic exoticisms and distorted foreign phrases, in particular from Italian: "totti frotti, Włoch Tęsknotti" ("tutti frutti, the Italian Melancutti," as translated by Madeline and Steven Levine). Finally, Barańczak also praised "Ball at the Opera" for dismantling the whole into parts: "There is a striking domination of pars pro toto—a particularly effective means of smashing the panoramic picture into little pieces." Barańczak, "Taking Revenge on Language," 244.

59. Barańczak, "Taking Revenge on Language," 244.

60. Barańczak, "Goodbye, Samizdat," 65.

61. Barańczak called this type of review a "bezecenzja." The term conflated the Polish "recenzja" (review) and "bezecny" (wicked) in a pun hinting at the disapproving approach to the reviewed book. Not exactly a precedent in Barańczak's output at that point, the critical genre of "wicked review" brings to mind his popular *Książki najgorsze* (The Worst Books) (1981), a collection of courageous reviews debunking valueless literature promulgated in the official circulation for propaganda reasons.

62. Barańczak, "Jak bliźniak z bliźniakiem."

63. The previously mentioned collection *Pegaz zdębiał* (2015) focused, as the subtitle had it, on the intersection between "nonsense poetry and everyday life." Some critics noticed later that Barańczak's experiments in fact very consciously and critically engaged with the status quo and surrounding reality, for instance Michniewicz, "Iha-ha!" Already in 1996, Jan Gondowicz argued that Barańczak's book could not be treated as politically innocent, in the same way that Russian futurism and Julian Tuwim's nonsense poetry combined linguistic experimentalism with political activism. According to him, in that case, too, Barańczak's "Pegasus reached out its tentacles" in certain directions. Gondowicz, "Pegaz wysuwa macki."

64. Barańczak, *Pegaz zdębiał*, 194.

65. Barańczak, "Jak bliźniak z bliźniakiem," 62; and Barańczak, *Pegaz zdębiał*, 196.

66. Barańczak, "Jak bliźniak z bliźniakiem."

67. The abbreviation alluded to the ZChN, namely the Zjednoczenie Chrześcijańsko-Narodowe (Christian National Union), a Christian right-wing political party founded in 1989.

68. Barańczak, "Jak bliźniak z bliźniakiem," 62.

69. The surname Kłapczyński probably alluded to the identical twins Lech and Jarosław Kaczyński, who were politically active and aligned with Lech Wałęsa at the time. Later, Lech Kaczyński became Poland's president and died in an infamous 2010 plane crash; Jarosław was Poland's prime minister and is currently the leader of the right-wing Law and Justice Party (PiS).

70. See Haltof, *The Cinema of Krzysztof Kieślowski*, 119.

71. Barańczak, *Pegaz zdębiał*, 198.

72. Barańczak, *Pegaz zdębiał*, 204.

73. Barańczak, *Pegaz zdębiał*, 207.

74. Barańczak, *Pegaz zdębiał*, 201–2.

75. Barańczak, *Podróż zimowa*, 42.

4. Winding the Clockwork Orange Three Times

1. Burgess, *A Clockwork Orange* (original), 148.

2. Tuziak, "Przypadki pewnej pomarańczy," 10.

3. Stiller, "Kilka słów od tłumacza," 217.

4. Stiller, "Co dał nam los," 1.

5. Wróblewski, "Trudny charakter pisarza," 5; and Siedlecka, *Kryptonim "Liryka,"* 26.

6. Stiller wrote critical reviews of literary translations of the famous cycle "Table and Scissors" ("Stół i nożyce").

7. Stiller's version R was first published as a supplement to the science fiction magazine *Fantastyka*. Burgess, *Mechaniczna pomarańcza* [Wersja R, two parts].

8. Following Stiller's death in 2016, the two versions were published in a single volume as a "special edition": Burgess, *Mechaniczna pomarańcza: Edycja specjalna*.

9. Stiller repeatedly referred to the work-in-progress Germanized version in both his translator's comments and his interviews. Critics and readers often referred to the upcoming version N in their articles, reviews, and blogs, for instance Cetera, "Translating the Translated," 109; Kubińska and Kubiński, "Osobliwy przypadek," 74; Wierzbińska, "Burgess Translated in Polish," 19; M. M., "Anthony Burgess," 16; Blogrys, "Pomarańcza Tony'ego"; and Marzec, "1001 drobiazgów o książkach i czytaniu."

10. Stiller, "Kilka sprężyn z nakręcanej pomarańczy [1991]," 142.

11. Burgess, *Mechaniczna pomarańcza* [Wersja R], back cover.

12. Burgess, *Nakręcana pomarańcza* [Wersja A], back cover.

13. Stiller, "Burgess a sprawa polska" (Burgess and the Polish Question) and "Kilka sprężyn z nakręcanej pomarańczy [1999]" (A Couple of Springs from the Wind-Up Orange), from version R; and Stiller, "Kilka słów od tłumacza" (A Few Words from the Translator), from version A. The two texts from version R combine passages from Stiller's prototype afterword to the 1991 edition. The later texts include threads absent from the 1991 version of Stiller's commentary, making it possible to trace the project's development.

14. Stiller, "Kilka słów od tłumacza," 217.

15. There were illegal editions in 1989 (Warsaw, Alternatywa) and 1990 (Kraków, ZRS), and an authorized version in 1991.

16. Stiller, "Kilka sprężyn z nakręcanej pomarańczy [1991]," 145.

17. Stiller, "Burgess a sprawa polska," 224.

18. Morrison, introduction to *A Clockwork Orange*.

19. Evans, "Nadsat: The Argot and Its Implications," 409.

20. Stiller, "Kilka sprężyn z nakręcanej pomarańczy [1991]," 138.

21. Among others, Stiller criticized the inconsistent construction of Nadsat, the plagiarizing of Joycean techniques, and the lack of any deeper social, political, or moral meaning in the experiment. Stiller, "Horror-Show, czyli bój się Pan jeża!"

22. However, there is no evidence of the censor's intervention recorded in the Central Archives of Modern Records in Warsaw (case number I.630.29.2016).

23. Stiller, "Kilka sprężyn z nakręcanej pomarańczy [1991]," 159.

24. Stiller, "Kilka sprężyn z nakręcanej pomarańczy [1991]."

25. Stiller, "Kilka sprężyn z nakręcanej pomarańczy [1991]," 145.

26. Wysocki, translator's note to *Anthony Burgess: Mechaniczna pomarańcza*.

27. Düring, "Obraz Związku Radzieckiego," 417–18.

28. *Literatura na świecie* published in 1978 extracts from Burgess's *Napoleon Symphony* (translated by Jarosław Anders). In 1986, the same magazine released Burgess's essay (translated by Elżbieta Pawełkiewicz) on George Orwell's *Nineteen Eighty-Four* alongside fragments from Orwell's minor works. That concession reflected censorship's more liberal attitude in years 1986–1987; see Looby, *Censorship, Translation and English Language Fiction*, 18.

29. Broński, "1985: Inny zmierzch zachodu," 30.

30. Stiller, "Horror-Show, czyli bój się Pan jeża!," 199.

31. Sadkowski, "Nie bójcie się mechanicznego jeża!"

32. Marcin Rzeszutkowski, in Czytelnicy i Fantastyka, "Sondaż VI: Ocena powieści," 66.

33. Stiller, "Kilka sprężyn z nakręcanej pomarańczy [1991]," 159; and Stiller, "Burgess a sprawa polska," 223.

34. Stiller, "Kilka sprężyn z nakręcanej pomarańczy [1991]."

35. Burgess, *Mechaniczna pomarańcza* [Wersja R], back cover.

36. Piotr Pieniążek, in Czytelnicy i Fantastyka, "Sondaż VI: Ocena powieści," 66–67.

37. Ironically, Stiller identified these versions as pirated copies. Stiller, "Kilka sprężyn z nakręcanej pomarańczy [1991]," 160.

38. Stiller's conflict with the *Literatura na świecie* editor inspired his resentment and efforts to publish his translation against all odds. He consequently quit the editorial board, accusing the magazine of failing in its role to promulgate foreign works freely. Stiller, "Do redaktora naczelnego," 345.

39. Batko, "Burgess: Groźny wizjoner," 65.

40. Stiller, "Burgess a sprawa polska," 224–25.

41. Stiller, translator's note to *Fantastyka*, no. 8.

42. Stiller, "Co dał nam los," 1.

43. Stiller, "Burgess a sprawa polska," 222.

44. Stiller, translator's note to *Fantastyka*, no. 8.

45. Stiller, "Kilka sprężyn z nakręcanej pomarańczy [1991]," 145.

46. Stiller, "Burgess a sprawa polska," 225.

47. Stiller, "Kilka sprężyn z nakręcanej pomarańczy [1991]," 145–46.

48. See Stiller, "Horror-Show, czyli bój się Pan jeża!," 192.

49. Stiller, "Kilka sprężyn z nakręcanej pomarańczy [1991]," 146. Following this argument, Stiller harshly criticized any other solutions he considered thoughtless and "absurdly mechanical," especially Cezary Michoński's 1987 Anglicized attempt.

50. Stiller, "Burgess a sprawa polska," 222.

51. Stiller, "Burgess a sprawa polska," 221.

52. Burgess, *A Clockwork Orange* (original), 91.

53. Stiller, "Burgess a sprawa polska," 221.

54. Burgess, *Mechaniczna pomarańcza* [Wersja R], 117.

55. Burgess, *Nakręcana pomarańcza* [Wersja A], 117.

56. Evans, "Nadsat: The Argot and Its Implications," 406; and Adams, *From Elvish to Klingon*, 69.

57. In a nutshell, the Polish-Russian combination played on inter-Slavic word formation, and syntactic and idiomatic calques. The "Ponglish" slang adopted noninflective forms; infinitive, auxiliary, and gerund constructions; definite articles; and plural endings. See Stiller, "Burgess a sprawa polska," 221–25.

58. Adams, *From Elvish to Klingon*, 69.

59. Burgess, *Mechaniczna pomarańcza* [Wersja R], 117; and Burgess, *Nakręcana pomarańcza* [Wersja A], 117.

60. Ułaszyn, *Język złodziejski*, 49–57.

61. Stiller, "Kilka sprężyn z nakręcanej pomarańczy [1991]," 151.

62. Wierzbińska, "Burgess Translated in Polish," 20.

63. Evans, "Nadsat: The Argot and Its Implications," 408; and Adams, *From Elvish to Klingon*, 69.

64. Stiller, "Kilka sprężyn z nakręcanej pomarańczy [1991]," 151.
65. Burgess, *Mechaniczna pomarańcza* [Wersja R], 177.
66. Burgess, *Nakręcana pomarańcza* [Wersja A], 177.
67. Burgess, *A Clockwork Orange* (original), 37.
68. Burgess, *Mechaniczna pomarańcza* [Wersja R], 45.
69. Burgess, *Nakręcana pomarańcza* [Wersja A], 46.
70. Stiller, "Kilka sprężyn z nakręcanej pomarańczy [1991]."
71. Stiller, "Kilka sprężyn z nakręcanej pomarańczy [1991]," 153–55.
72. Joyce, "Anna Livia Plurabella." This translation appeared in *Literatura na świecie* the year before Stiller's own unsuccessful 1974 publication of Burgess.
73. Most notably in Stefan Żeromski's *Syzyfowe prace* (1897), and in novels by Eliza Orzeszkowa and Józef Ignacy Kraszewski. See Brzezina, *Stylizacja rosyjska*.
74. Burgess, *Mechaniczna pomarańcza* [Wersja R], 7; and Burgess, *Nakręcana pomarańcza* [Wersja A], 7.
75. Burgess, *A Clockwork Orange* (original), 5.
76. Burgess, *Mechaniczna pomarańcza* [Wersja R], 68; and Burgess, *Nakręcana pomarańcza* [Wersja A], 68.
77. Burgess, *A Clockwork Orange* (original), 55.
78. Zawistowski, "Po nastajaszczy horror szoł."
79. Stiller, "Burgess a sprawa polska," 221.
80. Burgess, *A Clockwork Orange* (original), 18.
81. Burgess, *Mechaniczna pomarańcza* [Wersja R], 23; and Burgess, *Nakręcana pomarańcza* [Wersja A], 23.
82. Burgess, *A Clockwork Orange* (original), 19, 119.
83. Burgess, *Mechaniczna pomarańcza* [Wersja R], 24, 156; and Burgess, *Nakręcana pomarańcza* [Wersja A], 24, 156.
84. Burgess, *Mechaniczna pomarańcza* [Wersja R], 151, 189; 45, 152, 190ff.
85. Burgess, *Mechaniczna pomarańcza* [Wersja R], 85, 87, 88ff.
86. Bellos, *Is That a Fish in Your Ear?*, 36.
87. Czermińska, "On the Turning Point," 111.
88. See Tichomirowa, "Literatury łagrowej obszary nieodsłonięte," 97.
89. Herling-Grudziński, *Inny świat*, 16.
90. Skarga, *Po wyzwoleniu*, 203.
91. Bałtyn, "Przeciw społecznej inżynierii": "Russian has for ages played the role of a *rugatelnyi jazyk* [an abusive language]."
92. Michoński, "Kognitywne aspekty przekłady," 265; and Biegajło, "Three Different Versions of *A Clockwork Orange*," 140.
93. Janion, "Poland between the West and East." Maria Janion discusses in this context works such as Ryszard Kapuściński's *Imperium* (1993) and Dorota Masłowska's *Snow White and Russian Red* (*Wojna polsko-ruska pod flagą biało-czerwoną*, 2002). See also Janion's discussion in her *Niesamowita słowiańszczyzna* (Uncanny Slavdom), especially on "making ourselves more Western than Eastern," in Marta Figlerowicz's recently translated excerpt: Janion and Figlerowicz, "Uncanny Slavdom," 114.
94. Masłowska, *Snow White and Russian Red*, 74.

95. Zessin-Jurek, "Forgotten Memory?," 49.

96. Maciejewski, "Stereotyp Rosji i Rosjanina w polskiej literaturze," 192–93.

97. For different approaches to respective geographical areas, see Cavanagh, "Postcolonial Poland"; Thompson, *Imperial Knowledge*; Neumann, "Russia as Central Europe's Constituting Other"; and D. C. Moore, "Is the Post- in Postcolonial the Post- in Post-Soviet?"

98. Bojarska, "Muzyka a walka klas," 63.

99. Stiller, "Kilka sprężyn z nakręcanej pomarańczy [1991]," 155.

100. Jarzębski, "The Decade in Prose," 347–48.

101. Waszakowa, "Derywowane anglicyzmy," 96.

102. Waszakowa, "Derywowane anglicyzmy," 90.

103. Gruszczyński, "Robić zło"; and Kowalski, "Mechaniczna, czyli nakręcona," xliii.

104. See, e.g., Smółkowa, "Pokaż język."

105. Burgess, *Nakręcana pomarańcza* [Wersja A], 24. Compare this with instances of Nadsat in Burgess's original novel, 19: "pushing the old noga" (нога: leg), "good for smecks" (смех: laughter), "giggling like bezoomny" (безумный: insane), "viddy" (видеть: see), and "this cottage veshch" (вещь: thing); and in Burgess, *Mechaniczna pomarańcza* [Wersja R], 24: "wciskałem *girę*" (colloquial: leg), "osobna *dacza*" (дача: summer house), and "chichrali się jak *z uma szedłszy*" (participle of сойти с ума: go mad) (my emphasis).

106. This imitates the booming usage of "top" in Polish. Waszakowa, "Derywowane anglicyzmy," 98.

107. Stiller was very fond of this adaptation: Stiller, "Co robić z tą pomarańczą?," 88; and Stiller, "Słowa to małe piwko," 9.

108. Jarzębski, "Formy pesymizmu," 11–14. See also Czapliński, *Polska do wymiany*.

109. Goh, "'Clockwork' Language Reconsidered," 263.

110. Ray, "Alex Before and After," 482.

111. Burgess, "A Clockwork Orange Resucked," vi.

112. Burgess, "Nakręcana pomarańcza na nowo wyssana."

113. Burgess, *A Clockwork Orange* (original), 148.

114. Stiller, "Burgess a sprawa polska," 217.

115. Jarzębski, "The Conflict of Generations"; and Vassileva-Karagyozova, *Coming of Age under Martial Law*, 10.

116. Burgess, *Mechaniczna pomarańcza* [Wersja R], and Burgess, *Nakręcana pomarańcza* [Wersja A], 43, 100, 135, 137ff.

117. Burgess, *A Clockwork Orange* (original), 123, 126.

118. Burgess, *A Clockwork Orange* (original), 104.

119. Burgess, *Mechaniczna pomarańcza* [Wersja R], 137; and Burgess, *Nakręcana pomarańcza* [Wersja A], 137.

120. Burgess, *Mechaniczna pomarańcza* [Wersja R], back cover.

121. Stiller, "Co robić z tą pomarańczą?," 91–92.

122. Burgess, *A Clockwork Orange* (original), 42.

123. Burgess, *Nakręcana pomarańcza* [Wersja A], 53.

124. Burgess, *A Clockwork Orange* (original), 117.

125. Burgess, *Mechaniczna pomarańcza* [Wersja R], 154; and Burgess, *Nakręcana pomarańcza* [Wersja A], 154.

126. Stiller, "Kilka sprężyn z nakręcanej pomarańczy [1991]," 160.

127. Robert Stiller, interview, 2014, cited in Szymańska, "Miłość do trzech pomarańczy Roberta Stillera."

128. Burgess, *A Clockwork Orange* (original), 148.

129. Wierzbińska, "Burgess Translated in Polish," 19; and Ginter, "Powieść jako przygoda lingwistyczna," 188. Despite common criticism, it is unlikely that Stiller's strategy was a glitch due to its consistent distribution in relevant fragments and the absence of attempts to correct these "errors" in any of the reprintings.

130. Stiller, "Kilka sprężyn z nakręcanej pomarańczy [1999]," 200.

131. Burgess, *Mechaniczna pomarańcza* [Wersja R], 81–85; and Burgess, *Nakręcana pomarańcza* [Wersja A], 81–85.

132. Burgess, *A Clockwork Orange* (original), 63; Burgess, *Mechaniczna pomarańcza* [Wersja R], 81; and Burgess, *Nakręcana pomarańcza* [Wersja A], 81.

133. Burgess, *Nakręcana pomarańcza* [Wersja A], 81; and Burgess, *A Clockwork Orange* (original), 64.

134. Burgess, *Mechaniczna pomarańcza* [Wersja R], 85; and Burgess, *Nakręcana pomarańcza* [Wersja A], 85.

135. Isakowicz-Zaleski, *Księża wobec bezpieki*.

136. Daniel, "The Church-State Situation in Poland"; and Gowin, *Kościół w czasach wolności*, 52–87.

137. Robert Stiller, interview, 2014, cited in Szymańska, "Miłość do trzech pomarańczy Roberta Stillera."

138. Stiller, letter to the editors, *Nowe książki*, no. 4 (1997); Stiller, letter to the editors, *Nowe książki*, no. 7 (1997); Stiller, "Krzyżyk na ks. Chrostowskim," 6; and Robert Stiller, interview, 2014, cited in Szymańska, "Miłość do trzech pomarańczy Roberta Stillera." Stiller translated works by, for example, Eugen Drewermann, Karlheinz Deschner, and Horst Herrmann.

139. Cf. Burgess, *Mechaniczna pomarańcza* [Wersja R], 83; and Burgess, *Nakręcana pomarańcza* [Wersja A], 83; "grzdyl świętojebliwy" (sanctimonious squirt) (63), "świętojebliwiec" (fucked holier-than-thou) (84), "zafajdane muzyki świętojebliwe" (mucky sanctimonious music) (81), "hymn świętojebliwy" (fucked holier-than-thou hymn) (99), and "hymniszcze" (pejorative of "hymn") (81, 99).

140. Burgess, *Nakręcana pomarańcza* [Wersja A], 14, 67.

141. Stiller, "Kilka sprężyn z nakręcanej pomarańczy [1999]," 199.

142. Stiller, "Kilka sprężyn z nakręcanej pomarańczy [1991]," 151; Stiller, "Burgess a sprawa polska," 229; Stiller, "Co robić z tą pomarańczą?," 88; and Stiller, "Słowa to małe piwko," 9.

143. Stiller, "Kilka słów od tłumacza," 219.

144. Kubińska and Kubiński, "Osobliwy przypadek," 74.

145. Kopp, *Germany's Wild East*.

146. Robert Stiller, personal correspondence, April 7, 2016.

147. Burgess, *Sprężynowa pomarańcza* [Wersja N]. Cf. Stiller's excerpt and its discussion in Szymańska, "Miłość do trzech pomarańczy Roberta Stillera," 248–50.

148. Rödder, "Es gibt eine neue Angst vor Deutschland"; and Chwin, "Die Polen haben begründete Angst vor Auslöschung."

149. Burgess, *A Clockwork Orange* (original), 148.

150. Burgess, *Mechaniczna pomarańcza* [Wersja R], 193; and Burgess, *Nakręcana pomarańcza* [Wersja A], 193.

151. Burgess, *Sprężynowa pomarańcza* [Wersja N].

152. Stiller, "Słowa to małe piwko," 9.

153. Stiller, "Co robić z tą pomarańczą?," 88.

154. Cieślak, "Teatr ograniczonego zaufania," 15; and Pawłowski, "Nakręcana pomarańcza we Wrocławiu," 19.

5. Doing Brecht in Different Voices

1. Masłowski, "Brecht (dla) literatów."

2. Szaruga, "Poezje Brechta," 32.

3. All of them unanimously claim "Bertolt Brecht" to be the author of the book and list the four translators in brackets.

4. Kopacki, "Zanim," 6.

5. Wirth, *Siedem prób*, 65, 84.

6. Pijanowski, "Od wydawnictwa," 5.

7. Jan Kott, in Goliński et al., "Dwie rozmowy wokół Brechta," 110.

8. Rudnytska, "Translation and the Formation of the Soviet Canon," 61.

9. Gajek, "Wstęp. Brecht w Polsce," lxxiii, lxxxviii.

10. Krynicki, "Nazywać rzeczy po imieniu," 17.

11. Krynicki, "Nazywać rzeczy po imieniu."

12. Tadeusz Nyczek, in Goliński et al., "Dwie rozmowy wokół Brechta," 111.

13. For this reason, the domain of literary translation in the Soviet Union has been described as "a safe art," a "haven," and a textual "screen." See, e.g., Etkind, *Notes of a Non-Conspirator*, 146; Leighton, *Two Worlds, One Art*, 38; Loseff, *On the Beneficence of Censorship*, 77; and Baer, "Literary Translation and the Construction of a Soviet Intelligentsia," 155.

14. Valles, introduction to *Our Life Grows*, ix.

15. Szaruga, "Poezje Brechta," 31.

16. Brecht, *Gesammelte Werke in acht Bänden*, vol. 4, 1010. All Brecht's works in German will be quoted from this edition (henceforth *GW*). Unless otherwise indicated, English versions are provided in my (literal) translation.

17. Brecht, "Rozwiązanie."

18. Krynicki, "Podziękowanie," 142.

19. Luboń, *Przekraczanie obcości*, 213–15.

20. Ash, *The Polish Revolution*, 163.

21. The anthologies were: Stefan H. Kaszyński, ed., *W cieniu Lorelei: Antologia wierszy poetów Republiki Federalnej Niemiec* (1978); and Stefan H. Kaszyński and Eugeniusz Wachowiak, eds., *Antologia wierszy poetów Niemieckiej Republiki Demokratycznej* (1979). See Kornhauser, "Polityka i przekład," 243.

22. Kornhauser, "Polityka i przekład."

23. Stiller, "Brecht po polsku," 7. Four years later, Stiller managed to publish the most controversial poems from the performance by smuggling them into a 1986 children's book called *Rekin zęby ma na wierzchu* (*The Shark Has Its Teeth Outside / Und der Haifisch, der hat Zähne*).

Stiller's two other collections of Brecht's poetry in translation were both released by the official state publishing house in 1980 and 1988. The change in the thematic scope of the two could be seen as a touchstone of the political evolution from the period following the martial law of 1981 to the fall of communism in 1989. The ideologically monotonous image of Brecht the poet in the earlier book was slightly complicated toward the end of communism.

24. Stiller, "Brecht po polsku."

25. Goliński et al., "Dwie rozmowy wokół Brechta," 110.

26. Stiller, "Brecht po polsku," 7; and Krzemiński, "Efekt obcości," 70–71.

27. This statement refers primarily to Brecht's poetry in print and not the musical performances of his protest songs and ballads. The latter, for instance, were included by Kazik Staszewski, a leading rock musician known by his stage name Kazik, in his 2001 album *Kurt Weill's Melodies and Something Extra* (*Melodie Kurta Weill'a i coś ponadto*) in Roman Kołakowski's translations. Performing the ballad continued the subversive tradition of counterculture and was "a crucial component of memory" surrounding democratic protests even beyond the dissolution of the Polish People's Republic. See Bohlman, *Musical Solidarities*, 226.

28. Goliński et al., "Dwie rozmowy wokół Brechta," 121.

29. Czapliński, *Powrót centrali*, 41.

30. Hoffmann, "500 literatur, 500 światów," 152–53.

31. Adamczyk-Garbowska, "Sztuka przekładu," 172.

32. For instance, the then Democratic Party member and now controversial conservative politician Janusz Korwin-Mikke famously waged disputes with Robert Stiller over Polish translations of Lewis Carroll's "Jabberwocky" in a 1980 issue. Korwin-Mikke even presented his own poetic rendering in support of his arguments. Korwin-Mikke, "Stiller i inni."

33. This included, for instance, a fragment of James Joyce's *Ulysses* by Maciej Słomczyński and Józef Czechowicz published in 1973 on even and uneven pages, respectively, and an excerpt from Gustave Flaubert's *Madame Bovary* by Magdalena Tulli and Ryszard Engelking placed next to each other using the same convention in 2003 with an added introductory remark: "times two" ("razy dwa"). Joyce, *Ulisses* [fragment]; and Flaubert, *Pani Bovary* [fragment].

34. Simon, *Nauka o rzeczach (Czołówka)* [fragment].

35. Sadkowski, "Znamię trudności."

36. Sadkowski, "Znamię trudności," 352.

37. Stiller, "Przekład jako własność niczyja," 333–35.

38. Stiller, "Przekład jako własność niczyja," 335.

39. Leśniewska, "Projekt wydania całych *Kwiatów zła*," 351–52.

40. Bieńkowski, "W sprawie Baudelaire'a," 357.

41. Waczków, "Ryzyko."

42. Lewin, "O przekładzie 'Lorelei,'" 354. This strand featured examples such as Heinrich Heine's "Lorelei" in Robert Stiller's and Leopold Lewin's versions placed in parallel in 1981; Arthur Rimbaud's "The Drunken Boat" ("Le bateau ivre") in three renderings by Zenon Miriam Przesmycki, Adam Ważyk, and Józef Waczków, printed in 1982 one after another; and Alexander Pushkin's "Prophet" ("Пророк") in four renderings by Józef Łobodowski, Julian Tuwim, and twice by Witold Chwalewik (in versions of 1950 and 1968) grouped together in 1987 to expose diverse "shades abundant in the text." See Heine, "Lorelei"; Rimbaud, "Statek pijany"; and Puszkin, "Prorok."

43. Barańczak et al., "Boski Dante (po polsku)."

44. Dante Alighieri, "Piekło: Pieśń II."

45. For example, T. S. Eliot's double "Animula" in the 1980 selection of Krzysztof Karasek and Krzysztof Boczkowski; the 1991 presentation of Ezra Pound's poetry with "Canto I" bifurcating into Andrzej Sosnowski's and Leszek Engelking's readings; and the 2009 sample of C. K. Williams's writing with the poem "A Negro Woman" in Krystyna Dąbrowska's and Andrzej Szuba's separate interpretations. See Eliot, "Animula"; Pound, "Pieśń I"; and Williams, "Murzynka."

46. Karasek, "Od tłumacza," 245.

47. Jakub Ekier and Andrzej Kopacki's 1998 selection from Durs Grünbein with "Skull Base Lesson" ("Schädelbasislektion") in their distinct renderings; the 2006 double take on Gottfried Benn's "Never Lonelier" ("Einsamer nie") by Jacek St. Buras and Andrzej Kopacki; and four selections of Bertolt Brecht's lyrical works by Jacek St. Buras, Jakub Ekier, Andrzej Kopacki, and Piotr Sommer. See Grünbein, "Lekcja podstawy czaszki"; Benn, "Nigdy samotniej"; Brecht, "Wiersze"; and Brecht, "Utwory śpiewane z *Opery za trzy grosze*."

48. Buras, "Pod urokiem buntownika," 47.

49. Buras, "Pod urokiem buntownika," 50.

50. Ekier, "Ani czyjś, ani swój, ani jeden," 76, 81, 85.

51. Brecht, *GW*, 744; see also Ekier, "Ani czyjś, ani swój, ani jeden," 63.

52. Kopacki, "Śliwa pod okiem," 127–28.

53. Kopacki, "Śliwa pod okiem," 127.

54. Brecht, *GW*, 647.

55. Both Lech Pijanowski and Robert Stiller opt for the standard "leaves" ("liście"). Brecht, *Wiersze wybrane*, 41; and Brecht, *Postylla domowa*, 299.

56. Kopacki, "Śliwa pod okiem," 138.

57. Stiller, *Kilka słów o przekładach*, 8.

58. Sommer, "Tak, czyli jak?," 165.

59. Sommer, "Literatura jest tłumaczeniem," 14.

60. The textual base for Sommer's translation is John Willett and Ralph Manheim's 1976 edition of Brecht's poetry, *Poems 1913–1956*. However, the final version was also lightly edited by Kopacki. Piotr Sommer, personal correspondence, November 26, 2015.

61. Sommer, "Tak, czyli jak?," 166.

62. Sommer, "Tłumacząc miniatury Charlesa Reznikoffa," 233.

63. Wat, "If the Word 'Exists,'" 23.

64. Sommer, "Tak, czyli jak?," 168.

65. Wat, "If the Word 'Exists.'"

66. Sommer, "Tkać i pruć," 12.

67. Cf. Niżyńska, "The Impossibility of Shrugging One's Shoulders," 466.

68. Sommer, "Według Brechta." Copyright © 1986 by Piotr Sommer; reproduced with permission. The English version is my literal translation from the Polish.

69. Ekier, "Ani czyjś, ani swój, ani jeden," 83.

70. Buras, "Pod urokiem buntownika," 50.

71. Kopacki, "Śliwa pod okiem," 127.

72. Ekier, "Ani czyjś, ani swój, ani jeden," 86; and Kopacki, "Śliwa pod okiem," 129. See also Mościcki, "Ten cały Brecht: Przekłady i szkice."

73. E.g., Ekier, "Ani czyjś, ani swój, ani jeden," 77, 85.

74. E.g., Ekier, "Ani czyjś, ani swój, ani jeden," 83.

75. See more on the two renderings of this poem in Polish in Szymańska, "Ten cały Brecht (Burasa, Ekiera, Kopackiego i Sommera)."

76. This poem exists in different versions. In its format of a stand-alone poem ("Die Ballade vom ertrunkenen Mädchen") from *Hauspostille* (1927), it was later included in *Das Berliner Requiem* (1928). Read alongside songs such as "Grabschrift" and "Red Rosa" from the latter work, the ballad was often interpreted as the story of Rosa Luxemburg (Schebera, *Kurt Weill: An Illustrated Life*, 131). It initially appeared in 1919–1920 in Brecht's play *Baal* under the title "Vom ertrunkenen Mädchen," commenting on the story of Johanna, an innocent virgin seduced and then rejected by Baal, who consequently drowned herself in the river. See Brown, "Reading 'The Drowned Girl,'" 84.

77. Owen, "Voicing the Drowned Girl," 781; and Nägele, "Phantom of a Corpse."

78. Knopf, *Gelegentlich: Poesie*, 86; and Parker, *Bertolt Brecht: A Literary Life*, 387.

79. Thomson, *The Poetry of Brecht*, 103.

80. Whitaker, *Brecht's Poetry: A Critical Study*, 98.

81. Brecht, *GW*, 519. Copyright © 1993 Bertolt-Brecht-Erben/Suhrkamp Verlag; reproduced with permission.

82. Brecht, *Poems 1913–1956*, 225. Copyright © 1964, 1976 by Bertolt-Brecht-Erben/Suhrkamp Verlag. Used by permission of Liveright Publishing Corporation.

83. Brecht, "Wyłącznie przez ten zamęt," 57. Copyright © 1993 Bertolt-Brecht-Erben/Suhrkamp Verlag; reproduced with permission.

84. Brecht, "Wyłącznie z powodu narastającego nieporządku," 150. Copyright © 1993 Bertolt-Brecht-Erben/Suhrkamp Verlag; reproduced with permission.

85. In Polish, it also brings to mind Julian Tuwim's parody of the bourgeois talk of "horrible burghers" in his poem "Residents" ("Mieszkańcy") from 1933: "And again they say that Ford...that cinema...that God...that Russia...radio, sport, war" ("I znowu mówią, że Ford...że kino.../ Że Bóg...że Rosja...radio, sport, wojna"). Tuwim, "Mieszkańcy," 182.

86. Ekier, "Ani czyjś, ani swój, ani jeden," 80.

87. Ekier, "Ani czyjś, ani swój, ani jeden," 85.

88. This is for the German "was den Menschen rund macht und menschlich" ("what makes a man round and human").

89. Sommer, "Tak, czyli jak?," 174.

90. Sommer, "Tak, czyli jak?," 166.

91. Sommer, "Tak, czyli jak?," 167.

92. Kopacki, "Zanim," 5–6.

93. Przybylak, "Bertolt Brecht," 6.

94. See endnote 76 of this chapter.

95. Bentley, "Critical Views on *The Good Woman of Sezuan*," 49.

96. Bentley, "Critical Views on *The Good Woman of Sezuan*." Brecht was a rather traditional proponent of literal translation for publication as opposed to free adaptations for stage.

97. Brecht, *Brecht on Theatre*, 91.

98. Silberman, Giles, and Kuhn, introduction to *Brecht on Theatre*, 5.

99. Silberman, Giles, and Kuhn, introduction to *Brecht on Theatre*.

100. Jameson, *Brecht and Method*, 89–99.
101. Brecht, *Brecht on Theatre*, 70.
102. Brecht, *Brecht on Theatre*, 71.
103. Kopacki, "Zanim," 5.
104. Brecht, *Brecht on Theatre*, 92.

Conclusion

1. See Van Heuckelom, *Polish Migrants in European Film*, 109–12; Paszylk, *The Pleasure and Pain of Cult Horror Films*, 163; and Haltof, *The Cinema of Krzysztof Kieślowski*, 119.
2. Cetera, "Sztuka przekładu."
3. Rudolf and Alenowicz, "Słowo od redaktorów przekładu," 11; and Rudolf, "Wielogłosowa powieść w translatorskim wielogłosie."
4. Heydel, "Tłumaczenie jako wojna światów?," 334.
5. Heydel, "Dialog światów."
6. In recent years, many translation scholars have underscored the subversive power of literary translation to question established orders, hierarchies, and inequalities with respect to gender and sexual orientation as well as cultural and economic circulation between major and minor cultures. See, for instance, Von Flotow and Kamal, *The Routledge Handbook of Translation, Feminism and Gender*; Spurlin, "The Gender and Queer Politics of Translation: Literary, Historical, and Cultural Approaches," special issue of *Comparative Literature Studies*; Apter, *The Translation Zone: A New Comparative Literature*; and M. Baker, *Translation and Conflict: A Narrative Account*. This subversive strand has also found many practical realizations in the realm of experimental translation. For example, American translators such as David Cameron in *Flowers of Bad* (2007) and Christian Hawkey in *Ventrakl* (2010) ostentatiously deformed their texts to protest against the technologically driven warfare, capitalist exploitation, and aggressive politics of the United States. For other examples, see Lily Robert-Foley's "The Politics of Experimental Translation" as well as her discussion of two cases of machine-aided translation multiples in *Experimental Translation: The Work of Translation in the Age of Algorithmic Production*; Camille Bloomfield's "Deep Dante" (2021), composed of Dante translation variants from the dropdown menu of DeepL; and Mónica de la Torre's *Repetition Nineteen* (2020), featuring "Equivalencias Equivalences," a cycle of twenty-five English translations of her own Spanish-English poem using different procedures including Google Translate, Google Translate's voice recognition application, and her smartphone's autocorrect function, among others. In the Polish context, two mechanically aided deformations of Alfred Jarry's *Ubu Roi, ou, les Polonais* have been published with the established avant-garde press Ha!art, the first by three acknowledged translators, Aleksandra Małecka, Piotr Marecki, and Google Translate (2015); and the second "prompted" in GPT-4o by Jan K. Argasiński and entitled *Ubu GPT* (2024). According to Małecka and Marecki's manifesto, they turned the original absurdist satire on Ubu's tyranny in Poland into a critique of the pathologies of the free market's cultural production with its lukewarm quality and slapdash pace. Małecka and Marecki, "Ubu Król przepuszczony przez Tłumacza Google."
7. Rancière, "The Politics of Literature," 14.

BIBLIOGRAPHY

Adamczyk-Garbowska, Monika. "Sztuka przekładu." *Akcent*, no. 4 (2003): 172–73.

Adamiec, Witold, and Barbara Kołodziejczyk. "Rynek książki w Polsce." *Elektroniczny biuletyn informacyjny bibliotekarzy* 10 (2001). https://www.ebib.pl/2001/28/. Accessed May 5, 2023.

Adams, Michael. *From Elvish to Klingon: Exploring Invented Languages*. Oxford: Oxford University Press, 2011.

Anderson, Porter. "Nielsen Reports Translated Literature in the UK Grew 5.5 Percent in 2018." *Publishing Perspectives*, March 6, 2019. https://publishingperspectives.com/2019/03/nielsen-reports-translated-literature-in-uk-grows-5-percent-in-2018-booker/. Accessed June 6, 2022.

Appiah, Kwame Anthony. "Thick Translation." *Callaloo* 16, no. 4 (Autumn 1993): 808–19.

Apter, Emily. "Translation with No Original: Scandals of Textual Reproduction." In *Nation, Language, and the Ethics of Translation*, edited by Sandra Bermann and Michael Wood, 159–74. Princeton, NJ: Princeton University Press, 2005.

Apter, Emily. *The Translation Zone: A New Comparative Literature*. Princeton, NJ: Princeton University Press, 2005.

Ash, Timothy Garton. *The Polish Revolution: Solidarity*. 3rd ed. New Haven, CT: Yale University Press, 2002.

Baer, Brian James. "Literary Translation and the Construction of a Soviet Intelligentsia." In *Translation, Resistance, Activism*, edited by Maria Tymoczko, 149–67. Amherst: University of Massachusetts Press, 2010.

Baer, Brian James. "Translating Queer Texts in Soviet Russia: A Case Study in Productive Censorship." *Translation Studies* 4, no. 1 (2011): 21–40.

Baker, Mona. *Translation and Conflict: A Narrative Account*. Abingdon, UK: Routledge, 2006.

Baker, Sir Richard. *Cato Variegatus*. London: printed by Anne Griffin, sold by Anne Bowler, 1636.

Baldwin, Peter. *The Copyright Wars: Three Centuries of Trans-Atlantic Battle*. Princeton, NJ: Princeton University Press, 2016.

Bałtyn, Hanna. "Przeciw społecznej inżynierii." In *Anthony Burgess: Mechaniczna pomarańcza*. Spectator's brochure. Teatr im. Stefana Jaracza, Łódź, 1991.

Barańczak, Stanisław. "Annus Mirabilis." *Salmagundi*, nos. 85–86 (Winter–Spring 1990): 5–11.

Barańczak, Stanisław. *Bóg, Trąba i Ojczyzna: Słoń a Sprawa Polska oczami poetów od Reja do Rymkiewicza*. Kraków: Znak, 1995.

Barańczak, Stanisław. *Breathing under Water and Other East European Essays*. Cambridge, MA: Harvard University Press, 1990.

Barańczak, Stanisław. *Dziennik poranny: Wiersze 1967–1971*. Poznań: Wydawnictwo Poznańskie, 1972.
Barańczak, Stanisław. *Etyka i poetyka*. Paris: Instytut Literacki, 1979.
Barańczak, Stanisław. "Goodbye, Samizdat." *Wilson Quarterly* 14, no. 2 (Spring 1990): 59–66.
Barańczak, Stanisław. Introduction to *Polish Poetry of the Last Two Decades of Communist Rule: Spoiling Cannibals' Fun*, edited by Stanisław Barańczak and Clare Cavanagh, 1–13. Evanston, IL: Northwestern University Press, 1991.
Barańczak, Stanisław. "Jak bliźniak z bliźniakiem: Dwugłos braci Kłapczyńskich o twórczości Janusza Szpotańskiego." *Puls* 50, no. 3 (1991): 61–71.
Barańczak, Stanisław. *Jednym tchem*. Warsaw: Orientacja, 1970.
Barańczak, Stanisław. "Mały, lecz maksymalistyczny Manifest translatologiczny albo: Tłumaczenie się z tego, że tłumaczy się wiersze również w celu wytłumaczenia innym tłumaczom, iż dla większości tłumaczeń wierszy nie ma wytłumaczenia." *Teksty drugie* 3 (1990): 7–66.
Barańczak, Stanisław. "O przyjaciołach, tłumaczeniach, Ameryce i pisaniu wierszy." Interview by Piotr Szewc. *Nowe książki*, no. 1 (1998): 7–10.
Barańczak, Stanisław. "Oratorium Moratorium." *Puls* 51, no. 4 (1991): 38–42.
Barańczak, Stanisław. *Pegaz zdębiał: Poezja nonsensu a życie codzienne; Wprowadzenie w prywatną teorię gatunków*. London: Puls, 1995.
Barańczak, Stanisław. *Podróż zimowa: Wiersze do muzyka Franza Schuberta*. Poznań: Wydawnictwo a5, 1994.
Barańczak, Stanisław. "Poezja i duch Uogólnienia [1992]." In *Poezja i duch Uogólnienia: Wybór esejów 1970–1995*, 248–58. Kraków: Znak, 1996.
Barańczak, Stanisław. *Poezja i duch Uogólnienia: Wybór esejów 1970–1995*. Kraków: Znak, 1996.
Barańczak, Stanisław. "Proszę pokazać język: Trzydzieści lat później, czyli przygody słowa." *Teksty drugie* 1, no. 19 (1975): 72–85.
Barańczak, Stanisław. "A Small, but Maximalist Translatological Manifesto; or, An explanation of the fact that one also translates poetry with the aim of explaining to other translators that for most translations of poetry there is no explanation." Translated by Antonia Lloyd-Jones. In *Literature from Literature: Essays on Literary Translation*, edited by Kasia Szymanska and Magda Heydel, 137–200. Lausanne: Sdvig Press, 2020. http://ophen.org/pub-141728. Accessed February 18, 2021.
Barańczak, Stanisław. *Tablica z Macondo: Osiemnaście prób wytłumaczenia, po co i dlaczego się pisze*. London: Aneks, 1990.
Barańczak, Stanisław. "Taking Revenge on Language: Julian Tuwim's Ball at the Opera." *Slavic and East European Journal* 28, no. 2 (Summer 1984): 234–50.
Barańczak, Stanisław. "To Tell It All: Czeslaw Milosz's 'Six Lectures in Verse.'" *Harvard Review*, no. 4 (Spring 1993): 102–10.
Barańczak, Stanisław. *The Weight of the Body*. Chicago: Another Chicago Press, 1989.
Barańczak, Stanisław. *Zaufać nieufności: Osiem rozmów o sensie poezji*. Kraków: Biblioteka Nagłosu Wydawnictwo "M," 1993.
Barańczak, Stanisław, Jacek St. Buras, Zygmunt Kubiak, Tomasz Łubieński, Jarosław Mikołajewski, Piotr Sommer, and Anna Wasilewska. "Boski Dante (po polsku)." *Literatura na świecie*, no. 285 (1995): 2–45.

Barwin, Gary, and Derek Beaulieu. *Frogments from the Frag Pool: Haiku after Bashō.* Toronto: Mercury Press, 2005.

Bates, John M. "From a State Monopoly to a Free Market of Ideas? Censorship in Poland, 1976–1989." In *Critical Studies: Censorship and Cultural Regulation in the Modern Age,* edited by Beate Müller, 141–67. Amsterdam: Rodopi, 2004.

Batko, Zbigniew. "Burgess: Groźny wizjoner." *Nowa Fantastyka,* no. 1 (1994): 65.

Bazzana, Kevin. *Wondrous Strange: The Life and Art of Glenn Gould.* Oxford: Oxford University Press, 2005.

Bellos, David. *Is That a Fish in Your Ear? Translation and the Meaning of Everything.* New York: Farrar, Straus and Giroux, 2011.

Benn, Gottfried. "Nigdy samotniej." Translated by Jacek Stanisław Buras and Andrzej Kopacki. *Literatura na świecie,* nos. 418–419 (2006): 9–10, 59.

Bentley, Eric. "Critical Views on *The Good Woman of Sezuan*: On Translation and Adaptation." In *Bertolt Brecht: Comprehensive Research and Study Guide,* edited by Harold Bloom, 48–50. Broomall, PA: Chelsea House, 2002.

Bergvall, Caroline. "VIA (36 Dante Translations)." In *Against Expression: An Anthology of Conceptual Writing,* edited by Craig Dworkin and Kenneth Goldsmith, 81–86. Evanston, IL: Northwestern University Press, 2011.

Bergvall, Caroline. "VIA: 48 Dante Variations." In *Fig,* 64–71. Cambridge: Salt Publishing, 2005.

Bergvall, Caroline, with Ciarán Maher. "VIA (48 Dante Translations) Mix w Fractals." https://soundcloud.com/carolinebergvall/via-48-dante-translations-mix. Accessed March 27, 2024.

Bermann, Sandra. "Performing Translation." In *A Companion to Translation Studies,* edited by Sandra Bermann and Catherine Porter, 285–97. Chichester, W. Susx., England: John Wiley and Sons, 2014.

Bernofsky, Susan, Bonnie Chau, Jonathan Cohen, et al. "The 2023 Manifesto on Literary Translation." PEN America, 2023. https://pen.org/report/translation-manifesto/. Accessed January 25, 2024.

Beylin, Marek. "Patriotyczna poprawność." *Dialog,* no. 8 (1996): 147–49.

Biegajło, Bartłomiej. "Three Different Versions of *A Clockwork Orange* in the Polish Cultural Milieu." *Acta Philologica* 39 (2011): 136–42.

Bieńkowski, Zbigniew. "W sprawie Baudelaire'a." *Literatura na świecie,* no. 164 (1985): 354–57.

Blogrys. "Pomarańcza Tony'ego." August 1, 2009. https://blogrys.wordpress.com/2009/08/01/pomarancza-tonyego/. Accessed May 8, 2015.

Bloomfield, Camille. "Deep Dante." *Ridondante: L'Oplepo per il sommo, Biblioteca Oplepiana,* no. 49 (2021). https://camillebloomfield.com/deep-dante/. Accessed November 11, 2024.

Bloomfield, Camille, Rachel Galvin, and Pablo Martín Ruiz. "Acts de fundación de l'Outranspo." *MLN* 131, no. 4 (September 2016): 985–92.

Bloomfield, Camille, and Lily Robert-Foley. "Tweetranslating Trump: Outranspo's 'Bad Translations' of Trump's Tweets." *Contemporary French and Francophone Studies* 21, no. 5 (October 2017): 469–76.

Boethius, Anicius Manlius Severinus. *Troost-medecijne-wynckel der zedighe wysheyt.* Translated by Adrianus de Buck. Bruges: Lucas vanden Kerchove Boekdrukker, 1653.

Bohlman, Andrea F. *Musical Solidarities: Political Action and Music in Late Twentieth-Century Poland*. Oxford: Oxford University Press, 2020.
Bojarska, Anna. "Muzyka a walka klas." *Nowe książki*, nos. 2–3 (1992): 61–63.
Bök, Christian. *Eunoia*. Toronto: Coach House Books, 2001.
Bök, Christian. "Five Translations of Arthur Rimbaud's 'Voyelles.'" In *Eunoia*, rev. ed., 84–85. Toronto: Coach House Books, 2009.
Borkent, Mike. "At the Limits of Translation? Visual Poetry and Bashō's Multimodal Frog." *Translation and Literature* 25, no. 2 (Summer 2016): 189–212.
Borodo, Michał. *Translation, Globalization and Younger Audiences: The Situation in Poland*. Oxford: Peter Lang, 2017.
Brammall, Sheldon. "Translation Kits." *Cambridge Quarterly* 50, no. 2 (June 2021): 194–98.
Brecht, Bertolt. "An die Nachgeborenen / To Those Born Later." Translated by Team Translation (John Willett, Ralph Manheim, and Erich Fried). In *Bertolt Brecht: Poetry and Prose*, edited by Reinhold Grimm and Caroline Molina y Vedia, 70–79. New York: Continuum, 2003.
Brecht, Bertolt. *Brecht on Theatre: The Development of an Aesthetic*. Edited and translated by John Willett. London: Methuen, 1964.
Brecht, Bertolt. *Gesammelte Werke in acht Bänden*. Vol. 4. Frankfurt am Main: Suhrkamp Verlag, 1967.
Brecht, Bertolt. *Poems 1913–1956*. Edited by John Willett and Ralph Manheim. London: Methuen, 1976.
Brecht, Bertolt. *Postylla domowa*. Translated by Robert Stiller. Warsaw: Państwowy Instytut Wydawniczy, 1988.
Brecht, Bertolt. "Rozwiązanie." Translated by Ryszard Krynicki. *Region Środkowo-Wschodni NSZZ "Solidarność": Biuletyn związkowy* 35 (1981): 1.
Brecht, Bertolt. "Utwory śpiewane z *Opery za trzy grosze*." Translated by Jacek St. Buras. *Literatura na świecie*, nos. 418–419 (2006): 167–75, 219–43, 285–303, 325–32.
Brecht, Bertolt. "Wiersze." Translated by Jakub Ekier, Andrzej Kopacki, and Piotr Sommer. *Literatura na świecie*, nos. 418–419 (2006): 167–75, 219–43, 285–303, 325–32.
Brecht, Bertolt. *Wiersze wybrane*. Translated by Lech Pijanowski. Warsaw: Państwowy Instytut Wydawniczy, 1954.
Brecht, Bertolt. "Wyłącznie przez ten zamęt." Translated by Jakub Ekier. In *Ten cały Brecht*, edited by Andrzej Kopacki, translated by Jacek St. Buras, Jakub Ekier, Andrzej Kopacki, and Piotr Sommer, 57. Wrocław: Biuro Literackie, 2012.
Brecht, Bertolt. "Wyłącznie z powodu narastającego nieporządku." Translated by Piotr Sommer. In *Ten cały Brecht*, edited by Andrzej Kopacki, translated by Jacek St. Buras, Jakub Ekier, Andrzej Kopacki, and Piotr Sommer, 150. Wrocław: Biuro Literackie, 2012.
Briggs, Kate. *This Little Art*. London: Fitzcarraldo Editions, 2017.
Broński, Maciej (aka Wojciech Skalmowski). "1985: Inny zmierzch zachodu." *Przegląd Poznański* 1 (1988). Reprinted from *Kultura paryska* 3, no. 450 (1985): 127–30.
Brown, Hilda M. "Reading 'The Drowned Girl': A Brecht Poem and Its Contexts." In *Empedocles' Shoe: Essays on Brecht's Poetry*, edited by Tom Kuhn and Karen Leeder, 71–88. London: Methuen, 2002.
Brzezina, Maria. *Stylizacja rosyjska: Stylizacja językowa i inne ewokanty rosyjskości w utworach literackich ukazujących okres zaborów*. Warsaw: Energeia, 1997.

Brzostowska-Tereszkiewicz, Tamara. *Modernist Translation: An Eastern European Perspective; Models, Semantics, Functions*. Frankfurt am Main: Peter Lang, 2016.

Büchler, Alexandra, and Giulia Trentacosti. "Publishing Translated Literature in the United Kingdom and Ireland 1990–2012, Statistical Report." Literature across Frontiers, May 2015. https://www.lit-across-frontiers.org/wp-content/uploads/2013/03/Translation-Statistics-Study_Update_May2015.pdf. Accessed June 6, 2022.

Buras, Jacek St. "Pod urokiem buntownika." In *Ten cały Brecht*, edited by Andrzej Kopacki, translated by Jacek St. Buras, Jakub Ekier, Andrzej Kopacki, and Piotr Sommer, 46–50. Wrocław: Biuro Literackie, 2012.

Burgess, Anthony. *A Clockwork Orange*. Harmondsworth, England: Penguin Books, 1982.

Burgess, Anthony. "A Clockwork Orange Resucked." In *A Clockwork Orange*, ix–xv. New York: W. W. Norton, 1986.

Burgess, Anthony. *Mechaniczna pomarańcza* [Wersja R]. Translated by Robert Stiller. Kraków: Etiuda, 1999.

Burgess, Anthony. *Mechaniczna pomarańcza* [Wersja R, two parts]. Translated by Robert Stiller. *Fantastyka*, no. 83 (1989): 1–47; and *Fantastyka*, no. 84 (1989): 48–88.

Burgess, Anthony. *Mechaniczna pomarańcza: Edycja specjalna*. Translated by Robert Stiller. Kraków: Vis-à-Vis Etiuda, 2017.

Burgess, Anthony. *Nakręcana pomarańcza* [Wersja A]. Translated by Robert Stiller. Kraków: Etiuda, 1999.

Burgess, Anthony. "Nakręcana pomarańcza na nowo wyssana." Translated by Robert Stiller. In Anthony Burgess, *Nakręcana pomarańcza* [Wersja A], 195–99. Kraków: Etiuda, 1999.

Burgess, Anthony. *Sprężynowa pomarańcza* [Wersja N]. Translated by Robert Stiller. Unpublished manuscript, 2016.

Burt, Stephen. *The Poem Is You: 60 Contemporary American Poems and How to Read Them*. Cambridge, MA: Belknap Press of Harvard University Press, 2016.

Cai, Zong-qi, and Shengqing Wu. "Introduction: Emotion, Patterning, and Visuality in Chinese Literary Thought and Beyond." *Journal of Chinese Literature and Culture* 6, no. 1 (April 2019): 1–14.

Cameron, David. *Flowers of Bad*. New York: Unbelievable Alligator; Ugly Duckling Presse, 2007.

Campbell, Madeleine, and Ricarda Vidal, eds. *The Experience of Translation: Materiality and Play in Experiential Translation*. Abingdon, UK: Routledge, 2024.

Carson, Anne. "A Fragment of Ibykos Translated Six Ways." *London Review of Books* 34, no. 21 (November 8, 2012): 42–43. https://www.lrb.co.uk/v34/n21/anne-carson/a-fragment-of-ibykos-translated-six-ways. Accessed March 15, 2014.

Carson, Anne. "Variations on the Right to Remain Silent." In *Nay Rather*, 4–41. London: Sylph Editions, 2014.

Casanova, Pascale. *The World Republic of Letters*. Translated by Malcolm DeBevoise. Cambridge, MA: Harvard University Press, 2007.

Cassin, Barbara, ed. *Dictionary of Untranslatables: A Philosophical Lexicon*. Translation edited by Emily Apter, Jacques Lezra, and Michael Wood. Princeton, NJ: Princeton University Press, 2014.

Cassin, Barbara, ed. *Vocabulaire européen des philosophies: Le dictionnaire des intraduisibles*. Paris: Éditions du Seuil; Dictionnaires Le Robert, 2004.

Cassin, Barbara, and Rebecca Walkowitz. "Translating the Untranslatable: An Interview with Barbara Cassin." *Public Books*, June 15, 2014. https://www.publicbooks.org/translating-the-untranslatable-an-interview-with-barbara-cassin/. Accessed March 15, 2020.

Cavanagh, Clare. "O *Chirurgicznej precyzji* Stanisława Barańczaka." *Zeszyty literackie*, no. 65 (1999): 153–66.

Cavanagh, Clare. "Postcolonial Poland." *Common Knowledge* 10, no. 1 (2004): 82–92.

Cayley, John. "The Translation of Process." *Amodern* 8 (2017), "Translation-Machination." http://amodern.net/article/the-translation-of-process/. Accessed March 20, 2020.

Cetera, Anna. *Enter Lear: The Translator's Part in Performance*. Warsaw: Warsaw University Press, 2008.

Cetera, Anna. "'Suit the Word to the Action': Shakespeare's *Richard II* (2004); A Case of (Meta)Translation?" In *Shakespeare in Europe: History and Memory*, edited by Marta Gibińska and Agnieszka Romanowska, 239–52. Kraków: Jagiellonian University Press, 2005.

Cetera, Anna. "Sztuka przekładu." *Kontakt: Dwutygodnik internetowy*, February 23, 2015. https://magazynkontakt.pl/prof-cetera-wlodarczyk-sztuka-przekladu/. Accessed May 15, 2017.

Cetera, Anna. "Translating the Translated: The Evergreen Classics Storm the Publishing Market Again." *Brno Studies in English* 35, no. 1 (2009): 103–14.

Cetera-Włodarczyk, Anna. "'The Gates of the Day': Shakespeare in the Post-Holocaust Poetry and Translation of Roman Brandstaetter." In *Perspectives on Shakespeare in Europe's Borderlands*, edited by Mădălina Nicolaescu, Oana-Alis Zaharia, and Andrei Nae, 105–26. Bucharest: University of Bucharest Press, 2020.

Cetera-Włodarczyk, Anna. "Shakespeare in Purgatory: (Re)Writing the History of the Post-War Reception." *Theatralia* 24, no. 1 (March 2021): 17–32.

Cheesman, Tom, Kevin Flanagan, and Stephan Thiel. "Version Variation Visualization: Translation Array Prototype 1." Cronfa, Swansea University, 2012. https://cronfa.swan.ac.uk/Record/cronfa11958. Accessed September 21, 2020.

Cheesman, Tom, Kevin Flanagan, Stephan Thiel, Jan Rybicki, Robert S. Laramee, Jonathan Hope, and Avraham Roos. "Multi-Retranslation Corpora: Visibility, Variation, Value, and Virtue." *Digital Scholarship in the Humanities* 32, no. 4 (December 2017): 739–60.

Chuang Tzu, Allison Cobb, Jen Coleman, and Burton Watson. "Come Out of Works: A Physical Translation." *Chain* 10 (2003): 45–50.

Chwin, Stefan. "Die Polen haben begründete Angst vor Auslöschung." *Die Welt*, November 6, 2015. https://www.welt.de/kultur/article148497066/Die-Polen-haben-begruendete-Angst-vor-Ausloeschung.html. Accessed May 30, 2016.

Cieślak, Jacek. "Teatr ograniczonego zaufania." *Rzeczpospolita*, no. 287 (2005): 15.

Cobb, Allison, and Jen Coleman. Translators' note to "Come Out of Works: A Physical Translation." *Chain* 10 (2003): 50–51.

Collins, Martha. Introduction to *Into English: Poems, Translations, Commentaries*, edited by Martha Collins and Kevin Prufer, vii–xi. Minneapolis: Graywolf Press, 2017.

Collins, Martha, and Kevin Prufer, eds. *Into English: Poems, Translations, Commentaries*. Minneapolis: Graywolf Press, 2017.

Cook, Nicholas. *Beyond the Score: Music as Performance*. Oxford: Oxford University Press, 2013.

Cooperson, Michael. "Note on the Translation." In *Impostures: Fifty Rogue's Tales Translated Fifty Ways*, by al-Ḥarīrī, xxix–xlv. New York: New York University Press, 2020.

Croft, Jennifer, and Mark Haddon. "#TranslatorsOnTheCover: Sign the Open Letter." Society of Authors, September 30, 2021. https://www2.societyofauthors.org/translators-on-the-cover/. Accessed October 1, 2021.

Cronin, Michael. *Translation in the Digital Age*. Abingdon, UK: Routledge, 2013.

Czapliński, Przemysław. *Polska do wymiany: Późna nowoczesność i nasze wielkie narracje*. Warsaw: W.A.B., 2009.

Czapliński, Przemysław. *Powrót centrali: Literatura w nowej rzeczywistości*. Kraków: Wydawnictwo Literackie, 2007.

Czermińska, Małgorzata. "On the Turning Point: Polish Prose, 1989–1995." *Canadian Slavonic Papers* 39, nos. 1–2 (March–June 1997): 109–22.

Czytelnicy i Fantastyka. "Sondaż VI: Ocena powieści." *Nowa Fantastyka*, no. 1 (1990): 66–67.

Dąmbska-Prokop, Urszula. "Tłumacz-kanibal?" *Między oryginałem a przekładem* 3 (1997): 71–78.

Daniel, Krystyna. "The Church-State Situation in Poland after the Collapse of Communism." *Brigham Young University Law Review*, no. 2 (1995): 401–19.

Dante Alighieri. "Piekło: Pieśń II." Translated by Stanisław Barańczak, Tomasz Łubieński, Julian Korsak, Antoni Stanisławski, J. M. Michał Kowalski, Alina Świderska, and Edward Porębowicz. *Literatura na świecie*, no. 285 (1995): 46–61, 96–133.

Dante Alighieri and Caroline Bergvall. "VIA (48 Dante Variations)." *Chain* 10 (Fall 2003): 55–59.

Dawidowicz-Chymkowska, Olga. "Zestawienia retrospektywne 1944–2017." In *Rynek wydawniczy w liczbach*. Warsaw: Biblioteka Narodowa, 2017.

Dayan, Peter. "Different Music, Same Condition: Hofstadter and Lyotard." *Thinking Verse* 2 (2012): 9–26.

Deane-Cox, Sharon. *Retranslation: Translation, Literature and Reinterpretation*. London: Bloomsbury, 2014.

De la Torre, Mónica. *Repetition Nineteen*. Brooklyn: Nightboat Books, 2020.

Deleuze, Gilles, and Félix Guattari. *A Thousand Plateaus: Capitalism and Schizophrenia*. Translated by Brian Massumi. Minneapolis: University of Minnesota Press, 1987.

Deleuze, Gilles, and Félix Guattari. "What Is a Minor Literature?" Translated by Robert Brinkley. *Mississippi Review* 11, no. 3 (Winter–Spring 1983): 13–33.

Dembeck, Till. "Oberflächenübersetzung: The Poetics and Cultural Politics of Homophonic Translation." *Critical Multilingualism Studies* 3, no. 1 (2005): 7–25.

Derrida, Jacques. "What Is a 'Relevant' Translation?" Translated by Lawrence Venuti. *Critical Inquiry* 27, no. 2 (Winter 2001): 174–200.

Dobrołęcki, Piotr, Kuba Frołow, Łukasz Gołębiewski, Joanna Hetman-Krajewska, Ewa Tenderenda-Ożóg, Tomasz Nowak, and Piotr Miodunka. "Raport o stanie kultury 'Przemysł książki.'" Warsaw: Ministry of Culture and National Heritage of Poland, 2008.

Draesner, Ulrike, and Tom Cheesman, trans. *Twin Spin: 17 Shakespeare Sonnets Radically Translated by Ulrike Draesner and Radically Back-Translated by Tom Cheesman*. Oxford: Taylor Institution Library, 2016.

Duncan, Dennis. *The Oulipo and Modern Thought*. Oxford: Oxford University Press, 2019.

Duncan, Dennis. "Translating Constrained Literature." *Translation Studies* 12, no. 1 (April 2019): 124–26.

Dunne, Conor Brendan. "Prismatic Translation 2.0: A (Potential) Future for Avant-Garde Translation." In *Avant-Garde Translation*, edited by Alexandra Lukes, 121–46. Leiden: Brill, 2023.

Düring, Michael. "Obraz Związku Radzieckiego w prozie Tadeusza Konwickiego." In *Obraz Rosji w literaturze polskiej*, edited by Jerzy Fiećko and Krzysztof Trybuś, 409–22. Poznań: Poznańskiego Towarzystwa Przyjaciół Nauk, 2012.

Dworkin, Craig, and Kenneth Goldsmith, eds. *Against Expression: An Anthology of Conceptual Writing*. Evanston, IL: Northwestern University Press, 2011.

Edmond, Jacob. *Make It the Same: Poetry in the Age of Global Media*. New York: Columbia University Press, 2019.

Ekier, Jakub. "Ani czyjś, ani swój, ani jeden." In *Ten cały Brecht*, edited by Andrzej Kopacki, translated by Jacek St. Buras, Jakub Ekier, Andrzej Kopacki, and Piotr Sommer, 76–89. Wrocław: Biuro Literackie, 2012.

Eliot, T. S. "Animula." Translated by Krzysztof Karasek and Krzysztof Boczkowski. *Literatura na świecie*, no. 110 (1980): 243, 247.

Emmerich, Karen. *Literary Translation and the Making of Originals*. London: Bloomsbury, 2017.

Encyclopaedia Britannica. "La Marseillaise: French National Anthem." February 12, 2024. https://www.britannica.com/topic/La-Marseillaise. Accessed February 16, 2024.

Encyklopedia PWN. "Wydawnictwa polskie." https://encyklopedia.pwn.pl/haslo/wydawnictwo;4012022.html. Accessed May 5, 2023.

Etkind, Efim. *Notes of a Non-Conspirator*. Translated by Peter France. Oxford: Oxford University Press, 1978.

Etkind, Efim. "Le problème de la métatraduction." *Revue d'esthétique* 12 (1986): 17–22.

Evans, Robert O. "Nadsat: The Argot and Its Implications in Anthony Burgess' *A Clockwork Orange*." *Journal of Modern Literature* 1, no. 3 (March 1971): 406–10.

Fernández Long, Hilario. "Lengua y poesía china: Poesía de la Dinastía Tang." *Diario de Poesía* 10, no. 39 (September 1996): 32–33.

Flaubert, Gustave. *Pani Bovary* [fragment]. Translated by Magdalena Tulli and Ryszard Engelking. *Literatura na świecie*, nos. 1–2 (2003): 97–143.

Fordoński, Krzysztof. "Polski przekład literacki w warunkach wolnego rynku: Spojrzenie nieobiektywne, prowokacyjne i stronnicze." *Przekładaniec: A Journal of Literary Translation*, no. 7 (Spring–Summer 2000): 131–49.

Gajek, Konrad. "Wstęp. Brecht w Polsce." In *Dramaty*, by Bertolt Brecht, iii–lxxxix. Wrocław: Zakład im. Ossolińskich, 1976.

Ginczanka, Zuzanna, and Joanna Trzeciak Huss. "Poems Translated from the Polish and Introduced by Joanna Trzeciak Huss: Side Commentary, and: Senses, and: Declaration, and: Joyful Mythology, and: Pride, and: Ascension of the Earth, and: At Sea." *Hopkins Review* 15, no. 3 (Summer 2022): 167–75.

Ginter, Anna. "Powieść jako przygoda lingwistyczna: *A Clockwork Orange* A. Burgessa w przekładach na język polski i rosyjski." *Acta Universitatis Lodziensis: Folia Linguistica Rossica* 2 (2006): 175–91.

Goh, Robbie B. H. "'Clockwork' Language Reconsidered: Iconicity and Narrative in Anthony Burgess's *A Clockwork Orange*." *Journal of Narrative Theory* 30, no. 2 (Summer 2000): 263–80.

Goldsmith, Kenneth. "Why Conceptual Writing? Why Now?" In *Against Expression: An Anthology of Conceptual Writing*, edited by Craig Dworkin and Kenneth Goldsmith, xvii–xxii. Evanston, IL: Northwestern University Press, 2011.

Goliński, Jerzy, Jerzy Koenig, Jan Kott, Tadeusz Nyczek, Ireneusz Krzemiński, and Krzysztof Wolicki. "Dwie rozmowy wokół Brechta." *Dialog* 37, no. 7 (1999): 109–22.

Gondowicz, Jan. "Pegaz wysuwa macki." *Gazeta wyborcza*, no. 30 (February 5, 1996): 15.

Göransson, Johannes. "Toward a Sensationalistic Theory of Translation." *Evening Will Come: A Monthly Journal of Poetics*, no. 51 (March 2015). https://www.thevolta-org.zulaufdesign.com/ewc51-jgoransson-p1.html. Accessed September 7, 2024.

Górnikiewicz, Joanna. "L'image de la rose dans les douze traductions polonaises du 'Petit Prince' d'Antoine de Saint-Exupéry." In *Le Petit Prince et les amis au pays des traductions: Études dédiées à Urszula Dąmbska-Prokop*, edited by Joanna Górnikiewicz, Iwona Piechnik, and Marcela Świątkowska, 128–47. Kraków: Księgarnia Akademicka, 2012.

Gowin, Jarosław. *Kościół w czasach wolności 1989–1999*. Kraków: Znak, 1999.

Grass, Delphine. *Translation as Creative-Critical Practice*. Cambridge: Cambridge University Press, 2023.

Grass, Delphine, and Lily Robert-Foley. "The Translation Memoir: An Introduction." *Life Writing* 21, no. 1 (2024): 1–9.

Grünbein, Durs. "Lekcja podstawy czaszki." Translated by Jakub Ekier and Andrzej Kopacki. *Literatura na świecie*, no. 320 (1998): 5–9.

Gruszczyński, Piotr. "Robić zło." *Tygodnik powszechny* 20 (2005): 22.

Hahn, Daniel. *Catching Fire: A Translation Diary*. Edinburgh: Charco Press, 2022.

Haltof, Marek. *The Cinema of Krzysztof Kieślowski: Variations on Destiny and Chance*. New York: Wallflower Press, 2004.

Ḥarīrī, al-. *Impostures: Fifty Rogue's Tales Translated Fifty Ways*. Translated and edited by Michael Cooperson. New York: New York University Press, 2020.

Harvey, Rosalind. "On Anne Carson, 'Nay Rather.'" *Times Literary Supplement*, no. 5789 (March 14, 2014): 27.

Havel, Rudolf, and Alois Bejblík. *Havran: Šestnáct českých překladů*. Prague: Odeon, 1985.

Haven, Cynthia L., ed. *Czesław Miłosz: Conversations*. Jackson: University Press of Mississippi, 2006.

Haven, Cynthia L. "Shaman and Poet Stanisław Barańczak (1946–2014)—'A Fantastic Genius, Indeed.'" *Book Haven*, October 25, 2015. http://bookhaven.stanford.edu/2015/10/shaman-and-poet-stanislaw-baranczak-1946-2014-a-fantastic-genius-indeed/. Accessed March 10, 2020.

Hawkes, David. *A Little Primer of Tu Fu*. Oxford: Oxford University Press, 1967.

Hawkey, Christian. Preface to *Ventrakl*, 5–9. New York: Ugly Duckling Presse, 2013.

Hayot, Eric R. J. "The Strange Case of Araki Yasusada: Author, Object." *PMLA* 120, no. 1 (January 2005): 66–81.

Heilbron, Johan, and Gisèle Sapiro. "Translation: Economic and Sociological Perspectives." In *The Palgrave Handbook of Economics and Language*, edited by Victor Ginsburgh and Shlomo Weber, 373–402. Basingstoke, Hants., England: Palgrave Macmillan, 2016.

Heine, Heinrich. "Lorelei." Translated by Robert Stiller and Leopold Lewin. *Literatura na świecie*, no. 120 (1981): 356–57.

Herling-Grudziński, Gustaw. *Inny świat: Zapiski sowieckie.* Warsaw: Czytelnik, 1992.
Hermans, Theo. *The Conference of the Tongues.* Manchester: St. Jerome Publishing, 2007.
Hermans, Theo. *Metatranslation: Essays on Translation and Translation Studies.* Abingdon, UK: Routledge, 2023.
Heydel, Magda. "Dialog światów." *Tygodnik powszechny,* December 17, 2012. https://www.tygodnikpowszechny.pl/dialog-swiatow-18080. Accessed April 15, 2014.
Heydel, Magda. "Od Donne'a do Lennona." *Tygodnik powszechny,* January 4, 2015, 70–73.
Heydel, Magda. "Tłumaczenie jako wojna światów?" *Przekładaniec: A Journal of Literary Translation,* nos. 22–23 (2009): 333–40.
Heydel, Magda. "*Wybacz, że znowu zawracam Ci głowę*: Rzut oka na wybrane listy Stanisława Barańczaka do Czesława Miłosza." In *Ameryka Barańczaka,* edited by Sylwia Karolak and Ewa Rajewska, 31–52. Kraków: Universitas, 2018.
Hiley, Jim. *Theatre at Work: The Story of the National Theatre's Production of Brecht's "Galileo."* London: Routledge and Kegan Paul, 1981.
Hoffmann, Krzysztof. "500 literatur, 500 światów." *Czas kultury,* no. 4 (2013): 151–55.
Hofstadter, Douglas R. *Rhapsody on a Theme by Clément Marot.* Cedar City, UT: Grace A. Tanner Center for Human Values, 1996.
Hofstadter, Douglas R. *Le Ton beau de Marot: In Praise of the Music of Language.* New York: Basic Books, 1997.
Holca, Irina. "Sawako Nakayasu Eats Sagawa Chika: Translation, Poetry, and (Post)Modernism." *Japanese Studies* 41, no. 3 (2021): 379–94.
Hoover, Paul. *Sonnet 56.* TrenchArt: The Maneuvers Series. Los Angeles: Les Figues Press, 2009.
Horáček, Josef. "Pedantry and Play: The Zukofsky *Catullus.*" *Comparative Literature Studies* 51, no. 1 (2014): 106–31.
Hsiao, Li-Ling. "Wang Wei's and Su Shi's Conceptions of 'Painting within Poetry.'" *Southeast Review of Asian Studies* 35 (2013): 178–89.
Hsu, Hua. "When White Poets Pretend to Be Asian." *New Yorker,* September 9, 2015. https://www.newyorker.com/books/page-turner/when-white-poets-pretend-to-be-asian. Accessed March 15, 2019.
Hubert, Rosario. *Disoriented Disciplines: China, Latin America, and the Shape of World Literature.* Evanston, IL: Northwestern University Press, 2024.
Hur, Anton. "An Interview with Anton Hur." By Jimin Kang. *Oxonian Review,* May 24, 2022. https://oxonianreview.com/articles/an-interview-with-anton-hur. Accessed March 17, 2023.
Isakowicz-Zaleski, Tadeusz. *Księża wobec bezpieki na przykładzie archidiecezji krakowskiej.* Kraków: Znak, 2007.
Jacobs, Adriana X. "Extreme Translation." In *Prismatic Translation,* edited by Matthew Reynolds, 154–70. Oxford: Legenda, 2019.
Jacobs, Adriana X. "The Go-Betweens: Leah Goldberg, Yehuda Amichai, and the Figure of the Poet-Translator." In *A Companion to Translation Studies,* edited by Sandra Bermann and Catherine Porter, 479–91. Chichester, W. Susx., England: John Wiley and Sons, 2014.
Jameson, Fredric. *Brecht and Method.* London: Verso, 1998.
Jandl, Ernst. *Reft and Light: Poems by Ernst Jandl with Multiple Versions by American Poets.* Edited and translated by Rosmarie Waldrop et al. Providence, RI: Burning Deck, 2000.

Janion, Maria. "Poland between the West and East." Translated by Anna Warso. *Teksty drugie* 1 (2014): 13–33.

Janion, Maria, and Marta Figlerowicz. "Uncanny Slavdom." *PMLA* 138, no. 1 (January 2023): 110–26.

Jarniewicz, Jerzy. "After Babel: Translation and Mistranslation in Contemporary British Poetry." *European Journal of English Studies* 6, no. 1 (2002): 87–104.

Jarzębski, Jerzy. "The Conflict of Generations in Contemporary Polish Prose." In *Polish Literature in Transformation*, edited by Ursula Phillips, 25–34. Zurich: LIT Verlag, 2013.

Jarzębski, Jerzy. "The Decade in Prose." Translated by Karen Underhill. *Chicago Review* 46, nos. 3–4 (January 2000): 344–56.

Jarzębski, Jerzy. "Formy pesymizmu." In *Ćwiczenia z rozpaczy: Pesymizm w prozie polskiej po 1985 roku*, edited by Jerzy Jarzębski and Jakub Momro, 11–23. Kraków: Universitas, 2011.

Jędrzejewski, Jan. "The Polish Translations of Thomas Hardy." *Thomas Hardy Journal* 7, no. 1 (February 1991): 50–62.

Jerome (Hieronymus), Eusebius Sophronius. "Who Was the First Lying Author?" Translated by Moses Hadas. In *Western Translation Theory: From Herodotus to Nietzsche*, edited by Douglas Robinson, 30. Manchester: St. Jerome Publishing, 1997.

Joyce, James. "Anna Livia Plurabella." Translated by Maciej Słomczyński. *Literatura na świecie*, no. 25 (1973): 242–67.

Joyce, James. *Ulisses* [fragment]. Translated by Maciej Słomczyński and Józef Czechowicz. *Literatura na świecie*, no. 25 (1973): 242–67.

Kaczorowska, Monika. *Przekład jako kontynuacja twórczości własnej: Na przykładzie wybranych translacji Stanisława Barańczaka z języka angielskiego*. Kraków: Universitas, 2011.

Kalmar, Ivan. *White but Not Quite: Central Europe's Illiberal Revolt*. Bristol: Bristol University Press, 2022.

Kandziora, Jerzy. *Ocalony w gmachu wiersza: O poezji Stanisława Barańczaka*. Warsaw: Instytut Badań Literackich Polskiej Akademii Nauk, 2007.

Karasek, Krzysztof. "Od tłumacza." *Literatura na świecie*, no. 110 (1980): 244–45.

Karkowski, Czesław. "Niepoważne dokonania poważnego poety." *Polish Review*, April 25, 1996, 16.

Kaszyński, Stefan H., ed. *W cieniu Lorelei: Antologia wierszy poetów Republiki Federalnej Niemiec*. Poznań: Wydawnictwo Poznańskie, 1978.

Kaszyński, Stefan H., and Wachowiak Eugeniusz, eds. *Antologia wierszy poetów Niemieckiej Republiki Demokratycznej*. Poznań: Wydawnictwo Poznańskie, 1979.

Knopf, Jan. *Gelegentlich: Poesie; Ein Essay über die Lyrik Bertolt Brechts*. Frankfurt am Main: Suhrkamp Verlag, 1996.

Kopacki, Andrzej. "Śliwa pod okiem." In *Ten cały Brecht*, edited by Andrzej Kopacki, translated by Jacek St. Buras, Jakub Ekier, Andrzej Kopacki, and Piotr Sommer, 127–38. Wrocław: Biuro Literackie, 2012.

Kopacki, Andrzej. "Zanim." In *Ten cały Brecht*, edited by Andrzej Kopacki, translated by Jacek St. Buras, Jakub Ekier, Andrzej Kopacki, and Piotr Sommer, 5–7. Wrocław: Biuro Literackie, 2012.

Kopp, Kristin. *Germany's Wild East: Constructing Poland as Colonial Space*. Ann Arbor: University of Michigan Press, 2012.

Kornhauser, Julian. "Polityka i przekład." In *Polnische und deutsche Poesie in modernen Übersetzungen*, edited by Ulrike Jekutsch and Andrzej Sulikowski, 243–49. Szczecin: PPH Zapol Dmochowski Sobczyk, 2002.

Korwin-Mikke, Janusz. "Stiller i inni." *Literatura na świecie*, no. 111 (1980): 347–53.

Kowalski, Marek Arpad. "Mechaniczna, czyli nakręcona." *Najwyższy czas!* 37 (2006): xliii.

Kronfeld, Chana. *On the Margins of Modernism: Decentering Literary Dynamics*. Berkeley: University of California Press, 1996.

Krynicki, Ryszard. "Nazywać rzeczy po imieniu." Interview by Grażyna Banaszkiewicz. In *Gdybym wiedział: Rozmowy z Ryszardem Krynickim*, edited by Anna Krzywania, 17–38. Wrocław: Biuro Literackie, 2015.

Krynicki, Ryszard. "Podziękowanie." *Zeszyty literackie* 3, no. 71 (2000): 142–44.

Krzemiński, Adam. "Efekt obcości." *Dialog* 43, no. 2 (1998): 70–76.

Kubińska, Olga, and Wojciech Kubiński. "Osobliwy przypadek dwóch polskich przekładów *A Clockwork Orange*: Wycieczka w kulturowe uinnienie." In *Przekładając nieprzekładalne*, edited by Olga Kubińska and Wojciech Kubiński, 67–76. Gdańsk: University of Gdańsk Press, 2004.

Lee, Tong King. *Experimentalism in Translation: Exploring Play in Poetics*. Cambridge: Cambridge University Press, 2022.

Lee, Tong King. "Translation and Copyright: Towards a Distributed View of Originality and Authorship." *The Translator* 26, no. 3 (2020): 241–56.

Legault, Paul. "Who Is Writing Is the Translator: A Review of *Ventrakl*." *Jacket2*, June 28, 2011. https://jacket2.org/reviews/who-writing-translator. Accessed March 15, 2019.

Leighton, Lauren G. *Two Worlds, One Art: On Literary Translation in Russia and America*. DeKalb: Northern Illinois University Press, 1991.

Leśniewska, Maria. "Projekt wydania całych *Kwiatów zła* w serii dwujęzycznej Wydawnictwa Literackiego." *Literatura na świecie*, no. 164 (1985): 350–53.

Levý, Jiří. *The Art of Translation*. Translated by Patrick Corness. Edited by Zuzana Jettmarová. Amsterdam: John Benjamins, 2011.

Lewin, Leopold. "O przekładzie 'Lorelei.'" *Literatura na świecie*, no. 120 (1981): 352–54.

Lindseth, Jon A., and Alan Tannenbaum, eds. *Alice in a World of Wonderlands: The Translations of Lewis Carroll's Masterpiece*. Vol. 2, *Back-Translations*. New Castle, DE: Oak Knoll Press, 2015.

Loffredo, Eugenia, and Manuela Perteghella. "The Genesis of the Project: A Translational Journey." In *One Poem in Search of a Translator: Rewriting "Les Fenêtres" by Apollinaire*, edited by Eugenia Loffredo and Manuela Perteghella, 13–27. Oxford: Peter Lang 2009.

Loffredo, Eugenia, and Manuela Perteghella, eds. *One Poem in Search of a Translator: Rewriting "Les Fenêtres" by Apollinaire*. Oxford: Peter Lang, 2009.

Looby, Robert. *Censorship, Translation and English Language Fiction in People's Poland, 1944–1989*. Leiden: Brill Rodopi, 2015.

Looby, Robert. "Underground Fiction Translation in People's Poland, 1976–89." In *Translation under Communism*, edited by Christopher Rundle, Anne Lange, and Daniele Monticelli, 379–409. Cham, Switzerland: Palgrave Macmillan, 2022.

Loseff, Lev. *On the Beneficence of Censorship: Aesopian Language in Modern Russian Literature*. Translated by Jane Bobko. Munich: Otto Sanger, 1984.

Luboń, Arkadiusz. *Przekraczanie obcości: Problemy przekładu w programach i twórczości poetów Nowej Fali*. Rzeszów: Wydawnictwo Uniwersytetu Rzeszowskiego, 2013.

Lukes, Alexandra, ed. *Avant-Garde Translation*. Leiden: Brill, 2023.

M. M. "Anthony Burgess." *Gazeta wyborcza*, no. 240 (2003): 15–24.

Maciejewski, Janusz. "Stereotyp Rosji i Rosjanina w polskiej literaturze i świadomości społecznej." *Więź* 2 (1998): 183–97.

Makaryk, Irena. "Russia and the Former Soviet Union." In *The Oxford Companion to Shakespeare*, 2nd ed., edited by Michael Dobson, Stanley Wells, Will Sharpe, and Erin Sullivan, 474–76. Oxford: Oxford University Press, 2015.

Małecka, Aleksandra, and Piotr Marecki. "Ubu Król przepuszczony przez Tłumacza Google: Co z tego wyszło?" Interview by Łukasz Grzesiczak. *Gazeta wyborcza*, no. 13 (January 18, 2016). https://krakow.wyborcza.pl/krakow/1,44425,19491231,ubu-krol-przepuszczony-przez-tlumacza-google-co-z-tego-wyszlo.html. Accessed February 1, 2016.

Marzec, Jowita. "1001 drobiazgów o książkach i czytaniu." Lubimyczytać, March 9, 2019. http://lubimyczytac.pl/aktualnosci/publicystyka/11610/1001-drobiazgow-o-ksiazkach-i-czytaniu. Accessed May 8, 2015.

Masłowska, Dorota. *Snow White and Russian Red*. Translated by Benjamin Paloff. New York: Grove Atlantic, 2006.

Masłowski, Paweł. "Brecht (dla) literatów: O najnowszych przekładach wierszy poety." *Kultura liberalna*, no. 176 (May 22, 2012). https://kulturaliberalna.pl/2012/05/22/maslowski-brecht-dla-literatow-o-najnowszych-przekladach-wierszy-poety/. Accessed January 12, 2023.

Matheson, William. "Ten Variations on Bashō's 'Pond and Frog' Haiku." In *One Hundred Frogs: From Renga to Haiku to English*, by Hiroaki Sato, 170–72. New York: Weatherhill, 1983.

Mathews, Harry. "35 Variations on a Theme from Shakespeare." *Shiny* 9–10 (1999): 97–101.

McCaffery, Steve. *The Basho Variations*. Toronto: Book*hug Press, 2007.

McCullough, Christopher J. "From Brecht to Brechtian: Estrangement and Appropriation." In *The Politics of Theatre and Drama*, edited by Graham Holderness, 120–33. London: Palgrave Macmillan, 1992.

Michniewicz, Agnieszka. "Iha-ha!" *Podteksty: Czasopismo kulturalnonaukowe* 2, no. 20 (2010). http://katalog.czasopism.pl/index.php/Podteksty_2_(20)_2010. Accessed January 7, 2013.

Michoński, Cezary. "Kognitywne aspekty przekłady na podstawie tłumaczenia neologizmów w powieści Anthony Burgessa *Mechaniczna pomarańcza*." In *Język a kultura*, edited by Iwona Nowakowska-Kempna, 261–78. Wrocław: Wiedza o Kulturze, 1992.

Miłosz, Czesław. "Stanisław Barańczak (born 1946)." In *Postwar Polish Poetry*, 3rd ed., edited by Czesław Miłosz, 183. Berkeley: University of California Press, 1983.

Moc, Anna. "Nowe polskie prawo autorskie a kolejne tłumaczenia na naszym rynku wydawniczym, czyli przygody Pinocchia lub Pinokia." *Między oryginałem a przekładem* 3 (1997): 181–89.

Monk, Ian. "35 Variations on a Theme from Translatology." *MLN* 131, no. 4 (September 2016): 993–97.

Moore, David Chioni. "Is the Post- in Postcolonial the Post- in Post-Soviet? Toward a Global Postcolonial Critique." *PMLA* 116, no. 1 (January 2001): 111–28.

Moore, Nicholas. *Spleen: Thirty-One Versions of Baudelaire's "Je suis comme le roi."* London: Blacksuede Book Press; Menard Press, 1973.

Morawiec, Elżbieta. "Paskudna książka Barańczaka." *Tygodnik Solidarność*, no. 37 (1995): 16.

Morrison, Blake. Introduction to *A Clockwork Orange*, by Anthony Burgess, vii–xxiv. Harmondsworth, England: Penguin Books, 1982.

Mościcki, Paweł. "Ten cały Brecht: Przekłady i szkice." *Dwutygodnik*, no. 80 (2012). https://www.dwutygodnik.com/artykul/3460-ten-caly-brecht-przeklady-i-szkice.html. Accessed January 13, 2013.

Nabokov, Vladimir. "Problems of Translation: *Onegin* in English." *Partisan Review* 22, no. 4 (Fall 1955): 469–512.

Nägele, Rainer. "Phantom of a Corpse: Ophelia from Rimbaud to Brecht." *MLN* 117, no. 5 (December 2002): 1069–82.

Nakayasu, Sawako. "I Choose to Eat and Sleep." *Poetry Foundation Blog*, November 26, 2014. https://www.poetryfoundation.org/featured-blogger/71710/i-choose-to-eat-and-sleep. Accessed May 19, 2016.

Nakayasu, Sawako. "An Interview on Sawako Nakayasu and Sagawa Chika's 'Mouth Eats Color: Translations, Anti-Translations, and Originals' (Rogue Factorial, 2011)." By Thomas Fink. *Galatea Resurrects (A Poetry Engagement)*, no. 18, May 18, 2012. http://galatearesurrection18.blogspot.co.uk/2012/05/thomas-fink-interviews-sawako-nakayasu.html. Accessed May 15, 2017.

Nakayasu, Sawako. "An Interview with Sawako Nakayasu." By Lindsey Webb. *Asymptote*, July 15, 2016. http://www.asymptotejournal.com/interview/an-interview-sawako-nakayasu/. Accessed May 15, 2017.

Nakayasu, Sawako. Introduction to *The Collected Poems of Chika Sagawa*, i–xv. Translated by Sawako Nakayasu. Ann Arbor, MI: Canarium Books, 2015.

Nakayasu, Sawako. Introduction to *The Collected Poems of Chika Sagawa*, xi–xxv. Translated by Sawako Nakayasu. New York: Modern Library, 2020.

Nakayasu, Sawako, with Chika Sagawa. *Mouth: Eats Color; Sagawa Chika Translations, Anti-Translations, and Originals*. Tokyo: Rogue Factorial, 2011.

Neumann, Iver B. "Russia as Central Europe's Constituting Other." *East European Politics and Societies* 7, no. 2 (Spring 1993): 349–69.

Nicolaescu, Mădălina. "Translations of Shakespeare in Romania—Going from Local to Global?" *Perspectives* 20, no. 3 (2012): 285–96.

Niżyńska, Joanna. "The Impossibility of Shrugging One's Shoulders: O'Harists, O'Hara, and Post-1989 Polish Poetry." *Slavic Review* 66, no. 3 (2007): 463–83.

Owen, Ruth J. "Voicing the Drowned Girl: Poems by Hilde Domin, Ulla Hahn, Sarah Kirsch, and Barbara Köhler in the German Tradition of Representing Ophelia." *Modern Language Review* 102, no. 3 (July 2007): 781–92.

Parker, Stephen. *Bertolt Brecht: A Literary Life*. London: Bloomsbury, 2014.

Paszkiet, Sławomir. *Raport o sytuacji tłumaczy literackich w Polsce*. Kraków: Polish Book Institute, 2011.

Paszylk, Bartłomiej. *The Pleasure and Pain of Cult Horror Films: An Historical Survey*. Jefferson, NC: McFarland, 2009.

Pawłowski, Roman. "Nakręcana pomarańcza we Wrocławiu: Przemoc nasza powszednia." *Gazeta wyborcza*, no. 95 (2005): 19.

Paz, Octavio, Jacques S. Roubaud, Eduardo Sanguineti, and Charles Tomlinson. *Renga: A Chain of Poems*. New York: George Braziller, 1971.

Perloff, Marjorie. "The Oulipo Factor: The Procedural Poetics of Christian Bök and Caroline Bergvall." *Jacket*, no. 23 (August 2003). http://jacketmagazine.com/23/perlof-oulip.html. Accessed December 15, 2013.

Perloff, Marjorie. *Unoriginal Genius: Poetry by Other Means in the New Century*. Chicago: University of Chicago Press, 2010.

Piechowski, Jerzy. "Chichot przed lustrem." *Ład*, no. 51 (1995): 7.

Pijanowski, Lech. "Od wydawnictwa." In *Wiersze wybrane*, by Bertolt Brecht, edited and translated by Lech Pijanowski, 5. Warsaw: Państwowy Instytut Wydawniczy, 1954.

Pokorn, Nike K. *Post-Socialist Translation Practices: Ideological Struggle in Children's Literature*. Amsterdam: John Benjamins, 2012.

Polish Book Institute. "The Polish Book Market." Reports, 2006–2016. https://instytutksiazki.pl/en/polish-book-market,7,reports,18.html. Accessed June 6, 2022.

Pound, Ezra. "Pieśń I." Translated by Andrzej Sosnowski and Leszek Engelking. *Literatura na świecie*, no. 234 (1991): 46–51.

Pożar, Przemysław. "Panowie i państwo na Szekspirze: Czesław Miłosz and Roman Brandstaetter jako tłumacze Szekspirowskich dzieł w Polskiej Rzeczpospolitej Ludowej." *Przekładaniec: A Journal of Literary Translation*, no. 45 (2022): 110–32.

Prynne, J. H. "Difficulties in the Translation of 'Difficult' Poems." *Cambridge Literary Review* 1, no. 3 (Easter, 2010): 151–66.

Przybylak, Feliks. "Bertolt Brecht." *Akcent*, no. 6 (1998): 6.

Puszkin, Aleksander. "Prorok." Translated by Józef Łobodowski, Julian Tuwim, and Witold Chwalewik. *Literatura na świecie*, no. 186 (1987): 373–75.

Pym, Anthony. *Method in Translation History*. Manchester: St. Jerome Publishing, 1998.

Queneau, Raymond. *Exercices de style*. Paris: Éditions Gallimard, 1947.

Rambelli, Paolo. "Pseudotranslation." In *Routledge Encyclopedia of Translation Studies*, 3rd ed., edited by Mona Baker and Gabriela Saldanha, 441–45. Abingdon, UK: Routledge, 2020.

Rancière, Jacques. "The Politics of Literature." *SubStance* 33, no. 1 (2004): 10–24.

Ray, Philip E. "Alex Before and After: A New Approach to Burgess's *A Clockwork Orange*." *Modern Fiction Studies* 27, no. 3 (1981): 479–87.

Reichert, Klaus, and Fritz Senn, eds. *Finnegans Wake: Gesammelte Annäherungen*. Frankfurt am Main: Suhrkamp Verlag, 1989.

Reynolds, Matthew. *The Poetry of Translation: From Chaucer & Petrarch to Homer & Logue*. Oxford: Oxford University Press, 2012.

Reynolds, Matthew, "Prismatic Jane Eyre." 2016–2020. https://prismaticjaneeyre.org/. Accessed September 21, 2020.

Reynolds, Matthew, et al. *Prismatic Jane Eyre: Close-Reading a World Novel across Languages*. Cambridge: Open Book Publishers, 2023.

Richards, I. A. *Mencius on the Mind: Experiments in Multiple Definition*. Edited by John Constable. London: Kegan Paul, Trench, Trübner, 1932.

Rimbaud, Artur. "Statek pijany." Translated by Zenon Miriam Przesmycki, Adam Ważyk, and Józef Waczków. *Literatura na świecie*, no. 132 (1982): 290–300.

Robert-Foley, Lily. *Experimental Translation: The Work of Translation in the Age of Algorithmic Production*. London: Goldsmiths Press, 2024.

Robert-Foley, Lily. "The Politics of Experimental Translation: Potentialities and Preoccupations." *English: The Journal of the English Association* 69, no. 267 (Winter 2020): 401–19.

Robinson, Douglas. *The Experimental Translator*. Cham, Switzerland: Palgrave Macmillan, 2023.

Robinson, Douglas. "Philo Judeus." In *Western Translation Theory: From Herodotus to Nietzsche*, edited by Douglas Robinson, 12–13. Manchester: St. Jerome Publishing, 1997.

Robinson, Douglas. *The Translator's Turn*. Baltimore: Johns Hopkins University Press, 1991.

Rödder, Andreas. "Es gibt eine neue Angst vor Deutschland." Interview by Jan D. Walter and Catherine Martens. Deustche Welle, November 18, 2018. https://www.dw.com/de/r%C3%B6dder-es-gibt-eine-neue-angst-vor-deutschland/a-46341234. Accessed June 18, 2019.

Romanowski, Andrzej. "Granice śmiechu." *Tygodnik powszechny*, no. 32 (1995): 14.

Rose, Adrienne H. K. "Retranslating Ibykos and Li Bai: Experimental, Rhizomatic, Multi-Media Transformations." *Intertexts* 19, nos. 1–2 (2015): 83–98.

Rosenthal, Mira. "Czesław Miłosz's Polish School of Poetry in English Translation." *Przekładaniec: A Journal of Literary Translation*, no. 25 (2011): 221–28.

Rudnytska, Nataliia. "Translation and the Formation of the Soviet Canon of World Literature." In *Translation under Communism*, edited by Christopher Rundle, Anne Lange, and Daniele Monticelli, 39–71. Cham, Switzerland: Palgrave Macmillan, 2022.

Rudolf, Krzysztof Filip. "Wielogłosowa powieść w translatorskim wielogłosie, czyli *Anglicy na pokładzie* Matthew Kneale'a." *Przekładaniec: A Journal of Literary Translation*, no. 32 (2016): 128–44.

Rudolf, Krzysztof Filip, and Michał Alenowicz. "Słowo od redaktorów przekładu." In *Anglicy na pokładzie*, by Matthew Kneale, translated by Michał Alenowicz et al., 11. Gdańsk: Wiatr od Morza, 2014.

Rundle, Christopher, Anne Lange, and Daniele Monticelli, eds. *Translation under Communism*. Cham, Switzerland: Palgrave Macmillan, 2022.

Rutgers Radical Translation Collective. "Project Details." Rutgers University, School of Arts and Sciences. https://translation.rutgers.edu/project-details/648-rutgers-radical-translation-collective. Accessed February 10, 2024.

Sadkowski, Wacław. "Nie bójcie się mechanicznego jeża! Glosa do pamfletu Roberta Stillera." *Literatura na świecie* 2, no. 34 (1974): 203–7.

Sadkowski, Wacław. "Znamię trudności." *Literatura na świecie*, no. 196 (1987): 351–53.

Sato, Hiroaki. *One Hundred Frogs: From Renga to Haiku to English*. New York: Weatherhill, 1983.

Saussy, Haun. *Great Walls of Discourse and Other Adventures in Cultural China*. Cambridge, MA: Harvard University Press, 2001.

Schebera, Jürgen. *Kurt Weill: An Illustrated Life*. Translated by Caroline K. Murphy. New Haven, CT: Yale University Press, 1995.

Schulte, Rainer, ed. *Comparative Perspectives: An Anthology of Multiple Translations*. New York: American Heritage Custom Publishing Group, 1994.

Schulte, Rainer. "Profile: The Göttingen Approach to Translation Studies." *Translation Review* 53, no. 1 (1997): 1–4.

Scott, Clive. *Literary Translation and the Rediscovery of Reading*. Cambridge: Cambridge University Press, 2012.

Scott, Clive. *Translating the Perception of Text: Literary Translation and Phenomenology*. Oxford: Legenda, 2012.

Siedlecka, Joanna. *Kryptonim "Liryka": Bezpieka wobec literatów*. Warsaw: Prószyńska i S-ka, 2009.

Silberman, Marc, Steve Giles, and Tom Kuhn. Introduction to *Brecht on Theatre*, by Bertolt Brecht, 3rd ed., 1–7. London: Bloomsbury, 2015.

Simon, Claude. *Nauka o rzeczach (Czołówka)* [fragment]. Translated by Zofia Chądzyńska and Beata Geppert. *Literatura na świecie*, nos. 184–185 (1986): 132–36.

Skarga, Barbara (aka Wiktoria Kraśniewska). *Po wyzwoleniu… 1944–1956*. Poznań: W drodze, 1990.

Sławiński, Janusz. "Trzeci obieg." In *Słownik terminów literackich*, edited by Michał Głowiński, Teresa Kostkiewiczowa, Aleksandra Okopień-Sławińska, and Janusz Sławiński, 593. Wrocław: Zakład Narodowy im. Ossolińskich, 2000.

Smith, Helen. "Matter in the Margins." In *Thresholds of Translation: Paratexts, Print, and Cultural Exchange in Early Modern Britain (1473–1660)*, edited by Marie-Alice Belle and Brenda M. Hosington, 27–50. Cham, Switzerland: Palgrave Macmillan, 2018.

Smółkowa, Teresa. "Pokaż język." Interview by Mariusz Szczygieł. *Gazeta wyborcza*, no. 34 (1995). https://wyborcza.pl/duzyformat/7,127290,12676670,pokaz-jezyk.html. Accessed February 3, 2014.

Śniecikowska, Beata. "'Niepoważna' twórczość Stanisława Barańczaka—czy *Pegaz zdębiał z Chirurgiczną precyzją*?" *Fraza*, nos. 1–2 (2000): 243–53.

Sobolewski, Tadeusz. "Poetics of Chance (Krzysztof Kieślowski)." In *Being Poland: A New History of Polish Literature and Culture Since 1918*, edited by Tamara Trojanowska, Joanna Niżyńska, and Przemysław Czapliński, with the assistance of Agnieszka Polakowska, 723–28. Toronto: University of Toronto Press, 2018.

Som, Brandon. *The Tribute Horse*. Brooklyn: Nightboat Books, 2014.

Sommer, Piotr. "Literatura jest tłumaczeniem (rozmowa z Ryszardem Krynickim, Bronisławem Majem, Czesławem Miłoszem, Piotrem Sommerem i Marianem Stalą." *Na głos*, no. 11 (1993): 13–27.

Sommer, Piotr. "Tak, czyli jak? (O kilkunastu zdaniach B. B.)." In *Ten cały Brecht*, edited by Andrzej Kopacki, translated by Jacek St. Buras, Jakub Ekier, Andrzej Kopacki, and Piotr Sommer, 165–75. Wrocław: Biuro Literackie, 2012.

Sommer, Piotr. "Tkać i pruć." *Tygodnik powszechny*, no. 16 (2002): 12.

Sommer, Piotr. "Tłumacząc miniatury Charlesa Reznikoffa." In *Po stykach*, 220–40. Gdańsk: Słowo/Obraz Terytoria, 2005.

Sommer, Piotr. "Według Brechta." In *Czynnik liryczny*, 48. Kraków: Oficyna Wydawnicza, 1986. Reprinted in *Za pozwoleniem*, nos. 11–12 (1988): 1.

Southerden, Francesca. "The Voice Astray: Caroline Bergvall's Dante." *Postmedieval: A Journal of Medieval Cultural Studies* 15 (2024): 87–117. https://doi.org/10.1057/s41280-023-00299-7 . Accessed February 23, 2024.

Spišiaková, Eva. *Queering Translation History: Shakespeare's Sonnets in Czech and Slovak Transformations*. New York: Routledge, 2021.

Spurlin, William J., ed. "The Gender and Queer Politics of Translation: Literary, Historical, and Cultural Approaches." Special issue, *Comparative Literature Studies* 51, no. 2 (2014).

Stala, Marian. "Barańczak w krainie słoni." *Plus Minus*, no. 36 (1995): 12.

Staniewska, Anna. "Maciej Słomczyński vs. William Shakespeare." *Puls* 24 (1984–1985): 126–40.

Stiller, Robert. "Brecht po polsku, czyli cwaniactwo i tchórzostwo." *Wiadomości kulturalne*, no. 6 (1998): 7.
Stiller, Robert. "Burgess a sprawa polska." In Anthony Burgess, *Mechaniczna pomarańcza* [Wersja R], translated by Robert Stiller, 219–39. Kraków: Etiuda 1999.
Stiller, Robert. "Co dał nam los." Interview. *Życie Warszawy*, no. 214 (1991): 1.
Stiller, Robert. "Co robić z tą pomarańczą?" *Notatnik teatralny*, no. 38 (2005): 86–91.
Stiller, Robert. "Do redaktora naczelnego (6 maja 1980)." *Literatura na świecie*, no. 110 (1980): 345.
Stiller, Robert. "Horror-Show, czyli bój się Pan jeża!" *Literatura na świecie*, no. 34 (1974): 186–201.
Stiller, Robert. "Kilka słów od tłumacza." In Anthony Burgess, *Nakręcana pomarańcza* [Wersja A], translated by Robert Stiller, 217–18. Kraków: Etiuda 1999.
Stiller, Robert. *Kilka słów o przekładach za trzy grosze*. Lublin: Teatr im. J. Ostrewy, 1986.
Stiller, Robert. "Kilka sprężyn z nakręcanej pomarańczy [1991]." In Anthony Burgess, *Mechaniczna pomarańcza* [Wersja R], translated by Robert Stiller, 134–60. Warsaw: Wema, 1991.
Stiller, Robert. "Kilka sprężyn z nakręcanej pomarańczy [1999]." In Anthony Burgess, *Mechaniczna pomarańcza* [Wersja R], translated by Robert Stiller, 191–218. Kraków: Etiuda 1999.
Stiller, Robert. "Krzyżyk na ks. Chrostowskim." *Trybuna*, no. 137 (1998): 6.
Stiller, Robert. Letter to the editors. *Nowe książki*, no. 4 (1997): 81.
Stiller, Robert. Letter to the editors. *Nowe książki*, no. 7 (1997): 73.
Stiller, Robert. "Przekład jako własność niczyja." *Literatura na świecie*, no. 72 (1977): 322–35.
Stiller, Robert. "Słowa to małe piwko." Interview by Małgorzata Matuszewska. *Gazeta wyborcza*, no. 95 (2005): 9.
Stiller, Robert. Translator's note. *Fantastyka*, no. 8 (1989): 2.
Szaruga, Leszek. "Idiotyzm doskonałości." *Opcje*, no. 1 (1996): 138–39.
Szaruga, Leszek. "Poezje Brechta." *Nowe książki*, no. 11 (2012): 31–32.
Szczęsna, Joanna. "Poeta oburęczny, czyli przypadek Stanisława Barańczaka." In *Pegaz zdębiał: Poezja nonsensu a życie codzienne; Wprowadzenie w prywatną teorię gatunków*, by Stanisław Barańczak, 5–78. Warsaw: Agora, 2017.
Szymanska, Kasia. "Can Mirrors Be Said to Have Memories? A Polish Katerina Brac Looks Back at Her English Reflection." *PMLA* 132, no. 2 (March 2017): 427–33.
Szymanska, Kasia. "'Into English': A Collection of World Literature That Debunks Age-Old Translation Myths." *Words without Borders*, December 2017. https://www.wordswithoutborders.org/book-review/into-english-a-collection-of-world-literature-that-debunks-age-old-myth. Accessed December 29, 2017.
Szymańska, Katarzyna. "Miłość do trzech pomarańczy Roberta Stillera." *Przekładaniec: A Journal of Literary Translation*, no. 33 (2016): 235–52.
Szymanska, Kasia. "A Second Nature: Barańczak Translates Barańczak for America." *Slavic and East European Journal* 64, no. 3 (Fall 2020): 475–96.
Szymańska, Kasia. "Stanisław Barańczak: Between Autonomy and Support." In *Going East: Discovering New and Alternative Traditions in Translation Studies*, edited by Larisa Schippel and Cornelia Zwischenberger, 449–68. Berlin: Frank and Timme, 2016.
Szymańska, Katarzyna. "Ten cały Brecht (Burasa, Ekiera, Kopackiego i Sommera), czyli rzecz o metaprzekładzie literackim." In *Strategie translatorskie od modernizmu do (post)*

postmodernizmu, edited by Piotr Fast and Justyna Pisarska, 167–82. Katowice: Wydawnictwo Naukowe "Śląsk," 2014.
Tahir Gürçağlar, Şehnaz. "Pseudotranslation on the Margin of Fact and Fiction." In *A Companion to Translation Studies*, edited by Sandra Bermann and Catherine Porter, 516–27. Chichester, W. Susx., England: John Wiley and Sons, 2014.
Tahir Gürçağlar, Şehnaz. "Retranslation." In *Routledge Encyclopedia of Translation Studies*, 3rd ed., edited by Mona Baker and Gabriela Saldanha, 484–89. Abingdon, UK: Routledge 2020.
Taylor, Karen L. *The Facts on File Companion to the French Novel*. New York: Facts on File, 2007.
Thalmayr, Andreas. *Das Wasserzeichen der Poésie*. Nördlingen, Germany: Greno, 1985.
Thirlwell, Adam, ed. *Multiples: 12 Stories in 18 Languages by 61 Authors*. London: Portobello Books, 2013.
Thompson, Ewa. *Imperial Knowledge: Russian Literature and Colonialism*. Westport, CT: Greenwood Press, 2000.
Thomson, Philip. *The Poetry of Brecht: Seven Studies*. Chapel Hill: University of North Carolina Press, 1989.
Three Percent. "Three Percent: A Resource for International Literature at the University of Rochester." http://www.rochester.edu/College/translation/threepercent/. Accessed March 23, 2019.
Tichomirowa, Wiktoria. "Literatury łagrowej obszary nieodsłonięte: Kulturowe oblicza Innego." *Teksty drugie* 4 (2008): 90–100.
Tivnan, Tom. "Translated Fiction Enjoys Golden Age as Manga Surge Boosts Sector to Record High." *The Bookseller*, March 13, 2022. https://www.thebookseller.com/features/translated-fiction-enjoys-golden-age-as-manga-surge-boosts-sector-to-record-high. Accessed June 6, 2022.
Trotman, Nat. "Found in Translation." *Deutsche Guggenheim Magazine* 18 (Winter 2012): 4–17.
Trubicka, Hanna. "Stanisław Barańczak jako krytyk języka: Wokół dwóch esejów z tomu *Poezja i duch Uogólnienia*." *Przestrzenie teorii*, no. 16 (2011): 133–56.
Tuwim, Julian. "Ball at the Opera." Translated by Madeline G. Levine and Steven I. Levine. *Polish Review* 30, no. 1 (1985): 5–23.
Tuwim, Julian. "Mieszkańcy." In *Biblia cygańska i inne wiersze*, 182. Warsaw: J. Mortkowicz, 1933.
Tuziak, Andrzej. "Przypadki pewnej pomarańczy." *Tak i nie* 31 (1989): 10.
Tymoczko, Maria. "Post-Colonial Writing and Literary Translation." In *Post-Colonial Translation: Theory and Practice*, edited by Susan Bassnett and Harish Trivedi, 19–40. Abingdon, UK: Routledge, 1999.
Tymoczko, Maria. *Translation in a Postcolonial Context: Early Irish Literature in English Translation*. Manchester: St. Jerome Publishing, 1999.
Ułaszyn, Henryk. *Język złodziejski*. Łódź: Łódzkie Towarzystwo Naukowe, 1951.
Valles, Alissa. Introduction to *Our Life Grows*, by Ryszard Krynicki, translated by Alissa Valles, viii–xiii. New York: New York Review Books, 2018.
Van Heuckelom, Kris. *Polish Migrants in European Film, 1918–2017*. Cham, Switzerland: Palgrave Macmillan, 2019.

Vassileva-Karagyozova, Svetlana. *Coming of Age under Martial Law: The Initiation Novels of Poland's Last Communist Generation.* Rochester, NY: University of Rochester Press, 2015.

Venuti, Lawrence. *Contra Instrumentalism: A Translation Polemic.* Lincoln: University of Nebraska Press, 2019.

Venuti, Lawrence. "On a Universal Tendency to Debase Retranslations; or, The Instrumentalism of a Translation Fixation." *PMLA* 138, no. 3 (2023): 598–615.

Venuti, Lawrence. "Retranslations: The Creation of Value." In *Translation Changes Everything: Theory and Practice,* 96–115. Abingdon, UK: Routledge, 2013.

Venuti, Lawrence. *The Scandals of Translation: Towards an Ethics of Difference.* London: Routledge, 1998.

Venuti, Lawrence. "Spokesperson, Intellectual, and . . . More? On the New and Shifting Role of the Translator." *Literary Hub,* April 5, 2023. https://lithub.com/spokesperson-intellectual-and-more-on-the-new-and-shifting-role-of-the-translator/. Accessed April 6, 2023.

Venuti, Lawrence. *The Translator's Invisibility: A History of Translation.* Abingdon, UK: Routledge, 1995.

Venuti, Lawrence. *The Translator's Invisibility: A History of Translation.* 2nd ed. Abingdon, UK: Routledge, 2008.

Von Flotow, Luise, and Hala Kamal, eds. *The Routledge Handbook of Translation, Feminism and Gender.* Abingdon, UK: Routledge, 2020.

Waczków, Józef. "Ryzyko." *Literatura na świecie,* no. 164 (1985): 358–64.

Wade, Sidney. "13 Ways of Looking at Wang Wei." *Subtropics* 20–21 (Spring–Summer 2016): 174–78.

Waldrop, Rosmarie. Editor's note to *Reft and Light: Poems by Ernst Jandl with Multiple Versions by American Poets,* edited and translated by Rosmarie Waldrop et al., 8. Providence, RI: Burning Deck, 2000.

Walkowitz, Rebecca L. *Born Translated: The Contemporary Novel in an Age of World Literature.* New York: Columbia University Press, 2015.

Waszakowa, Krystyna. "Derywowane anglicyzmy jako wyraz ekspansji słownictwa potocznego i środowiskowego w języku mediów ostatniego ćwierćwiecza." *Slavia Meridionalis* 9 (2009): 89–102.

Wat, Aleksander. "If the Word 'Exists.'" Translated by Czesław Miłosz. In *Postwar Polish Poetry: An Anthology,* edited by Czesław Miłosz, 23. Berkeley: University of California Press, 1965.

Weinberger, Eliot, and Octavio Paz. *19 Ways of Looking at Wang Wei: How a Chinese Poem Is Translated.* New York: Moyer Bell, 1987.

Weinberger, Eliot, and Octavio Paz. *19 Ways of Looking at Wang Wei (with More Ways).* New York: New Directions, 2016.

Weissbort, Daniel. "His Own Translator: Joseph Brodsky." Review of *So Forth,* by Joseph Brodsky. *Translation and Literature* 7, no. 1 (1998): 101–12.

Wershler, Darren. Introduction to *Verse and Worse: Selected and New Poems of Steve McCaffery (1989–2009),* ix–xii. Waterloo, ON: Wilfrid Laurier University Press, 2010.

Whitaker, Peter. *Brecht's Poetry: A Critical Study.* Oxford: Clarendon Press, 1985.

Wierzbińska, Joanna. "Burgess Translated in Polish." *Anthony Burgess Newsletter* 7 (2004): 15–24.

Wilkins, Ernest H. "A Note on Translations of the *Divine Comedy* by Members of the Dante Society." *Annual Report of the Dante Society, with Accompanying Papers*, no. 75 (1957): 41–44.

Williams, C. K. "Murzynka." Translated by Krystyna Dąbrowska and Andrzej Szuba. *Literatura na świecie*, nos. 450–451 (2009): 88–89, 128.

Wirth, Adam. *Siedem prób*. Warsaw: Czytelnik, 1962.

Wolff, Larry. *Inventing Eastern Europe: The Map of Civilization on the Mind of the Enlightenment*. Stanford, CA: Stanford University Press, 1994.

Wróblewski, Andrzej. "Trudny charakter pisarza." *Życie Warszawy*, no. 30 (1989): 5.

Wysocki, Leszek. Translator's note to *Anthony Burgess: Mechaniczna pomarańcza*. Spectator's brochure. Teatr Ludowy, Kraków, 2011.

Zabalbeascoa, Patrick, and Montse Corrius. "How Spanish in an American Film is Rendered in Translation: Dubbing 'Butch Cassidy and the Sundance Kid' in Spain." *Perspectives* 22, no. 2 (August 2012): 255–70.

Zawistowski, Władysław. "Po nastajaszczy horror szoł." *Życie Warszawy*, no. 224 (1991): 7.

Zessin-Jurek, Lidia. "Forgotten Memory? Vicissitudes of the Gulag Remembrance in Poland." In *Life Writing and Politics of Memory in Eastern Europe*, edited by Simona Mitroiu, 45–65. New York: Palgrave Macmillan, 2015.

Zięba, Maciej. "Zapiski z kruchty: Wywołany do tablicy." *Tygodnik powszechny*, no. 37 (1995): 11.

INDEX

Figures are indicated by "f" following page numbers.

Ahmad, Aijaz, 5, 16
Allen, Esther, 170n2
All That Brecht (*Ten cały Brecht*): authorial credit for, 133–34, 189n3; as collaborative effort, 133, 135, 144, 157; cover of, 133, 134f; format of, 134, 140, 144–49; introduction to, 156–58; objectives of, 132, 144; shifting identities revealed in, 162; translation slams and, 150–58
Apollinaire, Guillaume, 16, 34
Appiah, Kwame Anthony, 170n13
Apter, Emily, 14
Aristeas, 1
Arndt, Walter, 45
Ash, Timothy Garton, 138
Asymptote (online journal), 10
avant-garde, 5, 33, 44, 47, 193n6

Bach, Johann Sebastian, 175n40
back-translation, 16
Baker, Richard, 18–20, 22, 30, 46
Balcerzan, Edward, 84
Barańczak, Stanisław: American persona of, 76–77, 179n8; on bezecenzja reviews, 183n61; *Breathing under Water and Other East European Essays*, 77; "The Confusion of Tongues," 180n13; correspondence with Miłosz, 75; on ethical role of poetry, 76; experimental genres and, 79, 180n20; *Fioletowa krowa*, 182n39; *A Fugitive from Utopia*, 77; *God, Trunk, Fatherland*, 80, 180–81n25; "Goodbye, Samizdat," 94; as Harvard University professor, 6, 75, 76, 78; homophonic translation multiples and, 76, 79–80, 82–93, 161–62, 182n58; on inner pluralism, 78, 180n13; "Like a twin with his twin," 94–98; manifestos of, 77, 79, 82, 180n18; New Wave movement and, 77, 180n24; nonsense poetry of, 79–80, 82, 180nn24–25, 183n63; *Pegaz zdębiał*, 180n20, 183n63; play based on works of, 78–79, 180n16; "Poetry and the Spirit of Generalization" speech, 76, 80–81; published translations of Anglophone poets, 79, 180n17; on sound, 82, 182n41; *Surgical Precision*, 181n36; twin-mirror metaphor and, 98; *The Weight of the Body*, 77, 179n5. *See also* "Oratorium Moratorium"
Barnstone, Willis, 58
Barwin, Gary, 32, 33
Bashō, Matsuo, 16, 32–34, 53
Bates, John M., 179n99
Baudelaire, Charles, 48, 58, 142, 170n2
Beaulieu, Derek, 32, 33
Beckett, Samuel, 38–39
Beethoven, Ludwig van, 85
Bellen, Martine, 32
Bellos, David, 3
Benjamin, Walter, 20
Bentley, Eric, 158

Bergvall, Caroline: *Drift*, 50; *Fig*, 25, 26, 172n46; as translation multiplier, 5; in "Translucinación" issue of *Chain* magazine, 32; "VIA: 48 Dante Variations," 19, 25–27, 28*f*, 49–53, 161, 172nn46–47, 172–73nn50–51
Bermann, Sandra, 172n46
Bernstein, Charles, 31–32, 44, 47
biases: aesthetic, 58; Brecht and, 132, 147, 151; class-based, 97; in English language, 43; ideological, 62; limitations of, 98; linguistic exclusion and, 48, 49; of Polish underground publishing, 69, 179n99; political, 154; in publishing industry, 48; racial, 49, 50, 174n6; in selection of variants, 59; xenophobia, 50
Bible, 1–3, 45
Blind Chance (film), 70–71, 72*f*, 73, 95, 162
Bloomfield, Camille, 56
Blyth, R. H., 33
Boethius, 171n22
Bök, Christian, 51, 175n31
Boodberg, Peter A., 21
Borges, Jorge Luis, 122
Borodo, Michał, 67
bpNichol, 33
Brecht, Bertolt: anticommunist translations of poetry by, 69; *Baal*, 192n76; *The Buckow Elegies and Other Poems*, 136; de-ideologization of works, 74; estate of, 67; FBI files of, 38–41; *Hauspostille*, 146, 192n76; instrumentalist readings of, 133, 140, 159, 164; on literal translation, 192n96; musical performances of protest songs, 190n27; New Wave movement and, 136; "On Speaking the Sentences," 147; "On the Drowned Girl," 150–51, 192n76; performance philosophy of, 158–59; "Solely Because of the Increasing Disorder," 150–56; "The Solution," 137, 138*f*; Stiller's translations of, 140, 146–47, 189–90n23, 191n55; *Svendborger Gedichte*, 145, 146; "Theatre for Pleasure or Theatre for Instruction," 159; "To Those Born After," 149; on V-effect, 158–60; "What Are You Waiting For?," 137–38, 138*f*; "When in My White Room at the Charité," 150. See also *All That Brecht*
Brexit referendum (2016), 166
Briggs, Kate, 171n19
Brodsky, Joseph, 67
Brontë, Charlotte, 10, 65, 67
Browne, Laynie, 32
Buck, Adrianus de, 171n22
Buras, Jacek St., 133, 144–45, 149–51, 158
Burgess, Anthony: correspondence with Stiller, 109; Nadsat language invented by, 104–5, 111, 125; *Napoleon Symphony*, 184n28; political mission of, 135. See also *A Clockwork Orange*
Burnett, Frances Hodgson, 67
Bush, George H. W., 81

Calvino, Italo, 29–30
Cameron, David, 45, 47, 193n6
Campos, Augusto de, 31
Carroll, Lewis, 16, 190n32
Carson, Anne, 38–42, 174n78
Casanova, Pascale, 6
Cassin, Barbara, 14, 176n43
Catholic Church, 84, 126–27
Cato, 18
Cavafy, C. P., 147
Cavanagh, Clare, 76, 181n36
censorship, 63–64, 68–70, 92–94, 105–7, 121, 162, 184n22
Cervantes, Miguel de, 46, 122
Cesarco, Alejandro, 5, 29–30, 31*f*
Cetera, Anna, 176n43
Chain (magazine), 31–32, 37–38, 172n46
chance operations, 44, 46
Chopin, Frédéric, 53, 54
Christian National Union, 183n67
Chuang Tzu, 37–38
Clark, T. J., 55
A Clockwork Orange (Burgess): antitotalitarian message of, 106; glossary of terms included in, 105, 111; Ludovico technique

in, 117, 123, 128; movie adaptation of, 103, 107; Nadsat language and, 104–5, 111, 125, 184n21, 187n105; repetitive patterns and recurring images in, 121; Stiller's triple translation project for, 8, 74; version N translation (*A Spring-Assisted Orange*), 100, 127–30, 129f, 184n9. *See also* version A translation; version R translation
Cobb, Allison, 37–38
Cohen, Sharmila, 45
Cold War, 9, 70, 73, 110, 130, 157, 162
Coleman, Jen, 37–38
Coleman, Ornette, 54
Collins, Martha, 57–59
Collodi, Carlo, 67
communist Poland: censorship in, 63–64, 68–70, 92–94, 105–7; labor camp (gulag) testimonies in, 114–16; state-run publishing in, 5, 62–66, 69; suppression of English-language literature in, 178n86; underground publishing in, 63, 68–69, 77, 105, 115, 132, 136, 148, 178–79n96, 179n99
conceptual moments, defined, 17
Cook, Nicholas, 54
Cooperson, Michael, 49
Copyright and Related Rights Act of 1994 (Poland), 67–68
Corrius, Montse, 176n43
Croatian War of Independence, 88
Croft, Jennifer, 57
Czechowicz, Józef, 190n33

Dante: *Divine Comedy*, 26, 30; *Inferno*, 16, 19, 25–30, 52–53, 143; selection for translation multiples, 5
Dayan, Peter, 24
Deane-Cox, Sharon, 59
Dejmek, Kazimierz, 107
Delaunay, Robert, 34
Deleuze, Gilles, 6, 60
democracy: barriers to, 167; capitalist, 119; emerging, 4, 8, 73–74, 80, 162; peaceful transformation into, 91; postcommunist, 62, 73–74; Western, 9, 92

Derrida, Jacques, 15–17, 44, 97, 171n19
Deschner, Karlheinz, 188n138
dialogue of difference approach, 59
Dickinson, Emily, 45
Diepeveen, Leonard, 47
diPalma, Ray, 32
discrimination. *See* biases
Divided Britain (film), 166
Döblin, Alfred, 159
Donne, John, 38–41
Dostoyevsky, Fyodor, 65, 67
The Double Life of Véronique (film), 95–96, 162
Drewermann, Eugen, 188n138
Drunken Boat (website), 10, 170n2
Dubois, Gérard, 73f
Dunayevsky, Isaak, 85
Duncan, Dennis, 176n46
Dunne, Conor Brendan, 173n63
Dworkin, Craig, 172nn46–47

Edmond, Jacob, 44, 50
Ekier, Jakub, 133, 145–46, 149–51, 153–56
Eliot, T. S., 143
Ellis, Steve, 27
Eltit, Diamela, 170–71n15
Emmerich, Karen, 12
Engelking, Ryszard, 190n33
English language: biases within, 43; fixed concepts of, 13; global, 4, 5, 7, 36, 49, 50, 61, 147; incompatibility between Latin and, 18; monolingual boundaries of, 49; percentage of translations published yearly, 4, 169n6; phonetic imitations of words in, 118; Polish youth attracted to, 108, 112; as vehicular language, 14
English-language translation multiples: of classical texts, 12, 16, 18, 25, 27; demand for airtime and visibility, 43; diversity of languages involved in, 5; ethno-specific varieties among, 49–50; racially biased representations in, 174n6
Enzensberger, Hans Magnus, 171n22
equivalence. *See* translation equivalence

ethics: of anticommunist dissident writing, 149; of poetry, 76; of postcolonial translations, 170n13; in postcommunist Poland, 62, 71, 94, 96; of translation multiples, 7, 60–61, 71, 74, 94, 135, 142–44, 165
ethnic conflicts, 81, 88, 91
Etkind, Efim, 176n43
European Union (EU), 74, 85, 127, 129
experimental translation, 7, 11–12, 16, 35, 42, 44–50, 56, 79, 193n6

Fantastyka (magazine), 105–7, 183n7
fascism, 91, 93, 135, 151
Fernández Long, Hilario, 171n26
Figlerowicz, Marta, 186n93
Fink, Thomas, 47
Flaubert, Gustave, 65, 67, 190n33
Fleurs du mal (website), 10, 170n2
Fluxus movement, 44
Foer, Jonathan Safran, 45
Fordoński, Krzysztof, 178n81
fourth wall illusion, 7, 160
framing devices, 52, 175n35
Frank, Armin Paul, 170n4
freedom of speech, 162, 179n99
Friedlander, Benjamin, 32

Galvin, Rachel, 56, 170n2
generalization, spirit of, 76, 80–81, 98
Gibbon, Edward, 30
Gibbons, Reginald, 179n5
Ginczanka, Zuzanna, 15
global English, 4, 5, 7, 36, 49, 61, 147
Goldsmith, Kenneth, 44, 172nn46–47
Gondowicz, Jan, 183n63
Göttingen Project, 170n4
Gould, Glenn, 54, 175n39
Grass, Günter, 66
Guattari, Félix, 6, 60
gulag (labor camps), 114–16

Haddon, Mark, 57
Hahn, Daniel, 15, 170–71n15

Halpern, Daniel, 16, 143
Haltof, Marek, 71
al-Ḥarīrī, 49
Harvey, Rosalind, 41
Hawkes, David, 13
Hawkey, Christian, 45–47, 193n6
Heaney, Seamus, 76–77, 173n51
Heine, Heinrich, 142, 190n42
Herbert, Zbigniew, 77
Herling-Grudziński, Gustaw, 115
Hermans, Theo, 176n43, 177n57
Herrmann, Horst, 188n138
Heydel, Magda, 78, 165
Hitler, Adolf, 145
hoaxes, literary, 46, 48, 94
Hofmann, Michael, 16, 143
Hofstadter, Carol, 23–24
Hofstadter, Douglas R., 19, 22–25, 51, 53, 59
Holca, Irina, 35
Holub, Miroslav, 147
Homer, 16
homophonic translation, 8, 44–46, 50, 176n43
homophonic translation multiples, 8, 73–74, 76, 79–80, 82–93, 161–62, 182n58
Hoover, Paul, 51
Horáček, Josef, 47
Horowitz, Vladimir, 53–54
Houédard, Dom Sylvester, 33
Howitt, Peter, 71
Hughes, Langston, 82
Huss, Joanna Trzeciak, 15

Ibycus, 5, 38–42
identities: group, 126; political, 138, 162; postcommunist, 116; shifting, 161–62, 164; of translators, 24, 26
instrumentalism, 133, 140, 159, 164, 176–77n56
International Translation Day, 57
intralingual translation, 45–46

Jameson, Fredric, 159
Jandl, Ernst, 5, 32–33, 44

Janion, Maria, 186n93
Janouch, Gustav, 38–40
Jerome, 1
Joan of Arc, 40
John of the Cross (saint), 58
John Paul II (pope), 181n25
Johnson, Kent, 45
Joyce, James, 67, 113, 173n54, 186n72, 190n33

Kaczorowska, Monika, 181–82n38
Kaczyński, Lech and Jarosław, 183n69
Kapuściński, Ryszard, 186n93
Karasek, Krzysztof, 143
Karkowski, Czesław, 180n24
Kieślowski, Krzysztof, 70–71, 72f, 73, 95–97, 162
Kirsanov, Semyon, 44
Klata, Jan, 119, 125, 131
Kliszko, Zenon, 107
Kneale, Matthew, 164
Kochanowski, Jan, 76–77
Konwicki, Tadeusz, 106, 113
Kopacki, Andrzej, 133, 146–47, 149–51, 156–58, 191n60
Kornhauser, Julian, 139
Korwin-Mikke, Janusz, 190n32
Kosiński, Jerzy, 69
Kraszewski, Józef Ignacy, 186n73
Kronfeld, Chana, 6
Krynicki, Ryszard, 136–37, 138f
Krynski, Jan, 179n5
Kubrick, Stanley, 103, 107
Kujawinski, Frank, 179n5
Kurosawa, Akira, 55, 73

labor camps (gulag), 114–16
L-A-N-G-U-A-G-E poets, 44
Lanthimos, Yorgos, 60–62
Larkin, Philip, 90
Lasdun, James, 16, 143
Law and Justice Party (PiS), 183n69
law of quantity, 15–17, 43–44, 171n19
Legault, Paul, 45, 46, 170n2

Legman, Gershon, 124
Leśniewska, Maria, 142
Levý, Jiří, 177n57
Lewin, Leopold, 190n42
Lezra, Jacques, 14
Li Bai, 50
Lindseth, Jon A., 16
literary hoaxes, 46, 48, 94
Literatura na świecie (Polish magazine): ethical agenda of, 142–44; extracts from Burgess's *Napoleon Symphony* in, 184n28; on merged translation, 142–43; as platform for circulating world literature in translation, 135; Stiller and, 100, 105, 106, 183n6, 185n38; translation multiples in, 8, 141–43, 164, 177n58, 190n33, 190n42; translation of Joyce's "Anna Livia Plurabella" in, 186n72
Literature across Frontiers, 169nn6–7
Łobodowski, Józef, 190n42
Loffredo, Eugenia, 5, 16, 34–35
London Underground, 39, 41–42
Looby, Robert, 69
Lourie, Richard, 179n5
Low, Jackson Mac, 44–45
Luboń, Arkadiusz, 138, 180n18
Luxemburg, Rosa, 150, 192n76

Macpherson, James, 46
Maguire, Robert A., 179n5
Maher, Ciarán, 25, 172n46
Mallarmé, Stéphane, 23
Man, Paul de, 97
Manheim, Ralph, 191n60
Marks, Alfred H., 33
Marot, Clément, 19, 22–25, 51
"La Marseillaise" (French national anthem), 8, 74, 84–92
Martín Ruiz, Pablo, 56
Masłowska, Dorota, 116, 186n93
Matheson, William, 33, 53
Mathews, Harry, 51
Mazowiecki, Tadeusz, 124
McCaffery, Steve, 32, 33, 53

A Mechanical Orange. See version R translation
metaliterature, 7, 55, 176n43
metatranslation, 55, 61, 176n43
Michoński, Cezary, 185n49
Mickiewicz, Adam, 107
Miłosz, Czesław, 75, 77, 80, 113
modernism, 5, 7, 35, 44, 45, 50–51, 142, 158
Monk, Ian, 56
monolingualism, 4, 36, 49, 50, 113, 165
Montesquieu, 46
Moore, Nicholas, 48
Moure, Erin, 170n2
Mozart, Wolfgang Amadeus, 82–83, 182n41
Müller, Wilhelm, 182n41
multilingualism, 32, 35–36, 49, 111–12
multimodal translation, 33, 34
music, thematic variations in, 22, 52–54
Myslovitz (music group), 131
myths: national, 80, 181n25; of the "original," 54; of posttransition miracle, 123; of Septuagint, 1; of translation, 4, 45

Nabokov, Vladimir, 15, 30
Nakayasu, Sawako: *The Collected Poems of Chika Sagawa*, 35; on experimental translation, 7, 47; *Mouth: Eats Color*, 35–36, 47; on one-to-one relationship, 36, 43; "Promenade," 35–37, 49, 52, 55, 161
Nash, Ogden, 82
nationalism, 81, 90, 91
New Wave movement, 77, 136, 139, 143, 147, 180n24
Nielsen BookScan reports, 169n6

"Oratorium Moratorium" (Barańczak): Beethoven's "Ode to Joy" and, 85, 87; communist/socialist song and, 85, 87, 92; on dialectic support for single viewpoints, 163; French national anthem "La Marseillaise" and, 8, 73–74, 84–92; Harmonia Mundi choir and, 84, 89–90, 92–93; as homophonic translation multiple, 8, 73–74, 76, 79–80, 84–93; *The Merry Widow* and, 85; reprinted version, 82, 92
Orwell, George, 81, 106, 184n28
Orzeszkowa, Eliza, 186n73
Osman, Jena, 37
O'Sullivan, Maggie, 34
Oulipo, 7, 32, 44, 51, 53, 56, 175n31, 176n46
Outranspo, 56, 176nn45–46
Ovid, 16, 143

Paktofonika (music group), 131
Paloff, Benjamin, 116
Parker, Dorothy, 82
Parsons, Thomas William, 173n51
Patterson, Cyril, 34
Patton, Julie, 32
Paz, Octavio, 16, 173n61
PEN America Translation Committee, 57
Penguin Classics' Poets in Translation, 11
Penkethman, John, 18
Perec, Georges, 51
Perloff, Marjorie, 44, 46, 51
Perry, Grayson, 166
Perteghella, Manuela, 5, 16, 34–35
Pessoa, Fernando, 48
Phillips, Carl, 58
Philo Judeus, 1–2
physical translation, 37–38
Pijanowski, Lech, 191n55
Pike, Warburton Mayer, 29*f*
PiS (Law and Justice Party), 183n69
Plato's curse, 54
Poe, Edgar Allan, 177n58
poetry and poetics: avant-garde, 5, 33; baroque manuals for, 171n22; conceptual, 19, 29, 33, 43, 94; ethical role of, 76; haiku, 16, 32–34, 53; metaphysical, 80, 181n28; modernist, 5, 35, 50–51; multilingual, 35–36; nonsense, 76, 79–80, 82, 180nn24–25, 183n63; polyphonic, 181n36; procedural, 51, 52; reiterative, 44; *renga*, 34, 173n61; Romantic, 27; sound in, 44; visual, 20–21, 31–33

Poland: accession to European Union, 74, 127; Balcerowicz Plan in, 118; Borderlands region of, 113; Catholic Church in, 84, 126–27; free-market publishing in, 4, 62–63, 66–68, 107; New Wave movement in, 77, 136, 139, 143, 147, 180n24; number of publishing houses in, 66, 178n81; partition of, 91, 111, 113, 116; percentage of translations published yearly, 4, 62, 169n7, 178n84; Poznań protests in (1956), 135; quota of Syrian refugees allotted to, 129; Roundtable Talks in, 73, 124; Russian language as viewed in, 115, 186n91; Solidarity movement in, 69–71, 73, 77, 80, 124, 132, 137–40, 147–48, 179n99; transition away from totalitarianism, 4, 62. *See also* communist Poland; postcommunist translation multiples

Polański, Roman, 162
Polish language, 79, 104, 108, 110, 128, 130
political tribalism, 8–9, 69, 71, 74, 81, 98, 166–67
Ponglish (language), 113, 117–19, 127, 185n57
Possession (film), 162
postcommunist translation multiples: Copyright Act and, 67–68; ethical resonance of, 71; homophonic, 84–93, 161–62; pluralist, 4–8, 61–63, 73–74, 165; subversive elements of, 6. See also *All That Brecht*; *A Clockwork Orange*; "Oratorium Moratorium"
Pound, Ezra, 21, 44
Poussin, Nicolas, 55
Powell, Bud, 54
prejudice. *See* biases
propaganda, 69, 77, 110, 123, 132, 137, 145, 183n61
Prufer, Kevin, 58
Przesmycki, Zenon Miriam, 190n42
Przybora, Jeremi, 80
pseudotranslation, 45, 46, 174n6, 174n8
publishing industry: biases within, 48; digital, 10–11, 31, 167; free-market, 4, 62–63, 66–68, 102, 107, 162–64; independent presses, 47, 105, 163; percentage of translations published yearly, 4, 62, 169nn6–7, 178n84; politics within, 59, 162; scholarly, 3, 6–7, 11–12, 170n6; single translations favored by, 43; state-run, 5, 62–66, 69, 105, 135, 163; translators' visibility in, 57; underground, 63, 68–69, 77, 105, 115, 132, 136, 148, 163, 178–79n96, 179n99

Puls (Polish magazine), 83, 94, 95
Purcell, Henry, 182n41
Pushkin, Alexander, 15, 190n42
Pym, Anthony, 176n53

Queneau, Raymond, 51–55

Rachmaninoff, Sergei, 22
racism, 49, 50, 174n6
Rancière, Jacques, 166
Rashomon effect, 55
Ravel, Maurice, 23
reading habits, 15, 28, 30, 33, 35, 164
Rees, Goronwy, 40
Reid, Christopher, 45
Reynolds, Matthew, 173n63
Reznikoff, Charles, 147
Richards, I. A., 12–14, 46
Rimbaud, Arthur, 170n2, 175n31, 190n42
Robert-Foley, Lily, 44
Robinson, Douglas, 38
Rose, Adrienne H. K., 176n55
Rudnytska, Nataliia, 64
Russian language, 99, 109–17, 186n91

Sachs, Jeffrey, 118
Sadkowski, Wacław, 141–42
Sagawa, Chika, 5, 35–36, 47, 49
Saint-Exupéry, Antoine de, 67
Satanowski, Jerzy, 180n16
Sato, Hiroaki, 5, 16, 32, 33, 53
Saussy, Haun, 21, 171n27
Schubert, Franz, 182n41
Schulte, Rainer, 170n6

Scott, Clive, 38
Senn, Fritz, 173n54
Septuagint, 1–3
Shakespeare, William, 10, 45, 51, 64–65, 151, 164, 176n43, 177n58
Shaw, Lytle, 32
Shklovsky, Viktor, 159
Simon, Claude, 141
Skarga, Barbara, 115
Słomczyński, Maciej, 65, 190n33
Słowacki, Juliusz, 181n25
Snyder, Gary, 21
Solzhenitsyn, Aleksandr, 114–15
Som, Brandon, 49–50
Sommer, Piotr, 133, 143, 147–51, 153–56, 191n60
Sorrell, Martin, 34
Soviet Union: collapse of, 61, 67, 76, 88; cultural and political influence of, 114; disrespect of individual minor nations, 87; labor camps (gulag) in, 114–16; translation in, 63–65, 169n13. *See also* Cold War
Spahr, Juliana, 37
speech, freedom of, 162, 179n99
Spicer, Jack, 45
spirit of generalization, 76, 80–81, 98
A Spring-Assisted Orange (version N translation), 100, 127–30, 129*f*, 184n9
Stasiuk, Andrzej, 113
Staszewski, Kazik, 190n27
Steiner, George, 48
Stevens, Wallace, 20
Stiller, Robert: Brecht translations, 140, 146–47, 189–90n23, 191n55; on Catholic Church, 126–27; correspondence with Burgess, 109; Heine translations, 142, 190n42; on levels of understanding, 108–9; *Literatura na świecie* and, 100, 105, 106, 183n6, 185n38; on merged translation, 142; Nadsat language and, 108–19, 125–27, 184n21; *A Pesky Orange* translation, 130; as Polish Jewish polyglot, 6, 100; skepticism regarding political narratives, 101; on translation multiples for critical reevaluation of past and present, 163; version N translation (*A Spring-Assisted Orange*), 100, 127–30, 129*f*, 184n9. *See also* version A translation; version R translation
Swensen, Cole, 58
Sze, Arthur, 58
Szirtes, George, 34
Szpotański, Janusz, 94–97
Szymborska, Wisława, 58, 76, 77

Tannenbaum, Alan, 16
Taylor, Karen L., 52
Telephone (online journal), 10, 31
The Tenant (film), 162
thematic variations, 22, 52–54, 82, 175n35
thick translation, 15, 170n13
Thirlwell, Adam, 16, 45
Three Percent program and database (University of Rochester), 56, 169n6
totalitarianism: as barrier to democracy, 167; cultural life under, 77; either/or binary and, 9; legacy of, 70, 74; rhetorical fallacies of, 165; transition away from, 4, 62
translation: back-translation, 16; canonization and, 63–66, 135, 163; cultural trends regarding, 6; as dialogue of the worlds, 165; diaries and memoirs of, 15, 170–71nn14–15; erasure techniques in, 45; experimental, 7, 11–12, 16, 35, 42, 44–50, 56, 79, 193n6; homophonic, 8, 44–46, 50, 176n43; illusions of, 3, 7, 62, 160, 165, 177n57; indirect, 23, 147; institutional constraints governing, 48–50; instrumentalist model of, 176–77n56; intralingual, 45–46; literal, 22, 23, 44, 192n96; literary vs. academic, 12–17; merged, 142–43; metaphor of, 53, 165; metatranslation, 55, 61, 176n43; multimodal, 33, 34; myths related to, 4, 45; norms of, 3, 40, 44, 46, 56; physical, 37–38; postcolonial approaches to, 170n13; pseudotranslation, 45, 46, 174n6, 174n8; retranslation, 3, 9, 21, 56, 59, 64, 165, 170n4, 176n43, 176n53; serial, 11, 19, 31–33; subversive power of, 193n6;

thick, 15, 170n13; transformative power of, 4, 36, 56

translation equivalence: law of quantity and, 15–17, 43–44, 171n19; limitations of, 51–52; one-to-one, 2, 7, 13–14, 36, 52, 56, 61–62; phonetic, 84, 87; somatic (physical), 38; variorum editions and, 12

translation multiples: artistic potential of, 2–3, 6; conceptual moments and, 17; for critical reevaluations of the past and present, 163; dialogue of difference approach to, 59; in digital publishing, 10–11, 31, 167; ethics of, 7, 60–61, 71, 74, 94, 135, 142–44, 165; homophonic, 8, 74, 76, 79–80, 82–93, 161–62, 182n58; in *Literatura na świecie*, 8, 141–43, 164, 177n58, 190n33, 190n42; machine-aided, 193n6; metacritical role of, 18, 55, 133, 151, 158, 166; pluralist, 4–8, 61–63, 73–74, 161, 164–67; polyphonic potential of, 164; reading habits redefined by, 28, 30, 33, 35, 164; in scholarly publishing, 3, 6–7, 11–12, 170n6; shifting identities and, 161–62; spatial relations and, 31, 34, 35; subversive potential of, 44, 50; texture of, 2, 6, 17, 19, 28, 31, 32; traditional studies of, 10–11, 170n4; V-effect in, 159, 160; visualization of, 28–35, 29f, 31f. *See also* English-language translation multiples; postcommunist translation multiples

translation slams, 150–58

translation studies (discipline), 56, 177n57

"Translucinación" (*Chain* magazine), 31–32, 37–38

tribalism, 8–9, 69, 71, 74, 81, 98, 166–67

Trump, Donald, 56

Tulli, Magdalena, 190n33

Tuwim, Julian, 93, 180n20, 182n58, 183n63, 190n42, 192n85

Twain, Mark, 67

twin-mirror metaphor, 98

Tykwer, Tom, 71–73

Tymoczko, Maria, 170n13

Urdu, Ghalib, 16

Valles, Alissa, 58

V-effect, 158–60

Venuti, Lawrence, 57, 67, 176–77nn56–57

version A translation (*A Wind-Up Orange*): afterword of, 103; book cover, 100, 101f; 102–3; circularity of, 121–25; creation and introduction of, 100, 103, 108; explanatory texts for, 103, 184n13; glossary of terms included in, 111; levels of understanding for, 108–9; Nadsat language and, 108–13, 116–19, 125–27; pursuit of the Western lifestyle in, 117; special edition with version R, 100, 102f; stage production of, 119, 120f, 125, 187n107

version N translation (*A Spring-Assisted Orange*), 100, 127–30, 129f, 184n9

version R translation (*A Mechanical Orange*): book cover, 100, 101f; 102–3; censorship of, 105–7; circularity of, 121–25; creation and introduction of, 99–100, 103–4; explanatory texts for, 103, 184n13; glossary of terms included in, 106, 111; illegal editions of, 105, 184n15, 185n37; levels of understanding for, 108–9; Nadsat language and, 108–16, 125–27; special edition with version A, 100, 102f; stage production of, 119, 120f; as supplement to *Fantastyka*, 105, 183n7

Virgil, 58

Vulgate Bible, 1

Waczków, Józef, 190n42

Wade, Sidney, 171n32

Waldrop, Rosmarie, 5, 32–33

Wałęsa, Lech, 80, 124, 137, 183n69

Walkowitz, Rebecca, 11, 19, 20, 31, 175n42

Wang Wei: "deer park" and, 16, 19, 21, 52; Fernández Long and, 171n26; selection for translation multiples, 5; Snyder and, 21; visuality and pictoriality in poetry of, 20, 171n30; Wade and, 171n32; Weinberger and, 16, 19–22, 59, 171n27, 175n42

Wat, Aleksander, 147–48

Watson, Burton, 37
Ważyk, Adam, 190n42
Weinberger, Eliot, 16, 19–22, 59, 171n27, 175n42
Wilkins, Ernest H., 26
Willett, John, 191n60
A Wind-Up Orange. *See* version A translation
Witold Chwalewik, 190n42
Wolf, Uljana, 31, 45
Wolff, Larry, 87
Wood, Michael, 14
Wright, Chantal, 16

xenophobia, 50

Yiddish language, 111–13, 128
Yugoslav wars, 81, 88

Zabalbeascoa, Patrick, 176n43
Zagajewski, Adam, 77
Zappulla, Elio, 27
Żeromski, Stefan, 186n73
Zukofsky, Louis and Celia, 44, 47
Żuławski, Andrzej, 162

TRANSLATION / TRANSNATION

Series Editor Emily Apter

Writing Outside the Nation by Azade Seyhan

Ambassadors of Culture: The Transamerican Origins of Latino Writing
   by Kirsten Silva Gruesz

The Literary Channel: The Inter-National Invention of the Novel edited
   by Margaret Cohen and Carolyn Dever

Experimental Nations: Or, the Invention of the Maghreb by Réda Bensmaïa

What Is World Literature? by David Damrosch

We, the People of Europe?: Reflections on Transnational Citizenship
   by Étienne Balibar

The Portable Bunyan: A Transnational History of "The Pilgrim's Progress"
   by Isabel Hofmeyr

Nation, Language, and the Ethics of Translation edited by Sandra Bermann
   and Michael Wood

Utopian Generations: The Political Horizon of Twentieth-Century Literature
   by Nicholas Brown

Guru English: South Asian Religion in a Cosmopolitan Language
   by Srinivas Aravamudan

Poetry of the Revolution: Marx, Manifestos, and the Avant-Gardes
   by Martin Puchner

The Translation Zone: A New Comparative Literature by Emily Apter

In Spite of Partition: Jews, Arabs, and the Limits of Separatist Imagination
   by Gil Z. Hochberg

*The Princeton Sourcebook in Comparative Literature: From the European
   Enlightenment to the Global Present* edited by David Damrosch,
   Natalie Melas, and Mbongiseni Buthelezi

The Spread of Novels: Translation and Prose Fiction in the Eighteenth Century
   by Mary Helen McMurran

The Novel and the Sea by Margaret Cohen

The Event of Postcolonial Shame by Timothy Bewes

Hamlet's Arab Journey: Shakespeare's Prince and Nasser's Ghost by Margaret Litvin

Archives of Authority: Empire, Culture, and the Cold War by Andrew N. Rubin

Security: Politics, Humanity, and the Philology of Care by John T. Hamilton

Dictionary of Untranslatables: A Philosophical Lexicon edited by Barbara Cassin

Learning Zulu: A Secret History of Language in South Africa by Mark Sanders

In the Shadow of World Literature: Sites of Reading in Colonial Egypt by Michael Allan

Leaks, Hacks, and Scandals: Arab Culture in the Digital Age by Tarek El-Ariss

City of Beginnings: Poetic Modernism in Beirut by Robyn Creswell

Vernacular English: Reading the Anglophone in Postcolonial India by Akshya Saxena

The Making of Barbarians: Chinese Literature and Multilingual Asia by Haun Saussy

Sacred Language, Vernacular Difference: Global Arabic and Counter-Imperial Literatures by Annette Damayanti Lienau

Literature's Refuge: Rewriting the Mediterranean Borderscape by William Stroebel

Translation Multiples: From Global Culture to Post-Communist Democracy by Kasia Szymanska

GPSR Authorized Representative: Easy Access System Europe - Mustamäe tee 50, 10621 Tallinn, Estonia, gpsr.requests@easproject.com